The Hawken Book

James A. Hawken (1916)
Photograph by George M. Edmondson,
Cleveland

THE HAWKEN BOOK

by William Donohue Ellis
and Nancy A. Schneider

The Cobham and Hatherton Press
Cleveland, Ohio
1990

The Hawken Book
Copyright © 1990 by William Donohue Ellis
    and Nancy A. Schneider
All rights reserved
ISBN 0-944125-13-1
First edition
Book design by William Donohue Ellis
    and Roderick Boyd Porter
Original photography by Kevin C. Vesely
Endpaper illustrations by Michael P. Sukys
Jacket design by Roderick Boyd Porter and
    Greg M. Oznowich: Watt, Roop & Co.
Research and appendix preparation by
    Christopher J. Pike
Typesetting by Delmas, Incorporated, of
    Ann Arbor, Michigan
Printing by Davies-Wing Company of Cleveland, Ohio
Binding by The Forest City Bookbindery of
    Cleveland, Ohio
The book has been printed on seventy-pound
    Mohawk Superfine paper.
Publication of *The Hawken Book*
    has been assisted by
    The Payne Fund.

Library of Congress Cataloging-in-Publication Data

Ellis, William Donohue.
    The Hawken book / W. D. Ellis and N. A. Schneider.
        p. cm.
    ISBN 0-944125-13-1 : $28.95
    1. Hawken School—History. I. Schneider, N. A.
(Nancy A.), 1950- II. Title.
LD7501.C625E44   1990
373.771'32—dc20   90-33730
                                                        CIP

The main purpose for which the
school exists is development of
character.

James A. Hawken

For any of us who find ourselves in charge of anything, I think this story of seventy-five years of survival and growth in the face of on-going emergencies is useful.

To me it says—no matter the crisis, renounce expediency and embrace principle.

John Sherwin, Jr., '53
President,
Board of Trustees 1987-1990

Foreword

JAMES HAWKEN and a few very gifted teachers came to Cleveland in 1915 to establish a small school for small boys with a very big goal, "that the better self shall prevail and each generation introduce its successor to a higher plane of life." His vision of the ideal "Hawken boy"* was of a young man of the highest integrity, educated rigorously in the standard curriculum of the time, with an added emphasis on the arts and physical education. These young scholar-athletes would be trained to enter adult life well equipped to serve their families and communities and to provide examples to the next generation.

Hawken's lofty aspirations were able to be understood and supported by the exceptional community that Cleveland had become by the turn of the century. Imbued from its Western Reserve heritage with the importance of education, the city had recently been enriched by people of diverse cultures and by many generations of industrial prosperity. Energetic and concerned citizens were building the great institutions for which Cleveland is now famous, including the Cleveland Orchestra and the Cleveland Museum of Art, as well as our beautiful public buildings and parks. The parents of those early boys stood behind Hawken ideologically and financially, and the school prospered.

Today Hawken School is a coeducational, twelve-grade school on two campuses with one hundred faculty and eight hundred students. It has proudly expanded its mission to include children from the various economic, religious, and racial backgrounds that

---

*See photograph of the sculpture of the ideal "Hawken boy" done by faculty sculptor Joseph C. Motto in the early days of the school (1922) at the beginning of the second section of illustrations.

make up our community. As was the case originally, it seeks to provide an outstanding education while developing the character of the student. There is strong emphasis on the individual, service to the community, and "Fair Play," Mr. Hawken's motto for daily life.

Alumni and parents owe a tremendous debt of gratitude to the extraordinary teachers who have led the school over the past seventy-five years. I hope those who read this book will agree that authors Bill Ellis and Nancy Schneider have told the Hawken story well, and will feel, as I do, rewarded by a sense of how exceptional the school and its history are, and recommitted to its important goals.

> Charles P. Bolton, '57
> Chairman of the Seventy-fifth
> Anniversary Celebration

Introduction

MOST SCHOOL HISTORIES are written on the occasion of a centennial. University-Liggett (Michigan), Buckingham, Browne, and Nichols (Massachusetts), and University School (Ohio), for example, all chose one-hundredth-year histories. Others, John Burroughs School in St. Louis, for instance, have occurred in the fiftieth year. For Hawken School the board of trustees' selection of the seventy-fifth year was appropriate. The time frame is brief enough to allow the historians direct access to those former students who are now in their golden years, who could serve as primary sources in recalling the school's earliest days; but long enough for an interpretation of the roots and flowering of a boys-only school, which, a half-century after its founding, would take three major risks: expansion of its mission to include secondary education, a second campus, and coeducation.

The board's choice of authors William Donohue Ellis and Nancy A. Schneider was also wise. Having no prior association with Hawken, they approached their assignment with the objectivity which all who had been involved in early discussions of a possible history had wanted. The consequence, for the Hawken community, is an immensely readable piece, the result of scores of interviews and painstaking analyses of hundreds of Hawken documents.

The Hawken Book will no doubt also wend its way into northeast Ohio public libraries and into offices and faculty rooms of other independent schools and organizations across the nation. All of this is fitting, for one can legitimately contend that a school with Hawken's unique history and national reputation has a responsibility to produce such a work.

Hawken owes much to Charles P. Bolton, '57, parent and trustee, who has chaired the school's seventy-fifth anniversary celebration. He has given caring direction to the anniversary year activities and to the history project itself.

We hope that you will enjoy and learn from *The Hawken Book*.

T. Douglas Stenberg
Headmaster

From the Authors

"COME QUICK!" The young stage hand rushed off stage yelling, "Mr. Stephens has been struck by thunder!"

Sterling (Bill) Hubbard, '29, recently told that to the son of Mr. Stephens, who conducted some interviews for this book. Hubbard explained that, when his class was staging *Wapping Wharf*, Charles R. Stephens, in his regular role of seeking perfection, told soft-spoken Flamen Ball to shake the sheet of tin that made the thunder "More vigorously! Vigorously! Get more out of it! Like this!" Grabbing the tin, Mr. Stephens demonstrated ferociously. The suspension beam for the tin gave 'way, hitting Stephens on the head, drawing blood and stunning him.

Too trivial a memory, it would seem, to represent a national institution building for seventy-five years ... until we note this combination of the humorous and the profound dominates the revenant impressions of Hawken. Where is the profound? The school's most distinguished teacher, concerned not only with academic excellence, but excellence in shaking a piece of tin ... vigorously ... coupled with Hubbard's next statement, *"Hawken made the greatest influence on my life."*

This last comment in nearly identical language came to us from dozens of alumni.

And that was the whole idea, as stated in James Hawken's opening brochure in 1915—"The raison d'etre is ... discover and lead out all that is best in the individual boy." In the school archives we saw that work time and again.

The Reader as Author

For every story told here, the alumnus and alumna reader will know a hundred more. In a saga involving perhaps eight thousand people over seventy-five years, omissions dominate this book. We suggest you use the blank pages at the back to write in those important events, and donate your book later to the Hawken hundredth-anniversary committee. As this book progresses, there will be less and less detail as the cast and the events proliferate from a school of nineteen boys to one approaching a thousand boys and girls and two campuses, a faculty and staff of two hundred, and a curriculum of one hundred courses.

Our Thanks to . . .

Sixty-two alumni, faculty, and trustees for extensive interview time.

Christopher J. Pike, '83, young Hawken alumnus and archivist who located and organized seventy-five years of materials into extremely accessible form, familiarized himself closely with the contents, and conducted interviews.

Charles L. Stephens, '46, emeritus director of the Middle School, for giving us in extensive interviews a sweeping overview at the outset and for later interviewing alumni and retired faculty for this work.

Meacham Hitchcock, '42, former trustee and present associate headmaster for development, for interviewing some alumni.

The chairman of the seventh-fifth anniversary committee, Charles P. Bolton, for facilitating the work.

Kermit J. Pike for his own critique and for coordinating the manuscript review by several reviewers and managing the manuscript phase to keep it on schedule.

Roderick Boyd Porter of the Cobham and Hatherton Press, for editing the manuscript and managing publication with his special style, including layout.

Headmaster T. Douglas Stenberg and the development office staff and to Mrs. Jackie Gillespie for hospitality while we worked on premises.

About Sources . . .

We avoid footnotes here. The sources are often cited right in the text. But, additionally, all print and correspondences are neatly filed and labeled in twenty-six drawers in the Hawken development office on the Gates Mills campus. An archival summary of categories, prepared by the archivist, appears in the appendix.

William Donohue Ellis
Nancy A. Schneider

Table of Contents

The Hawken Book, because the object of its consideration is a continuing, changing, and vibrant institution, cannot have dealt entirely with all the school's history since 1915. Hence, the authors and the publisher have provided space in the book's margins in which percipient readers may indite notes for future research and for subsequent attempts to record and interpret Hawken's history. There are also several blank note pages at the end of the volume for expanded comments. Readers may forward such remarks and observations, corrections, and the like to the publisher, the Cobham and Hatherton Press, at 1260 West Fourth Street, Cleveland, Ohio 44113.

The Hawken Book

Book I
The Concept

1. 1572 Ansel

"I BEGAN to seriously question my decision."

The whip-figured young New York math teacher's apprehension rose when he turned onto Cleveland's Ansel Road looking for 1572. In June 1916 Ansel Road radiated heat and traffic rumble, which struck him in contrast to wooded Hackley School campus in Tarrytown fronting the Hudson and backed by the Catskills ... from which he had resigned. He may have made a serious mistake.

The teacher, Charles R. Stephens, had made the deliberate decision that he was getting too comfortable at prestigious Hackley School. He should move around while young, build varied experience. He had accepted a post at this new school which a certain James Hawken had launched the previous year on Ansel Road, Cleveland. En route to the University of Wisconsin for more summer study, Stephens stopped off here for a first look.

He located 1572, an ordinary small frame house ... locked. Squinting through a road-dusted window he saw some small desks in the living room. He went out back and looked in the kitchen window. Must be the art classroom. He scanned the scuffed bare back yard, about fifty feet on a side. Must be the playground.

Very concerned, Stephens made his way back toward Euclid Avenue. There, by startling coincidence, he nearly bumped into a Dr. Campbell, under whom he had studied at Wisconsin, "To meet you here!"

When they got down to talking, Stephens later recounted, "I told him of the plunge I had taken and the depression I was feeling. By coincidence he knew of the school and the people behind it. 'Charles, I think you may be taking part in an interesting and possibly very important project.'"

Charles R. Stephens

Why?

As in most very important projects, the reason traces back to a man or woman with a certain conviction which magnetizes. In this case a James Albert Hawken.

Who is he?

Stephens knew the statistic Hawken. He had taught at Interlaken School at La Porte, Indiana, and at Newman Browning School in New York City. That leaves blank why professionals abandoned positions at such as Groton and Middlesex School in Concord, Massachusetts, to teach nineteen boys in a five-room house.*

Stephens went on to Wisconsin and returned to Ansel Road for duty in September. This second sight of the school told him something more about James Hawken. In just those few weeks the original building at 1572 Ansel had become the headmaster's house; the school was a few doors away at 1588, a larger house with a larger back yard and a barn.

Enrollment had nearly doubled, thirty-seven boys and four very strong new masters.

Jim Hawken was a very slim young man, wavy hair combed back, immaculate in dress, soft in voice, devoid of authoritative demeanor. People joined him as if in a cause.

However, Stephens at first was upset. He was assigned to teach first grade: "a woman's job."

Studying that faculty told more about Jim Hawken than studying Jim Hawken. There was a gifted sculptor teaching art, Joe Motto. There was Bill Phelan, who had an uncanny magic with boys and language studies. Those two, with Hawken, were the original 1915-16 faculty. New for 1917 was Mort Smeed, who would become legendary, a *Reader's Digest* "Most Unforgettable." George Sawyer, Ashley

*The first nineteen: first grade—William Boardman, Charles Bolton, Stevenson Burke, Norman Ingersoll, Roger Perkins, Dwight Smith, David Weir, William Weir. Third grade—Jack Baker, Patterson Bole, Stephens Chamberlin, Alvah Drake, Tom Grandin, Sherman Hayden, William Palmer, John Phillips, Barnard Prescott, John Teagle, James Weir.

Nagle, John Carney, and Charles Stephens, men who could teach just about anywhere they wished. Why were they here with Jim Hawken?

Who was Hawken?

The School Before the School

James Hawken was teaching at Browning School in New York in 1914. Five hundred miles to the west in Cleveland, in a barn on Euclid Avenue, five boys ages six to eight were being tutored. They were Pat Bole, John Teagle, Jim Weir, John Phillips, and Sherman Hayden.

Why a school for five boys? Some say that Mrs. Benjamin P. Bole and the mothers of the other boys, wanting top-flight education for their sons, hired Alcott Farrar Elwell to tutor them. However, Mrs. Robert M. Clements, sister of Frank and John Teagle, credits the fathers: "My father and Warren Hayden, Ben Bole and Dr. William Weir, wanting an alternative to University School, hired Elwell."

Another motive, perhaps buried too deep to be recognized, was the historic education concern of Connecticut Western Reserve descendants. While most frontier settlements hungered for schools, Connecticut Western Reserve settlers had a special intensity. The Reserve was retained in Ohio by Connecticut. When sold to the privately-owned Connecticut Land Company in 1796, Connecticut put the proceeds toward its schools—which these settlers were forced to leave. Not the classic farmer-woodsmen-frontiersmen, these reluctant settlers, inheritors of shares in the struggling Connecticut Land Company—lawyers, ministers, doctors, businessmen—were forced to come west to develop their lands to make them salable. Sixty-five of them (thirty-three percent) were Yale graduates. In 1823 young Seabury Ford and D. Witter walked all the way back east through the wilderness to Yale University. Since then a steady parade of Western Reserve settler descendants were prepared carefully to go east.

Elwell, as remembered by Hayden, was "a tall strongly built man with extremely blue eyes, tart Boston accent and graying hair. He was a clever artist and held the youngsters' attention by drawing super monsters on the blackboard while teaching geography."

Along with instruction, Elwell, twenty-eight, brought to the boys a storybook persona. Son of a sculptor, he lived as a boy in France and Germany, attended the famous Cambridge Latin in Massachusetts, became a counselor at Camp Mowgli in New Hampshire, which will touch Hawken history later (and by coincidence the present headmaster was once a counselor at Mowgli). In and out of Harvard University for financial reasons, he worked as a cook on a survey team in the Wyoming Badlands. He returned to Harvard, interrupted again for a tour in Mexico, and once again to come to Cleveland at the call of Roberta Bole.

Interpolating among remembered versions by Sherman Hayden, Frank Teagle, younger brother of John, and Helen Clements, it seems likely that in the middle of the 1914-15 school year other parents wanted their boys to join the original five, causing the tutoring to move to a house on East 102nd Street.

Suddenly Alcott Elwell resigned to return to Harvard in 1915. He will re-enter this account years later as Colonel Elwell.

Meanwhile Mrs. Roberta Bole, the former Roberta Holden, needed very quickly a replacement for him. Her sister-in-law was the mother of Dean Holden, who had been well-tutored by a certain James Hawken of New York.

James Hawken, born in Rochester, New York, was the youngest of the ten children of Albert and Anna Hawken. James, studying for the priesthood, left the church in a philosophical disagreement over confession and absolution. In 1912 he married Bertha Sapp of Danville, Ohio. She died in a car accident soon after the marriage.

The information about Hawken sparked the New York interview of the young teacher. Roberta Bole was a young matron of tremendous energy. Impressed with Hawken, she asked him to take Elwell's job as tutor. Hawken declined. She later urged him to reconsider. Again—no.

Hawken, however, had long daydreamed of a special type of school for boys which would be a kind of extension of the home, would have very small classes, would concentrate on development of character with paramount emphasis on the boy as an *individual*. This last concept is commonly espoused, but James Hawken envisioned it practiced in uncommon intensity, classes so small that the teachers could make a piercing discovery of the *uniqueness* of each boy, nurture his individual talents.

Hawken began to think that perhaps these women in Cleveland could implement his vision. He discussed his plan for such a school with Roberta Bole.

It was her turn—no. Emphatically, her group was not at all interested in founding another independent school in Cleveland.

She added, however, if Hawken wanted to start such a school, they would send their own sons and try to interest their friends in doing so. But no promises, no capital commitments. The Weirs were interested in funding his school, but did not have the means.

It was clearly understood—Hawken would be on his own. No hardware investment would be made by the Cleveland group beyond tuition for their own boys. The financial responsibility—strictly Hawken's.

Hawken agreed.

He quickly arranged for the house at 1572 Ansel Road and converted it with financial assistance of a good friend, Henry Sheffield. Three downstairs rooms became classrooms, two upstairs for teacher living quarters for Hawken, Phelan, and later, Motto. He recruited nineteen boys, basically for first and third grades. Hawken taught third grade, Phelan first grade. There were no hard boundaries between staff duties. All three taught, administered, cleaned the building, shoveled the snow, and tended furnace.

What separated this from a merely enthusiastic adventure were two special elements. The first was the dedication of the three young teachers to strict adherence to Hawken's vision. Amid the shoveling of coal and the sweeping and scrubbing these three kept paramount the high credo.

For the start of the 1916-17 year Jim Hawken spelled that out in miniscule type in a pocket-size booklet, in part:

> The raison d'etre of the school is two-fold: first, a firm conviction ... that until he has reached ... fifteen or sixteen a boy should have for his normal surroundings the home.... [The school] should be merely the extension of the home for ... such matters as can be done more conveniently and more effectively than by the family itself.
>
> The second consideration is ... that, just as truly as each individual boy has physical characteristics different from his companions, so truly does he possess individual talents ... powers, tastes, instincts and tendencies. And because of this there can be no real and efficient education where a general ... method of training is applied to a group of boys.
>
> The educator must have the opportunity to concentrate all his ability, his attention, his efforts on the individual boy before him in order to discover and to lead out all that is best.

The booklet briefly described methods: No more than eight boys under one master; curriculum designed to permit a boy at any time to enter another school without losing a grade; "parental suggestions and criticisms will be invited by the headmaster at the end of each term, but it is requested that such ... be withheld until that time."

The last instruction to parents was: "*The school exists for the boy. The Headmaster will be glad at all times to confer with parents and to answer any need the boys may have of him.*"

A later brochure listed the faculty:

James A. Hawken, William F. Phelan, Charles R. Stevens [Stephens], George Garfield Sawyer, Ashley Pierce Nagle, H.

Mortimer Smeed, and Joseph Motto.

In one sense Hawken summed up his character goal for the boys in two words—fair play.

At the new 1588 Ansel Road address, Hawken School taught five grades. The school office was the pantry. Mr. Motto's clay modeling room was the kitchen. There were two back rooms on the second floor used for "anything which came handy." The other rooms were classrooms.

The following year Hawken added a sixth grade. They joined a second-floor spare room to the lavatory to make an extra classroom, converted the former gym in the attic to a manual training shop. The barn became the gym.

They installed a tall flagpole in the front.

In 1919-20 they squeezed an eighth grade into a third floor room opening onto manual training. The second grade pre-empted Mr. Hawken's office. He moved to the faculty room.

Stephens began to understand the tug of the James Hawken magnet. When you talked to him he listened with burning focus and respect. "We were encouraged," Stephens wrote, "to be creative, to explore, to experiment so long as we kept in mind our obligation to the pupil to reach certain goals in the teaching process. I recall a Latin motto in large print under the glass top of Hawken's desk, *Maxima debetur puero reverentia*—The greatest reverence is due the boy. It meant among other things—don't waste his precious time in class with poorly prepared lessons or superficial experiments ..."

The second special element lifting this one-house school above its mundane quarters was a corps of parents with an unusually intense preoccupation with education as the mainspring of life. For example, Frances Bolton, mother of Charles, '27, went to the school daily for several weeks the first year. These parents valued Jim Hawken's attitude about his mission.

Just as Hawken required his teachers to find and develop the special qualities in each boy, his own quiet leadership did the same for his teachers. He told them, "Every master a headmaster." And they became so.

The two-way respect extended to all staff levels. One day a short, totally bald John Ciarlillo (as it was sometimes spelled) arrived on a bicycle to become half-day custodian. Falling under the James Hawken spell of respect, he tackled the job as if in charge of a cathedral and as if also responsible for the boys' development. He soon made the job full time. His strong profile, love, and brown-toothed garlic laugh comprise the single most vivid memory of many senior alumni.

But James Hawken had barely assembled his unusual staff when it was wiped out in the blast of a bugle call.

SCHOOL WITHOUT STAFF

They were enlistment-age teachers. Stephens and Smeed were to go into uniform in the spring of 1917. Phelan joined the American Field Service in France. Others later answered the call for "Over There."

At James Hawken's request Stephens first went to New York to interview potential staff for replacement. Of those interviewed, he recommended two to Hawken. One was Ross MacMahon, a tweedy and burly bear storied still in Hawken alumni meetings. Smeed, Phelan, and Stephens visited a school on Cleveland's Hough Avenue where they watched thirty motionless first graders entranced by an amazing teacher, Miss Luehrs. Tall and unselfconsciously beautiful, she radiated something compelling. She was hired to teach Hawken first grade; and for many an alumnus prior to the class of '48, Miss Luehrs *is* Hawken School.

Hawken viewed the World War I era as the worst in his life. With the exception of Miss Luehrs and Ross MacMahon, he felt he had to operate the school without top-notch staff. He seriously considered closing the school.

MARATHON FACULTY MEETINGS

The clearest focus on James Hawken comes not by looking at him straight on, but at his reflection in the staff. Even after the staff had the broadening experience of seeing "Paree" they still wanted to return to work with Jim Hawken. After the Armistice they wrote to see if there were places for them down on the farm.

By then there were new faculty members, of course, but Hawken took back all the veterans and increased enrollment.

Jim Hawken had taken an apartment near the school. With him lived Smeed, Motto and Carney. Across the street lived Phelan and Stephens. They all had breakfast and dinner at Hawken's home, accidentally creating an ongoing faculty meeting covering methods and theories of teaching, the curriculum and information about progress or problems of individual boys. It was, Stephens remembered, "a constant seminar in the making of a school, superior to a graduate course in education."

The young teachers were in awe of their own charge as stated in the small 1916 brochure, "To bring the boy up to date on the progress and achievements of man during centuries of living, all in the course of a few short years. We hope in his life, he will evolve a higher plane ... worth passing on to future generations." And they started the small boys early on those pretentious learning adventures. The written themes of small boys explore the French Revolution; Marco Polo's legacy; the use of art.

This small faculty carried a heavy classroom load compounded by playground duty, drama, music, shop, art and building equipment for teaching aids. And despite the presence of John Ciriralillo (as it is other times spelled), the faculty continued to man the mops, paint brushes, and snow shovels. They also supervised athletics. John Price, '36, remembers, "As a Hawken boy, if you had four limbs, you did athletics."

At lunch time the faculty walked the students to the art museum where along with lunch they absorbed the wonders of the art world. Teaching duty was dawn to dusk, followed by the on-going faculty meeting. A new young manual-training teacher arrived and soon announced to the headmaster, "I'm the manual training *teacher,* not the school carpenter."

Hawken mildly replied, "It won't be necessary. I always have John and Steve (Ciarlillo and Stephens)."

However, as a side glance at Hawken's supposedly soft leadership, it is noted that, despite real competence in the classroom, the new manual-training teacher was soon off the payroll.

The Hawken Rule Book

One aspect of Hawken's leadership, and one which the faculty admired, was the absence of a thick book of rules. The whole rule book, constitution, and bill of rights, were two words—Fair Play—which James Hawken commissioned Joe Motto to design into a sign to be hung in each room. No empty shibboleth, it was taken very seriously. Char Hickox, '31-I, remembers, "There was a fat effeminate boy whom we ridiculed one day. We lost our class 'Fair Play' sign for two weeks, and we smarted some."

The Hawken Report Card

The reporting was unique. These statements to parents were detailed biographical tracts, called "character reports." To write one of these lengthy documents, a teacher was forced to think long and deeply about each of his boys. These comprehensive essays were observations of the boy by the teacher as seen in class, in extracurricular action and in interaction with other boys. They identified incipient special abilities, nascent special interests and sensitivities. These were highly valued by parents, and upon reading them they could have little doubt that the one person in the world who knew their son best was that teacher.

There was a still greater if invisible merit to these reports, every one of them read by the headmaster: while they evaluated the boy, by side effect they evaluated the teacher.

Growing Pains

Because of Jim Hawken's particular style of leadership which encouraged staff initiative, the school at times developed more rapidly than the founder really favored. Opening in October of 1915 with just nineteen boys and three faculty, it doubled in school year 1916-17 to thirty-seven boys and seven faculty. Most of the nineteen boys in the first year were in grades one and three. That was deliberate. Hawken felt he could do more with the boys if he got them early, and a better school spirit would develop.

Pressure built up, however, to add more grades quickly to accommodate the advancing younger students and some older boys.

Grades one and two ended school at noon. Grades three, four and five in 1917 continued instruction and playground activity in the afternoon. Most boys went home for lunch. The others walked with masters to the Cleveland art museum tea room for lunch.

At 1588 Ansel Road the barn was used for chapel, drama, and manual training, but it was also for athletics.

1588 Ansel Road

"Shirts and Shoes! and Hurry It Up!"

Richard Inglis, '29, described that gym and Wally Wallace, the thin slope-shouldered gym teacher, yelling for the boys to change for athletic period, "And hurry it up!"

The two basketball baskets attached directly to the barn walls; no backboards. Two gymnastic rings and a climbing rope hung from the ridge pole above a few wrestling mats.

When the boys were changed Wally, just back from the war, blew his whistle, "Fall in!" There was a little infantry close-order drill followed by calisthenics—"arms at the thrust" and all that, to the unutterable boredom of boys waiting to be turned loose for basketball. There a boy could cut loose, the long shooters being stopped too often by Wally yelling,

"Pass! Don't shoot!"

There were no showers.

In spring the small backyard became "one of the strangest diamonds ever laid out," Inglis explains. "The barn wall ran along the baseline from second to third and the barn occupied most of left field." They moved the shortstop between first and second and three outfielders were in right field.

A ball hit between second and third base became a bank shot off the barn. So after a good hit the runner was shocked to find his own good hit had ricocheted to beat him to first base.

School policy was that every boy reaching a certain grade level must play football on an empty lot on Ansel Road. Inglis explains "there were those who reveled in this physical contact, and others whose concept involved only not getting in anybody's way."

Sports had been strictly intramural, but in 1919 the boys used the barn to train a basketball team to go interscholastic. They had just one off-campus game scheduled, Empire School. For this they practiced all season in the barn. Game time came. Final score 0-50. The school paper reported that although they lost, Jack Brayton, '25, played "a star game." In a later issue some wag asked, "What would the score have been if Brayton had not played such a star game?"

While the boys may have been shut out on the formal court, they were not beaten in the informal contests. Some boys arrived at school driven by parents, some by chauffeurs, some walked. "In those days" Charles Perkins, '24, remembers, "there was a gang on every street." He lived near Wade Park and East Boulevard. "Had to fight the 102nd Street gang on the way to school and on the way home."

But Jim Weir, '25, Charles's cousin and best friend, assembled his 84th Street gang, invaded 102nd Street gang territory "and threw them off the causeway into a frozen creek."

In that way the environment probably built character, but there were dangers on Ansel Road. Ambassador Myron T. Herrick's son, Myron, was fatally struck by a car in front of the school. Three other boys were injured by traffic.

Financial Time Bomb

Outstanding new private schools have a high failure rate. A good but undistinguished school will have a fairly level enrollment year to year, and can thus hold facilities and staff constant and plan its costs to fit revenue. An outstanding school, however, is under pressure to expand, requiring in turn expanding facilities and staff. Banks do not favor lending to schools for expansion.

Despite enrollment growth, Jim Hawken stuck to his rule, only eight boys per classroom. That boosted staff costs. But no matter how difficult the financing, Hawken would not water down his original concepts.

If the school was under pressure to expand, would not that provide the additional tuition revenue? The pressure was to add new higher grades to accommodate the advancing classes. But bringing in new students to fill the empty grades *behind* that advancing wave was difficult.

Many prospects could not pay the high tuition. Many others were loyal to University School and hostile toward the idea of a new boys' school. Still others took the view "we'll wait and watch." Some other parents considered Hawken a very temporary waiting room for their boys until a really established school could be found. Parents were not interested in financial involvement beyond tuition. It was Hawken's problem, Hawken's school. So Hawken struggled financially.

Twice, the annual tuition revenue actually covered the costs. When it did not, Hawken reduced his own salary and accepted financial help from his friend, Henry Sheffield, a wealthy lawyer, with a relaxed legal practice. Without Sheffield's financial support before 1918-19, Hawken later explained, the school could not have survived.

Henry Sheffield

Should Beggars Be Choosers?

The school needed a larger building. However, Henry Sheffield could not supply that, nor should he be expected to pick up the deficit regularly.

Practical men, watching, could see that you cannot safely leave a good institution like this school in the hands of a dreamer, however brilliant. And so a group of people went to James Hawken with a magnificent offer ... the use of a fine large property which would solve the facilities problem for years to come.

To the amazement of the offerers, Jim Hawken, in appreciative and courteous language—declined.

To startled colleagues he explained that, in accepting the gift, the faculty would give up too much control over education policy.

A man who turns down money is a worry.

In the form of that outstanding property, Hawken had turned down large dollars. Many a man of character has stood on principle and gone down to leave no footprints.

Who could understand a man like that?

Worldly men shook their heads. "Space to let" signs would soon surely appear at 1588 Ansel.

2. Declarations of Independence

The main purpose for which the school
exists is development of character.

James Hawken

IT JUST HAPPENED that in that original corps
of parents whose sons were the first Hawken class
was a young woman, Frances Bingham, who, along
with Roberta Bole, could exactly understand that special Hawken concern about losing control of basic
principles. She had a maverick understanding for
Hawken's independent stand.

Why?

The reason lay in her growing up; and that story,
with Bole's and Hawken's, becomes basic to the
school's history. Her father, Charles W. Bingham,
founder and head of the vital Standard Tool Company, was deeply involved beyond that in the whole
basic Cleveland industrial triangle—iron, coal, and
ships, compounded by civic work. Stern and aloof of
demeanor, he overawed Frances. Her mother, a loving parent, was very preoccupied handling her son
Oliver's serious endocarditis, requiring energy-con-
suming travel to climates which might help. Add the
fact that Frances, then short and stocky, stood somewhat in the shade of her sister, Betty. In the sprawl-
ing Perry mansion east of East 21st Street, built by
her great-grandfather on Millionaires' Row, Frances
felt alone.

Losing her mother when she was thirteen, Frances
fled to books, read hungrily, particularly the eastern
philosophers ... about self development. She also
fought loneliness with music, developing a career-po-
tential voice which would not be recognized until
years later when she no longer needed the boost. Her
father sent her on the chaperoned classic grand tour

of Europe. When she returned at sixteen he immediately sent her away again, this time to Miss Spence's School in New York City.

Following her debut in Cleveland she found that her group of debutante friends shared a special sense of mission about helping people trapped in life's sub-basement. They conceived a plan for working with Cleveland's doctorless health victims. Calling themselves the Brownies (a name they had used as girls) they approached Matilda Johnson, head of the Visiting Nurse Association in Cleveland. Could they help her?

Could they ever!

The first chore was clean and innocuous; make bandages. The girls requested deeper involvement. Therefore the next step changed many lives, including Frances's. Matilda Johnson said, "Get your parents' consent. They might not want this."

Frances did not ask; she knew he would refuse.

The young women next accompanied and assisted the Visiting Nurse Association on their slum rounds. Frances Bingham was assigned to bathe some small children. Matilda handed her scissors, "first you cut them out of their winter clothes." Softening crusted scales with oil, she watched beautiful children emerge. She concealed this work from her father.

She changed dressings on a variety of wounds, including knife stabs. She fed undernourished old men and women. She tended kids so housebound mothers could escape for an hour. She tended the bruises of battered women. She fed an undernourished, brilliant, thirty-five-year-old woman scientist who was huddled in rags in a basement suffering drug addiction.

She developed keen awareness of the world's grief and a towering admiration for nurses which would become important.

One morning at breakfast Charles Bingham said, "Frances, I want to talk to you in my study after breakfast."

The study had always been for Frances a forbidding chamber. Bingham asked her if it was true that she had been going around with visiting nurses?

"Yes, Father."

"Why . . . without asking me?"

"Because I knew you'd say no."

"Yes I would. But since you have done it, tell me about it."

He said she could continue. He probably did not know how far she would continue. That would lead to another confrontation.

So we later see Miss Bingham as a slim and graceful nineteen, standing before the board of Lakeside Nursing School at the request of board member Kate Hanna Ireland eloquently chastising their insufficient concern over mediocre training and quarters for nurses. Kate and Frances had chosen the moment as strategic because the nurses had just risen heroically to diphtheria and scarlet fever epidemics.

Her father, a member of the board, was present as Frances closed, "All I hope is you go up and see it (the nursing school and its living quarters), and I defy you to sleep well tonight!"

Following that, John D. Rockefeller financed a survey of nurses' training nationally, including Lakeside School.

At twenty-two Frances married her childhood friend, Chester C. Bolton; and this partnership of love and family enveloped an extended family of public service and education. In 1907 he was a young steel executive whose business acumen and financial expertise would later serve Hawken School as well as industry. During World War I he worked in Washington, highly placed on the munitions board.

One day Frances was on her way to call on the secretary of war to expedite final approval and action on creation of an army school of nursing. Powerful contention blocked this. The United States Army and the Red Cross wanted to use volunteer nurses' aides. Frances, then representing three national nursing organizations, wanted real fully-trained nurses for the war. A descendent of the Binghams, Perrys, and Paynes and wife of a Bolton, she was not timid of calling on fellow Clevelander, Newton D. Baker,

Frances Payne Bolton

to get the paperwork signed. However, she was shy of being seen on unannounced public business by her husband, who was suddenly walking toward her in a war department corridor. She stepped behind a pillar until he passed. From the secretary of war's anteroom she sent her message in to Baker. The response—he could not tend to it right away. Frances said she would wait. She sat three hours. And as a result, the army school of nursing was born before four o'clock that day.

This odyssey of independence brings her to age thirty-four, mother of three boys—Charles, Kenyon, and Oliver. While down with influenza pneumonia and not expected to live, she has just lost a fourth child, a one-day-old baby.

Short statured but now with a strikingly erect posture, she is a handsome woman, dark blond hair with a tinge of auburn brushed above the ears. Blue eyes come at the world straight on.

This is the woman who appreciates Jim Hawken's philosophical independence, akin to her own. Witness his memorandum to parents in which he adamantly counsels them to desist from giving parties at home for their sons, stop letting them go to the movies, and stop allowing absenteeism from school: *"Parents who are not in absolute sympathy with the school's aims, to my mind, ought to withdraw their boys from the school. James Hawken."*

Hawken wrote that at a time when he had enough trouble without inciting parent mutiny. His trained faculty had gone to war. His school was overcrowded and under-funded.

Frances Bolton, however, understood about the need to take a stand and hold it. She understood the need for independence to do this. Therefore she and Roberta Bole created a device in 1919 to let people help fund the school without buying any managerial rights. They established the Hawken School Endowment Association, which could receive gifts for the school, but had no official voice in school policy. First association members were Frances and Chester Bolton; Mrs. Benjamin Bole; Warren S. Hayden and

Jim Hawken's close friend, Henry Sheffield.

Bill Nash, '29, remembers Sheffield as a handsome, stately presence "but a nebulous and shadowy figure." In 1959, Jim Hawken wrote Charles Stephens that without Henry Sheffield's financial support on Ansel Road, there would have been no school.

* * *

Every reader is entitled to speculate—what would become of a school landlocked in a ten-room house?

However, what actually did happen was that the first gift received by the endowment association was from the Boltons, fourteen acres of farm land near their new home, Franchester, in then rural Lyndhurst. With the land came the promise of a new building. Both gifts in 1919 were from Chester and Frances Bolton who, with two generations of their direct descendants, would take a guardian role in this story to the present day.

The gifts were not to the school, but to the endowment association. Did these enormous gifts overwhelm the wall between endowment association and school? No. For example, the association chose Walter R. McCornack, architect for the Cleveland Board of Education, for building architect. However, the fundamental architect was James Hawken. Despite the growth boosters and the practical businessmen who had learned in industry to build oversize for expansion, James Hawken insisted on very small classrooms to implement his basic philosophy ... individual attention.

Change frightens people. Lyndhurst was way out in farm country. In 1921 it was a village; Mayfield, Cedar, and Richmond roads were narrow brick country roads. Shaker Heights did not even exist, Cleveland Heights was just starting to grow. Most Hawken families lived inboard of East 100th Street, on or near Euclid Avenue and in the University Circle area. How would parents get their children to school? Why Lyndhurst?

One reason was, of course, the land donation from the Boltons. Around this time Chester was developing his Franchester Farms in Lyndhurst. His neighbors included the Weirs and the Blossoms and the Mayfield Country Club. Donating the land adjacent to his property for the school might also encourage parents interested in sending their children to move from the city and help develop this area.

As the new building was scheduled to open in the fall of 1922 (details later) many parents began to get cold feet about sending their children so far from home. Some said they would withdraw their boys from the school.

3. Lyndhurst

> ... this talk will react on
> the good name of the school.
>
> Chester C. Bolton

CONSTRUCTION of the new school involved complex engineering and finance but even more complex emotion. For James Hawken it involved a combination of gratitude and mental chaos.

For Chester Bolton it meant deep involvement. He would become a major force in the school financial planning and administration. On the last day of 1919, he received from architect Walter R. McCornack a construction estimate for the new Hawken building prepared by Crowell & Little Construction ... $219,245.00.

McCornack felt that by ordering materials early and working on a time and materials basis twenty percent could be saved. If construction began in March and materials were ordered at once, he believed enough of the building would be finished by October to open school.

Jim Hawken's missionary feelings about the school surfaced in a letter he wrote to Chester Bolton in February 1920. The Hawken endowment association had offered a piece of land for the new school which Hawken had first approved. Later he recanted, believing the ground sloped too much but more seriously that it would soon be encircled by other development, defeating the concept of a school in the country creating its own environment. "I had rather relieve the Hawken School Endowment Association of all obligations to my school than accept ... a site ... inadequate for its purpose."

We get further revelation of Hawken's dedication and emotional state from another part of the letter.

"I'm sure I need not tell you how painful this business is to me and how I have had to summon all my courage to go through with it. If the SCHOOL were merely something that belonged to me and your generous endowment were a personal gift, my action would be quite different; but I have learned to look upon the school not as an experiment which I can work at or leave alone at will but a trust to which I must be faithful ... with all my efforts.

"I trust you will accept this statement as clear and frank as I can make, of my position as preface to a heart to heart talk with you."

Henry Sheffield, nonchalant and genial, deeply involved in the financial side, may have been more effective than Hawken in preserving his friend's educational objectives. His connection to the school was Jim Hawken. Easy going as Sheffield was in his relaxed lifestyle, he was financially alert and shrewd. In response to a letter from Chester Bolton, Sheffield returned from vacation (he and Hawken shared a vacation cottage on Deer Island, Maine) to tend to a financial emergency. Finding the fund flow running behind the construction bills, he told the contractor to give him a cost estimate of roofing over the work so it could stand the weather and also said to shut down the project temporarily.

Figures presented to him had shown overdrafts at the bank for payroll of ten thousand dollars, balance due on the July statement of twenty thousand dollars and non-cancelable obligations already incurred of forty thousand dollars. The amount needed to roof over the existing construction would be thirty thousand dollars.

The contractor told Sheffield that to stop construction would be a detriment to the building and cause financial loss. Sheffield's financial philosophy comes through in his August 5, 1920 letter to Chester Bolton (then on vacation at Prouts Neck, Maine): "I don't doubt that this is so, but feel that the danger of running into debt is paramount to anything else."

Sheffield's involvement was not merely managerial: "I today cashed $70,000 in my treasury certificates which, with the interest, amounted to $72,700 in order to take care of the payrolls and obligations above mentioned."

He writes that the architect and contractor were doing very good work but, "I feel very strongly that the work should cease at once before there is danger of funds being exhausted."

Chester Bolton requested from McCornack an updated cost estimate which came as close to angering a polite man as one can come. He wrote McCornack on August 14, 1920, in part, " ... your position and reputation are too well established to allow of any question; however with a paid clerk to assist you ... I could not understand how six months could have elapsed in which we had not heard that a difference of nearly 100% between estimate and cost was possible."

He reviewed McCornack's original statement that final cost could be under two hundred thousand dollars and restated, "Our limit today is $200,000, and therefore, it is absolutely a necessity that work be stopped and nothing done until we can get figures which will permit of our doing the work within that limit."

Chester Bolton had a high regard for Sheffield's judgment. In July of 1921 we find him writing to Sheffield for his opinion about resuming the work. He had gotten McCornack and the builder to revise estimates to an over-run of one hundred seventeen thousand dollars. While still a huge spread, Chester Bolton felt that if they waited longer to resume construction they would run into a predicted strike by the trades, delaying the building perhaps another year. "We have talked of this new building for two years and if something is not actually done in the near future, this talk will react on the good name of the School." To start the continuation, he proposed, "we arrange to borrow an additional $50,000 at one of the banks, which note Frances and I will be glad to endorse ... I await your wire advises."

Examination of Conscience
for the Teachers of Hawken School

Amid the chaos of design, construction, and financing of the new school building, James Hawken kept his eye on the central education concept. The heart of that as always was the teacher. Hence for the teacher he published a slim nine-page booklet on good paper, _An Examination of Conscience_.

It opened: "In establishing Hawken School one of the chief aims was to give to men and women who were genuinely consecrated to the work of education an opportunity to do real work unhampered by the mechanics of complicated systems; to surround teachers of the right spirit ... with conditions ... for the realization of the greatness of their vocation."

The pamphlet then asks Hawken teachers to measure "your thoughts and conduct at least once a week by the following standards." Just a few of them were:

Do you realize the dignity of your profession?

It is no exaggeration to assert that all the pressing problems ... of life are solved by right education. Do you believe this?

Are you vigilantly on watch for what is being written on your own special subject?

Do you read superior novels, essays, poems?

Do you hear good music? Visit art museums?

Do you realize the greatness of your opportunity in class?

Do you make careful lesson plans?

Are you exact in small matters of the class-room?

"Maxima debetur puero reverentia." Do you look with reverence upon the fine young spirits you are teaching?

The Hawken boy should be known for fair play .... Are you always his exemplar ...?

Is your classroom a place of cheerful but intense industry?

Do your boys come to you with their special problems?

Do you see that the boy himself studies or do you do most of the work for him?

How often do you make out a character card?

[On the playground] do you make the play an opportunity for showing pluck?

His questions increase over several pages in didactic specificity.

In a brochure aimed at prospective parents, Hawken explains some of the Hawken School philosophy: "The question of education is much simpler than we imagine, and most of what is written and spoken on the subject serves but to obscure that which is plain. Its object is to provide vigor and activity of body, mind and conscience. To this end the whole process of teaching and discipline should be made subservient."

A few paragraphs later: "My whole point is that spiritual qualities (Initiative, truthfulness, sincerity, courage, thoroughness, reverence, etc.) are infinitely more important to his present charm and future achievement than the most complete knowledge of writing, arithmetic, history, grammar, classics and natural science ....

"Tis not a body that we are training up, but a man, and we ought not to divide him."

If anyone ever had any doubts about Hawken's pluck in holding the school strictly to its founding principles, no matter how favored might be the student or the parent, note parts of the letter he felt forced to write to the major school benefactor:

November 22, 1921

My dear Mr. Bolton:

I am sorry to have to bother you with the matter of this letter but I can see no other way out of it.

The Saturday morning make-up period was instituted after much careful study and deliberation. It was not made effective until it had been brought to the attention of the boys and their parents .... You can imagine, then, the embarrassing position in which the school was placed when the only boy to fail to appear when he was requested to do so was Charley. The boys know that his failure was due to the fact that you did not see the wisdom of his coming.

It has had this result: In the eyes of the boys Charley is privileged because his parents are building a school for Mr. Hawken. In the minds of some parents ... it simply confirms the report that I have been bought by your wealth; and in the mind of Charley it can't help but undermine the authority of the school and consequently lessen the good the school can do for him ....

Charley's failure to appear on Saturday last and take his medicine with the other boys has created a most embarrassing situation for me and has given Charley a suggestion which is not for his good. I can't see any other course open to me but to ask Charley to report at nine a.m., December third, for the next Saturday make-up period .... The reputation of the school, the discipline of the school, and Charley's own standing in the school, I think, demand this.

     .... [E]ven so I do wish that you had sent Charley last Saturday and then had it out with me afterwards....

Sincerely yours,
James Hawken

The relationship between Chester Bolton and Jim Hawken had the strength of frank plain dealing with no beating around the semantics. This respectful candor fired both directions. On November 19, 1922, Bolton critiqued Hawken's financial management, and Hawken respected the other man's expertise:

December 15, 1922

My dear Mr. Bolton:

     ... I wish to say with all possible force that I unreservedly approved and accepted the system you installed for the operating department of the school. I feel that it is imperative that you should have a record of my absolute respect for and support of this system.

Hawken's long response concedes financial management failure, but beyond that the letter is further quoted here because it reveals, as no paraphrasing could, some other important nuances of the founder's state of mind during this quantum transition from Ansel Road:

     The present business management is a failure. My hands have been tied and I have been powerless to avoid mistakes or to effect remedies. It is aside from the question, perhaps, that I want you to know that I am almost completely discouraged.

Just what are we to do? There is one thing that we must not lose sight of. This is a very experimental year. In spite of our carefully studied-out budget I am convinced now that we cannot know what the operating expenses will be.... Relative to our past experiences, our expenses are enormous and our income per boy considerably less. I wish I could give you some insight into my mental state.... Now that you and Mrs. Bolton have taken over the responsibility of meeting the deficit ... running expenses keep piling up beyond your own careful estimate—when I consider these things I wonder whether I have not undertaken a task, if not beyond my ability, at any rate so inconsistent with my temperament as to destroy whatever genius I've had as the head of a boy's school. I find myself afraid and limited by fear. It may be that I have chosen a kind of education for our boys that is practically and from a financial point of view, too expensive. I am every day now fighting depression.

I don't wish to put any more burden on your shoulders nor am I trying to run away from an unpleasant task. I feel the school is my school only in the sense that I am the keeper of its ideals and must keep alive the spirit of the boys and its teachers.

... I hope you can give me some of your time for a meeting before the 20th, and then tell me frankly what you think are our weak points. At that meeting we may find a remedy for our poor business conditions.

Sincerely yours,
James Hawken

Miss Charlesworth, who was treasurer, resigned during this turmoil. A letter from her to Chester Bolton seems to indicate that she was financially very capable and was not given attention or support by Hawken to do the job she was well qualified to do.

Hawken was mostly absent during the summer and, when present, indecisive in financial matters.

MR. HAWKEN'S FINANCIAL MAN FRIDAY

On a Saturday morning in late December of 1922 Horace Aylard, a noticeably neat, noticeably proper young teller stood at his window at the Guardian Trust at East 105th and Euclid. As he remembers the event, "In walked a handsome, immaculately dressed man who seemed somewhat upset. He came to my window." The customer's problem, it developed, was that the Cleveland Trust branch across the street had mixed up his personal account, J. A. Hawken, with the account of Hawken School. So he wanted to open at Guardian a personal account.

Young Aylard proficiently opened the new account. When the signature cards were completed he commented, "Too bad to be working on a Saturday."

The new customer said, "Well, maybe you won't always have to work on Saturday."

Aylard thought no more about it until the following week when he was invited by the new customer to have lunch with him at the Union Club. "He called for me in a chauffeur driven car," Aylard remembers. "Jim Hawken did not drive."

Aylard explains, "Mr. Hawken [at this remove Aylard still only refers to him as "Mister"] hated money matters. Didn't want anything to do with it."

With a view to the possibility of Aylard becoming bursar, Hawken invited him to his office and then to look at the whole school plant. Horace Aylard remembers vividly, "Mr. Hawken's office had two stand-up telephones, and ferns and books."

Horace Aylard went to work as bursar, and made it his mission to see that Mister Hawken never had to get into the money matters. Aylard later became treasurer, attended the board meetings, and worked with Tom White and Liv Ireland and Henry Sheffield on the financial side. He held the post until 1942.

LYNDHURST

A classic colonial building made of Harvard brick rose in an open field in Lyndhurst, Ohio.

You'll remember there was rising parental resistance to moving out to the country. To counter, Mr. Hawken abruptly moved classes to the unfinished structure in the spring of 1922. Parents whose children were enrolled would not pull them mid-year; they would be fairly settled in by the end of the school year, and therefore would not have the summer months to think about changing schools. Thus the unusual birth date for the Lyndhurst campus—April 19.

During Easter vacation in the spring of 1922 the faculty moved school furniture to the new building, arranged transportation for students, and engaged a cook for noon meals.

The first and second grades moved to a house on East 96th Street. Frank Teagle, '32-I, John's young brother, remembers the younger boys did not have desks; they sat on the floor in a circle around Miss Luehrs.

The entire school was twelve faculty and one hundred students.

On April 19, 1922 the other grades, three through nine, and faculty boarded a trolley supplied by Cleveland and Eastern Interurban and rode to the country village of Lyndhurst. From the end of the car line they walked a mile to the new building, making jokes about the end of the world. Except for Jim Hawken and the dedicated Horace Aylard, this school had a sense of humor.

The memorable day was described by a student author in a later yearbook: "Over rickety duck boards in a sea of mud, we walked toward the beautiful building. Outside the building were piles of mud, lakes of mud and mud sandtraps for losing baseballs and smaller boys in."

The eighth graders looked away from the teacher in surprise one day to see an equally surprised horse sticking his head in the window.

The new campus was proof of the power of environment. Noticeably emphatic boost in morale of students and faculty occurred ... and a sense of Hawken as an institution.

The acreage around the school building gave competitive sports real space to develop.

On the fifteenth day of June a ceremony formally dedicated the new campus. Warren Hayden presided. His son, Sherman, then in the ninth grade, was in that first class of nineteen in 1915 and made an acceptance speech for these boys. Present as well were other Hawken pioneers, Jim, David, and William Weir; Patterson Bole; Charles Bolton, and Alvah Drake.

The estimate of this new building had been $219,245 with the possibility of coming in twenty percent below that. The final bill, however, was $377,363.

Beyond the land, the Boltons gave more than two hundred thousand dollars. That would be only a beginning.

ROBERTA BOLE

The move to Lyndhurst naturally raises thoughts of the founder. Why is she not prominent in the news of the move? First, she backed away from all news about herself. Secondly, she was very busy at that time, launching another major education innovation.

Five-foot-five-inch Roberta Bole became a giantess. Modest, even shy, always refusing to have her picture taken, she was electric, starting large new civic projects.

Roberta and Benjamin Patterson Boles

Bedeviled by a hundred enthusiasms—birds, trees, animals, education, art, music, theater, books—the days were cruelly too short to start every new venture. Extremely pretty, pale, blond, but too busy to be stylish, her projects were so large they required enlisting hundreds of people and several institutions. Her recruiting approaches were not assertive; instead gentle—but stubborn.

A hungry reader, she was largely self-educated. A remarkable childhood friendship with her brother

Albert Holden, built around birds and plants and animals, grew into a rare adult loyalty. It would later produce an heroic story of a sister's devotion and a distinguished national institution, the Holden Arboretum.

After founding Hawken School, she had another education urgency nagging her. A particular attitude in public schools troubled her deeply. Generally, top school administrators believed that the brilliant student will get along well enough in school and in life because of his brilliance. Therefore, the teacher should concentrate effort on the less able pupils. Roberta felt keenly that this priority deprived the gifted child of equal education in that it did not give equal attention to the potential of the gifted. She believed we were therefore wasting our brilliant young people who could be contributing great benefits to society. How many Edisons or Einsteins were we wasting for lack of proportionally suitable education?

She did not mean wealthy children; she meant that a special, advanced education for gifted children should be in the public schools.

She went to work on this by approaching many people but, importantly, the Women's City Club of Cleveland, enlisting their leverage.

As a result, the Cleveland board of education adopted and launched her concept as the Major Work Program, coordinated by Dorothy E. Norris. It began in 1921 with twenty-five high-IQ youngsters in grades four, five, and six at Denison School. Conversational French was included in the curriculum.

From that beginning, the program expanded to lower grades in other Cleveland public schools. Children with IQs of 125 and above were able to enter these Major Work classes. Visitors were startled to see the students learning French, German, and Russian, building working models of human organs, and grading each other's work. Fifth graders were assigned four books a week to read, eighth grade math studied the stock market.

So, while the private school she founded moved into the new Hawken building in the country, the Major Work Program she founded was starting in the city. It would blossom into a nationally emulated concept; and from Cleveland alone it would graduate thousands of young people who went on to distinguished careers in the professions and business. Not until the 1950s was it widely known that Major Work was a Roberta Bole project.

STRANGE COMBINATION

One of the amazing characteristics of the early Hawken faculty, which Toughy Smeed's son called "that marvelous accident of human chemistry," was a strange combination of tenderness and temper.

Charles R. Stephens, the math teacher who served until 1958-59, was notably gentle with boys, Char Hickox remembers: "He would help me find my rubbers so I wouldn't miss my bus." On the other hand he was known as the school's strictest disciplinarian. Al Conkey, '31-I, remembers Stephens "climbing onto the desk with flushed face and both hands cupped to the mouth yelling out the class rules." Ted deConingh, '44, remembers the day the whole class earned an historic one hundred percent on the homework. Stephens complimented them on it. The class, therefore, later approached him requesting a reward for that first-time accomplishment. Stephens answered, "Why should you be rewarded for doing exactly what is expected of you?" DeConingh said, "The lesson stuck with me for life."

David Weir, '27, remembers Stephens, "the boss," as "kindly but *very* firm. I remember clearly his statement, 'There are two reasons for not doing your homework: sickness and death ... preferably death.'"

"Stephens was kindly," John Price recalls, "but strict. When Herb Spring ['36] fell asleep in class Stephens flung an eraser at him which ricocheted off two walls and clonked Herb on the head. Tended to keep your attention in class."

John Finley, '38, remembers Stephens as very formal in class. He always stood. And he was demanding; if you could mentally skip one step in a math problem on the blackboard, he would not accept that.

That early faculty was extremely considerate of each other. Yet Morris Everett, Sr., '27, remembers that Carney's temper even exploded against his boss. Carney was generally considered the number-two man. Hawken phoned him during class time. After the call, Carney stormed down the hall to Hawken's office, "If you ever call me in class again, I quit!" Everett also recalls the day Carney threw David Weir out the classroom window into the bushes for throwing a blackboard eraser.

"Mr. Carney was full of heat lightning," Char Hickox remembers.

Ross MacMahon, described by John Price as that "big old Caledonian," would tirelessly create a year-long continued story about Captain Dingle for the boys riding the interurban to and from school. "However, if irritated in class, he would yell, 'Get out!' like Barrymore doing Scrooge."

The huge MacMahon, with the fearsome overhang of eyebrows, who would be at Hawken for decades, carried his favorite chair with him from class to class. Sterling Hubbard, '29, remembers the chair was "beat up and loose." Once the boys took the chair apart and reassembled it just barely. When MacMahon next sat down, "the chair totally collapsed. He asked us who did it. No one would squeal. So he kept us until six o'clock."

John H. McCarthy, the Jesuit trained Latin teacher with a percussive Celtic diction and reddish hair, looked to young Francis Silver, '30, like a Roman senator. He carried a wonderfully shabby and overstuffed book bag. He would not yell, but according to John Price, "he would grab you and shake you up, a no-nonsense teacher." Impatient for answers in class, he tapped his foot audibly; and if a succession of responders failed, he would turn exasperated to the star pupil, "Tell 'em, Benny [Schneider, '30]!"

Phelan, the French teacher, was especially short-fused. He once threw an ink well at a boy, missed, hit the wall, and splashed it. The school hung a map over it. Old boys lifted the edge of the map to show new boys "what Mr. Phelan is like."

By contrast, two of these pioneering teachers spread waves of tranquility. Toughy Smeed was absolutely unflappable. This man loved the classroom, as a later headmaster would say, "better than eating." He was totally confident of his way of handling boys. Not even the second toughest kid in school could make him blink.

MissLuehrs (the two words always elide like that) was part of this paradox. Commanding immense respect because of her tall beauty, she was, on the other hand, the gentlest of them all. If a six year old needed to be cuddled, he was enclosed in a caring arm and a faint bouquet of attar of roses.

Wally Wallace, phys-ed, was a great jokester. Mona Eckert, secretary to the headmaster (1923-32, between Louise Shroeder and Holly Prescott), remembers he called her from downtown where he had gone to instruct the primary boys, "I'll be late back to Lyndhurst for my other classes because I'm carrying the dead from the Cleveland Clinic fire to Cyrus Eaton's home."

"Oh s-u-r-r-e you are."

However, it was true. Wallace drove past the clinic, saw the painters trying to get a ladder up to the windows where smoke poured out. He braked his Ford, helped place the ladder and climbed up. When he reached the window a Dr. Phillips yelled, "Get the hell out of here! They're dying like flies in here!"

However, Wallace continued rescuing people.

He returned for his Lyndhurst classes, but was evacuated to the Bolton estate for a week to recover from smoke inhalation.

But Wallace's heroism was also good education for the boys by example.

James Hawken, of only medium height, walked tall. Aging alumni describe their boyhood impressions of him in the most extreme terms ... "a noble look" ... "saint-like" ... "piercing blue eyes riveted your attention." He would "put his hands on both sides of your face and draw you out and listen to you intently. He made you important." In fact the overwhelming final impression of Hawken by both faculty and students was that he created a climate of *respect.* It may have been the paramount distinguishing feature of the school.

He could not see a human being demeaned. Coming across a penalized boy assigned to sit the hall, Hawken said, "If it's embarrassing sitting here, why don't you go to the end of the hall by the encyclopedia and read. It will look like that's why you're out here."

The boys were not that gentle with each other. The line into chapel or dining room was occasionally blocked because Willie, '27, and Jim Weir, '25, were in another fight.

One morning Rigan McKinney, '26, walked up to Steven Burke, '27, and without announcement knocked him flat. The ensuing battle and its origin are widely known. In the Corrigan-McKinney Company (steel), both families owned forty-eight percent. Judge Burke, for his fee in putting the company together, had taken four percent of the stock. In a battle for control both families bid for Judge Burke's stock. The judge accepted the Corrigan's offer, giving them control. Rigan McKinney came to school upset.

Bill Nash remembers Price and Rigan McKinney were chauffeured to school in the only Mercedes the boys had seen. It had an open front seat.

Courtney Burton, '30, reigned for several years as the toughest kid. That was very good for the school in interscholastic sports, but hard on classmates. A new boy, Francis Silver, came to Hawken, particularly because in prior visits he found it "much friendlier than public school. A happy place, where you wouldn't have to fight for your space."

That was true, basically. But Courtney decided to challenge the new kid with a couple of test nudges that escalated to punches and counter punches which drew a crowd. Faculty broke it up, but Robert S.

"Hardtop" Adams, who felt Hawken boys were a little soft, thought it would be good to formalize this debate in the ring with gloves, which was done. Burton won.

However, possibly the most fondly remembered Hawken custom was the end of the day. As the boys left school, Mort Smeed shook hands with each Lower Schooler, and Charles Stephens with each Upper Schooler, exchanging a word with *each* boy. Then the boys shook hands with the headmaster. As Jim Ireland, '32-I, remembers, "so that no boy ended with a bad day." The custom continued through several headmasters and still continues in grades kindergarten through five.

4. "Trying To Get Up My Courage To Return"

GROWTH generates growth.

Achieving and settling into the new building should have earned for the staff and endowment association a pause to regroup.

Instead, as in any breakthrough, it opened up scores of new opportunity avenues which would not wait. The new quarters by themselves seemed to generate three years of innovations, not always to James Hawken's liking. And the new plant, with a kind of autonomy of its own, usurped some control from central administration.

For example, you will remember some parents' concern about getting their boys to a school so far away in the country. However, Eastern Traction Company provided one special trailer for Hawken students, the red car. Its schedule becomes relevant. It left Cedar Avenue and Stearns at 8:25, arriving Coventry 8:30 and Mayfield-Richmond 9:09, a mile hike from the campus. A return car for the younger grades brought boys home at 1:00 p.m., the older boys at 5:00. A master or two rode with the boys.

Notice this schedule in effect created four more Hawken assemblies, *off* campus. Hawken masters, being what they were, would not let that time be wasted. Hence we find several kinds of quasi-official school activity going on ... *away* from school. Suspenseful were Mr. MacMahon's ad-libbed marathon yarns of Captain Dingle. One teacher instructed the boys in playing bridge. Sometimes the boys entertained each other with improvised serializations, "Jake and his Bed Tick" and "Rex and His Back Scratcher."

Laudable? Certainly. But it became a significant part of Hawken life, not on campus; and we will see other activities grow out of the trolley rides.

As to the influence of the campus itself, grand open space gave room for the young animals to charge full force without running into the Ansel Road fence or the barn.

Additionally for any boy who wanted to grow flowers or vegetables, a ten-by-twelve-foot plot of ground was available, Chester Bolton overseeing.

Interestingly, before the lunch bell rang at twelve-thirty, the dining tables in the gym folded down out of the walls for lunch which ascended by dumb waiter from a basement kitchen. One master dined at each table of boys except the upper classman table where occasionally Jim Hawken sat.

Since most boys were accustomed at home to fine buildings, one might expect them to take the new building for granted. To the contrary, the first classes moving up from Ansel Road took a proprietary pride in it, as if they had built it. House committees were formed in each grade for putting the rooms in order with teaching materials stowed correctly.

This new school's grounds became a growth force by increasing the pressure to mount more interscholastic teams in more sports.

The tremendous outdoor space available for practice (coupled with larger enrollment) vastly improved sports practice and increased confidence in an area where confidence had once been shattered, witness the 1922 baseball season:

Hawken 15   Lyndhurst 1
Hawken 29   Lyndhurst 6
Hawken 9   S. Euclid 8
Hawken 14   Bratenahl 7

Interest in baseball rose and in 1923 the great Tris Speaker of the Cleveland Indians addressed assembly.

The football season was also successful.

Since the new theatre was largely designed by K. Elmo Lowe, it was logical for him to direct its first play, *Robin Hood*. In turn, the high professionalism of Lowe of the Cleveland Play House, which under his guidance would achieve national distinction, set a quality pace and high interest in Hawken productions which endures today.

Sports and the school plays were dominant activities because everyone was involved. Athletics were required, "unless you have a note from the doctor saying you're dead." In the plays, those who weren't in the cast were making costumes, building sets, printing programs and tickets or handling lighting, promotion or clean-up. Hiram Haydn wrote some of the scripts.

COMPETITION AS EDUCATOR

Jim Hawken's concept of life and of education had gentle overtones—collegial cooperation and fraternity—student to student, faculty to faculty and faculty to student. "A family" was his habitual phrasing.

However, the off-campus world is seldom thus. Hence among the boys in late 1922 arrived another concept ... competition.

Begin with a seemingly innocuous event.

Faculty member Glenn A. Dowling was riding home with the boys on the red car in the spring when he suggested a vote be taken on selecting some school colors. The next day, in a special election, the boys voted: Maroon and gray, four votes; blue and white, six; blue and gray, nine; red and gray, nineteen votes.

Red and Gray won. But the heraldry aspect of it was least important. The real effect grew from dividing the boys into the Reds and Grays. While not a totally original idea, it was very effective. All alumni remember which team they were on. Once enlisted, you were on that team for life. The competition permeated all activities. A point system developed:

An "A" for the month equalled two points; a "B" one; a "D" minus one, and an "E" minus two.

Points were earned for making first team in any sport or a position in any extracurricular activity.

The first elected captains of the Reds were Jim Weir and John Lincoln, '26; the Grays, Edward Maeder, '25, and Bob Cleveland, '26. The judgment of the electorate was prophetic as one watches the later careers of these natural leaders.

The first month the Grays won by eleven points. The competition ran so tight that, for example, the period ending January 31, 1924 tied at 625 points; the two highest individual scorers for October-November were Richard Inglis of the Grays, thirty-eight points; Ben Schneider, thirty-seven.

Competition tested the boys against the Fair Play banner. For example, at one point the Reds were deprived of the services of Jim McNabb, '25, for an extended period. Competing one man short, they petitioned faculty saying their score should be augmented at least by the average of the whole school. The Grays rejected this, counter-proposing: We'll give the Reds the monthly average of the lost student.

Vikings and Cyclops were later established as farm teams for the Reds and Grays.

Competing became a dominating and motivating force over the decades; and it cannot be denied that, as a case hardening around Jim Hawken's softer fraternal concept, it equipped generations of boys to go out into the competitive, sometimes hostile world ... and achieve.

Competition sparks were fanned by increasing numbers of honors and prizes. With no intent to document all these, a one-time look at the awards for one year is informative (June 14, 1923):

Head Boy, Jim Weir, '25, "contributed most to
    the school."
First Honors in Upper School,
    Sherman Hayden '24
Second Honors in Upper School,
    Kirke Lincoln '26
First Honors in Lower School,
    Richard Inglis '29
Second Honors in Lower School,
    Dudley Blossom '29
Scholar Athlete, Kirke Lincoln
Leadership in Fair Play, Age 3-7,
    Kenyon Bolton '30
History Prize, Patterson Bole '25
7th Grade Latin Prize, P. McKinney '28

6th Grade Latin Prize, Richard Inglis

Grade Honors:
    8th Stevenson Burke '27
    7th Price McKinney '28
    6th Richard Inglis '29
    5th Benny Schneider '30
    4th Fayette Brown '31
    3rd Herman Peck '32

Leadership medals:
    Price McKinney, Richard Hooker, Kenyon
    Bolton, Alex Brown, Winthrop Barnes, and
    William Osborne.

The effect of the new school plant was equally invigorating to faculty. A teacher no longer had to explain to friend, enemy, or himself that this was a real school with a special concept. It announced itself even though the primary grades in 1924 were still in town, moved from 2026 E. 96th Street to the parish house of Emmanuel Church at 8614 Euclid Avenue. (In 1929 primary moved to Lyndhurst.)

In the new location John Carney charged into class with even crisper manner, "Get ready to spell!" Charles Stephens lost nostalgia for the view from the Catskills above the Hudson.

Beginnings

Among the carpeted offices was a faculty room with tan and black drapes, a large table in the center for periodicals and wicker chairs. The room was lined with white bookcases. Here the masters read and conferred. Will this spoil a faculty accustomed to firing the boiler and shoveling snow?

On the contrary, the new teacher conference room became an idea incubator which crowded the next three years at Lyndhurst with beginnings.

In 1924 Phelan started the glee club.

The orchestra began.

Smeed started the Cartoon Club.

The debating society began.

The beginning: on the porch at 1572 Ansel Road

Clockwise (above): James A. Hawken and Fannie Luehrs; Miss Rowland; and Miss Luehrs, Mr. Motto, et al

Clockwise (upper left):
First Grade, June 1921 (top): Jimmy Ireland, Bill Osborne, and Stephen Blossom; (middle): Louis Baldwin, Henry Harvey, Everett Shoales, Timmy Perkins, Willard Brown, and Bee Peck; (bottom): Winthrop Barnes and John Harshaw
Circa 1921: Stephen Blossom embraces pals John Harshaw and Timmy Perkins
The primary department moved into this house at 2026 East 96th Street in the fall of 1922.
The first grade attending 1922-23 (left to right): Timmy Cheney, Jimmy Hoyt, Gilbert Humphrey, Robert Bishop, Teddy Brown, Franklin Bowler, Claude Peck, Edward Lenihan, and Frank White
Fayette Brown, with unidentified friend sneaking into the shot

Mr. Hawken (top photo) in class and Mr. Motto (bottom photo) and future sculptors

Mr. Phelan (top photo) in class; Miss Luehrs (bottom left photo) with first grade class; and (bottom right photo) the front stoop at East 96th was a popular place. Here Willard Brown reads to Billy Osborne (on his left) and Everett Shoales. Jimmy Ireland appears uninterested in the story.

The camera was ready in any weather. The winter shot features (left to right) Mason Williams, Billy Calfee, Hubbard Little, Malcolm Vilas, Jimmy Hoyt, Teddy Brown, and Henry Williams.

The newly completed school in the country

In progress (top and middle photos) and open for learning (bottom photo)

Fair Play

The building was not quite ready for them but the boys look ready for anything!

The courtyard and long-time resident, Pan

The sunlit chapel

Faculty meeting room

Mr. Hawken's office

The gymnasium

Typical classroom

Attention to detail is evident, even in the halls.

WOODIES!

The newspaper, *Hawken School Review* begun in 1921, became more sophisticated in 1922. It reported on the formation of three intramural baseball teams—Columbia, Bears, Indians.

It reported on three camps which Hawken boys attended and Hawken faculty staffed—Camps Mowana in Maine, Camp Chagrin, and Camp Mowgli in New Hampshire.

First Scholarships

An interesting situation triggered Hawken's first scholarships to outside boys. For the school year 1923-24, the eleventh grade had enough boys, but one boy was ready for twelfth grade, a senior class of one. While the particular boy may have been "in a class by himself," faculty felt more boys were needed to give competition to the lone senior. It could not recruit more paying students for the class; hence the school offered three full scholarships to boys from South Euclid, a Lyndhurst neighbor.

Year of Tumult
1924

This history cannot chronicle all faculty arrivals and departures, but 1924 requires it. Five new faculty arrived. William Baker signed on to teach French; A. Irwin Leishman came on for manual training, drawing and football; E. C. Pietsch for geography and science; Dorothy Leece for music. There also arrived the handsome square-jawed Latin and phys-ed teacher, John A. McCarthy. Via Latin he taught the power of muscle. Good teachers would come and go, but McCarthy soon joined the legendary permanent corps. Hawken graduates whom McCarthy had bruised came back to visit him for counsel for years to come.

Brand new "ancient traditions" started monthly. James Hawken hung the Head Boy panel in the chapel. Two names were on it—James Weir and Sherman Hayden.

The football team became more formalized with

a better schedule planned for next year, and they elected the right halfback, Char Bolton, captain; David Weir, manager.

FOUNTAINHEAD

Some of the newer people who assembled on June 8, 1924 did not really realize the full significance of this occasion until the youngest speaker, Sherman Hayden, '24, took the podium speaking to and for his classmates. "We are unique. We are the first graduating class ever sent out from Hawken School .... Some of us who are leaving today have been through the school from its infancy ... at 1572 Ansel Road .... And now for my classmates I must say good-bye, to you Mr. Hawken, and ... to this beautiful building and to these woods and fields." He closed, "No matter where we go ... let us give a good account of ourselves, for in so doing we are rendering the highest possible tribute to Hawken School."

Graduations are always significant, but this one left marks.

The Reds presented the school with the flag for the front lawn.

The young commencement speaker presented to the school the fountain for the courtyard. Seen as a fine decorative piece by the crowd, few knew then that it would become a magnetic and mystical centrum for alumni for decades.

Immediately following the graduation of this first class, the boys formed the Hawken Club (Alvah Drake, '25, president) which became the Hawken Alumni Association which would quickly grow to the point where it published *The Hawken School Alumni Bulletin,* Vol. 1, No. 1, 1927. A decade later there would be 187 members, 129 of whom would be active.

James Hawken witnessed the graduation of some boys who were in his very first class. Under his gentle, tender concept of education, how would these boys fare out in the world's rough and tumble? Were they motivated?

Hawken would watch over the years. What he saw

justified his tiny 1916 brochure ... "the raison d'etre of the school is the boy." He saw Jim Weir graduate from Harvard and become a skillful attorney. He saw Sherman Hayden mature and come back to take an active role in sustaining this school.

"Trying To Get Up My Courage To Return"

James A. Hawken, although only forty-two years of age, was physically drained from the intensity of the past half decade. Additionally he suffered a then incurable affliction, tic douloureux, which created pounding headaches. He planned a belated sabbatical leave in 1923. However, he postponed this because of the serious illness of his mother. She died that year.

On November 29, 1924 James Hawken sailed on the *S.S. Duitio* to Genoa. Carney moved to acting head.

Steve Blossom, '32-I, was taken to Europe that year. Suddenly in Paris he began yanking his parents toward a pedestrian he wanted them to meet. They didn't know why. Steve had spotted "Mr. Hawken." Steve recently explained why he and many of the boys thrived on the individual attention at Hawken. Many of the boys' parents, extremely occupied with major national careers or very active civic and social calendars, left the children in care of nurses and household staffs. This observation was repeated by several alumni.

From Italy, France, Switzerland, Hawken sent back to the faculty affectionate messages in his small, level handwriting on postcard photos of art museums and statues.

One mysterious line in a postcard from Switzerland to faculty member R. A. Slavin, *"Trying to get up my courage to return."*

The Shock

Jim Hawken did return.
He appeared reinvigorated.

Suddenly, however, at the close of the 1925-26 school year, James A. Hawken, still a young man—resigned.

Education professionals were aware of history; hundreds of educational institutions, seated much more firmly than Hawken School, exit when the founder exits.

Experienced faculty, friends, and parents knew that Hawken School had only a fingerhold on existence. Many beautiful private school buildings have been easily converted to hospitals, city halls, nursing homes, or corporate headquarters. Despite the new faces on the faculty, James Hawken and his original faculty corps had been the real spiritual—if not official—cement.

One more failed educational experiment would be only a small item in one day's very local newspaper.

5. Mr. Carney

THERE WERE emotional good-bye dinners in parent homes.

There were small faculty farewell get-togethers. There was one large faculty meeting on June 11, 1926, expressing tremendous gratitude to Hawken.

Health—was the opaque response to the overwhelming question. Why?

Jim Hawken, on the very best of terms with the endowment association, named Frances Bolton his successor in the proprietorship. You'll remember Hawken had to start the school himself, and was sole proprietor. Money and property were held in trust for the school by the association.

Jim Hawken promised to do the search for his successor as headmaster. Actually, he had long since been doing that, and he was leaning toward John Carney.

* * *

It becomes important to look at John Carney. At this distance we can only do that through the eyes of people who knew him. In doing so we find John Carney was not a monolithic personality like a Hawken or Smeed or MacMahon or Stephens. Carney was a different person to different people. Intense, serious, brisk, very precise, a bachelor in 1926, Carney was an English teacher with a sense of mission about the subject. "But he couldn't spell," grins Mona Eckert, secretary to the headmaster from 1923 to 1932.

To some boys Carney *was* the school.

To Edgar Taylor, '26, "John Carney was very important in my life. I stayed in contact for years." Taylor became a teacher.

Others found him as David Weir did, "calm and cool behind rimless glasses, colorless and remote except when mad."

On the other hand Francis Silver, who remembers

John J. Carney

Carney's speech as "especially crisp, clear, and pleasant in tone, with gray hair over a very youthful face," cites evidence that Carney would go to tremendous extremes to help a single boy. Francis' brother got in trouble because as student manager of athletic equipment he had the storage key. Some older boys, whose good opinion he coveted, inveigled him into getting out equipment for them after hours. The Silver boy was in major trouble with Carney. But as Francis tells it, "John Carney came to the house every morning in his Chevrolet for weeks to drive Dan to school and talk things out."

While some found John Carney distant and severe, Bill Nash, '29, considered him "much more of a mixer than Mr. Hawken."

Faculty member David Russell said, "He had a way of getting along with people. He never gave orders."

Apparently well before Hawken actually retired he had asked Carney if he would accept the post of headmaster. A paragraph or two would be enough of an answer for most men today. But, on January 13, 1926, John Carney required five pages, single-spaced, to reply. Although not essential to this narrative, parts are presented here because they reveal, in the midst of apparent closeness, a strangely stilted kind of respect. There are two pages of demurrer followed by these excerpts:

> In saying this I am vividly conscious that some of us are going to miss you—not only personally, but in our need for inspiration in our contact with the life of the School— John Carney most particularly—yet even this knowledge is now no longer influencing my thought. *I have come to the crossroads that you set before me, reluctantly, and with no little sorrow:* I agree wholly ... that you have finished your work here, that the time of departure has come—that you too, like Almustafa, the Prophet, have "climbed the hill without the city walls and looked seaward" and have beheld your "ships coming

with the mist."

Now John Carney carries this poem on for eight more stanzas, then returns to this:

I have only a word or two more—the first, about the actual "successor." If you are still unequivocally of the same mind that I am the one who should control the immediate future of the School, I am ready to accept the responsibility. But I should infinitely prefer that the wording of the "transfer" be such that I be named more as the representative of a group than as one individual. Life is so filled with the unexpected and Death is always so close at hand, that it seems to me too insecure a thing to convey to but one individual the future of our School.

Further than this, I feel that our parents and the public at large will have a greater sense of security of solidarity if you convey it to me as President of a Board of Trustees of my own choosing, or in some such manner. This, however, I am quite happy to leave for your decision.

I am curiously certain that you are simply awaiting my answer to your expressed desires, my release of you from the request to stand by until I could reach this point of decision which has now been reached; that if your bags are not already packed, they stand open; that another life is beckoning, and that your desire is pressing you on. Just what has convinced me of this I do not know—but the thought is ever present with me.

I know how keenly you feel that once a decision is reached no good comes from postponement of action, so that I realize that almost over night you will probably be gone.

This goes over to you by hand this morning. If you want to see me and will let me know sometime before 8:30 tomorrow, Fri-

day morning, I can re-arrange my appointments tomorrow afternoon so as to be here
at home between three and six. I need not
tell you that I shall be so glad to do this
should you desire it.

"If in the twilight of memory we should
meet once more, we shall speak again together and you shall sing to me a deeper
song.

"And if our hands should meet in another dream we shall build another tower in
the sky."

Etc.

* * *

John Carney couldn't stroll, only charge. His style
of leadership leaned less to colorful innovation. He
joylessly, but faithfully, attended the river of administrative chores. "He dressed like a banker," recalls
Sterling Hubbard. Of course Hubbard's opinion
could be biased, being himself a fun-loving type who
flew for the Army, Navy, and Pan Am, and brags
that he lasted at Yale, "two hours and ten minutes,
including lunch."

John Carney's real love was teaching. Concerning
the headmastership he told Mona Eckert, "this administration job I just don't like!"

When Jim Hawken walked out of the office
bound for California, he told Eckert, "I know Mr.
Carney won't write me about problems here, so you
tell me what's happening."

Carney commissioned Western Reserve University to make a sweeping survey of Hawken School to
see what improvements might be indicated, particularly on organizational lines.

David Russell remembers Carney as a headmaster
who gave powerful support to his faculty. Russell's
evidence is worthwhile here because it reveals much
more about the school. Russell came out of three and
a half years of Wharton School of Finance into the
credit department of Newman Stearns, sporting
equipment.

I didn't find the work that exciting. Got

a fellowship to Bexley Hall, Kenyon, to become a minister. After a year there ... Greek, history, and such ... I decided—not my calling. Came back to Western Reserve, took a masters in science, but didn't know what to do with it.

He was walking on East 84th Street near Euclid when he ran into an old friend, Mort Smeed.

Mort said, "You ever think of teaching?"

"No."

"Come out to Hawken and look around."

I went out and looked. Mr. Carney was the headmaster.

Later Mort called me, "We need a special science teacher in a hurry. Would you be interested in trying it?"

"Yes."

When I got out there, suddenly there was a vacancy in third grade. John Carney said, "If you'll take the third grade I'll raise the salary to $2,000."

Parents always wanted to talk to a prospective new teacher before hiring. So Russell was invited to several parents' homes for dinner, and passed the test.

Fifteen kids came to the third grade. They were high IQ hellions and full of steam. I could not control them—they just raised hell with me.

I went to John Carney and told him I couldn't do this. He said all I needed was a little more practice. "Go back and keep at it."

I explained that he didn't realize how bad it was, "Why the other day the whole class actually jumped out the window on me and escaped."

Carney said, "No Hawken class ever threw a teacher, and they're not going to throw you." Carney volunteered to come into the class and help. However, these hellions even defeated Carney.

Carney said that if Russell would stick it out, the school would come up with the money to send him to a six-week seminar at Western Reserve for teachers on the art of classroom teaching.

Well, I attended the seminar. Didn't get much out of it except one crucial point ... which stood me in good stead the rest of my career: Don't start a lesson with the subject you want to teach, start with a subject the boys want to learn.

As a result, Russell opened new subjects with a variety of props which led to the subject he was about to teach. For example, in opening a segment on math, he brought his own printing press into class. The boys were fascinated by the press, hardly realizing that typesetting is a very mathematic process. When he opened a segment on writing papers, he proposed they write papers they could print on the press, and sell as a class publication. For a science segment he brought a camera. He got into photography and the developing of the pictures from the negatives.

Russell got the boys to bring in items of interest. He remembers Scott Inkley, '36, later head of University Hospitals. As a boy, Scott loved nature, hated classes. On some occasions "I would send Scott out of the class into the woods to bring in specimens for the next science class ... frogs or whatever."

On another occasion, knowing that Thomas Edison had published a paper, Russell had the boys send a copy of the newspaper they wrote and published, *The Chronicle,* to Edison with a letter. The boys (fifth grade) were excited to receive an answer:

Dear Boys:—The Chronicle has been received. I think it very good. It was better than the little paper I published when I was a news boy on the Grand Trunk Railway.

Thomas Edison.

Other teachers also found Carney's strong backing important in their careers. Elmer Sipple, for example, a superb craftsman hired for manual training, suddenly developed a severe allergy to wood shavings and sawdust. Rather than let him go, Carney gave him a chance to move out of the shop into classroom teaching. Sipple added "and Mort Smeed who had a gift for teaching boys, and teachers as well, helped me enormously." Char Hickox remembers, "Sipple had a great savvy about people—knew which were good and which humbug."

Carney sustained the basic concepts seeded by Jim Hawken. For example, the Fair Play credo did not become outdated or diluted with cynicism. Malcolm Vilas, '33, admits "I still try to live by 'Fair Play' and I'm in the real estate business."

The credo was practiced on campus. Guthrie Bicknell, '30, remembers when Hawken was playing the Lyndhurst junior high football team and leading 13-0 at halftime. During the intermission Bud Humphrey, '32-II, asked coach Wally Wallace, "Do we have extra pairs of cleats in the storage room?"

"Sure, why?"

"Could we give the opponents cleats to even up the game? I'll pay for them."

The opposing team was pleased with the cleats. The fair play did not hurt Hawken—35-0.

John Carney sustained the tradition of the masters saying good night to each boy at day's end. However, in the mid-twenties there were a very large number of boys named Bill. At the end of the day that name was heard all over the school as the boys and teachers said good-night. Ross MacMahon was known to call any boy "Bill" if he forgot the student's real name.

Carney could be very gentle. One afternoon, Benny Schneider came running to Mr. Carney with eyes full of tears exclaiming, "Mr. Carney, I broke Junior Royal's head. Come quick."

Carney, with visions of the poor boy lying on the floor with his brains scattered under the chair, hastened to the gym, where Mr. Dowling was conducting a class.

"Come quick," cried Carney, "hurry." So Mr. Carney and Mr. Dowling, with Benny at their heels, hurried to the far end of the building where on the floor lay a disfigured hunk of clay that was once Mr. Motto's clay sketch of Junior Royal.

The headmaster did not laugh, but he did soothe Ben Schneider's worry.

Another adult source of comfort to boys was John Ciarllilo ("Trilio" to some). He comforted many a sobbing small boy hurt on the athletic field. He would brush them off, stand them up, put a hand on their shoulder, and sing to them a rousing "Giuseppe Garibaldi" until they smiled and trotted back to combat.

John Carney's leadership of the faculty was lauded by many teachers, most of whom cited the same characteristics—firm and very emphatic. However, one teacher had the impression "John Carney never quite got onto the job, as if not comfortable sitting at Jim Hawken's desk."

HAWKEN INCORPORATED

On June 19, 1929 a corps of Hawken friends the reader has largely already met incorporated as the Hawken School Corporation, separate from the Hawken School Endowment Association. The corporation charter was broad and detailed, but basically the purpose was to take over the functions of Jim Hawken's sole proprietorship. Hawken had moved to Santa Barbara, California, with Henry Sheffield, and technically still owned the school. To have the owner two thousand miles away was awkward. Hence the purpose of the new corporation was to operate Hawken School, to own and purchase property, hire and discharge staff, and do all other acts necessary to operations.

The feeling was that Jim Hawken would turn over all proprietary documents to the corporation; in fact he generously volunteered to do this. Awkwardly enough there was substantial delay in implementing transfer, and the board minutes dance a genteel ballet of correspondence around this.

The incorporators were James Hawken, Chester Bolton, Mrs. B. P. Bole, Asa Shiverick, Dr. Joel B. Hayden, Dr. Robert E. Vinson, Dr. Charlton Robinson, Mrs. William Weir, Sherman Hayden, Henry Sheffield; board of trustees: Hawken, Bolton, Vinson, Joel Hayden.

Nearly the first official act of the board was to give John Carney a sabbatical leave beginning October 1929.

Standing in for him as headmaster was Charles R. Stephens, now a veteran of that central faculty corps which built the school. We will see him step into the breach several times in the future.

ROAD BLOCK

An enrollment problem mounted to crisis proportions during Stephens's watch—parents taking their boys out of Hawken to go to eastern prep schools. It was long customary in Cleveland to take boys and girls out of local prep schools and send them to eastern prep schools for admission to eastern colleges. This did not hurt the lower Hawken grades. In the higher grades, however, when a boy returned to Hawken in the fall and found half his friends gone east, he and his parents as well felt forsaken. Further, trustees were beginning to feel that if Hawken could not overcome the role of half-way house to eastern schools, it would not survive.

Therefore, Stephens launched a series of parent meetings to reverse this trend. He felt that if he could get two consecutive seventh grade classes to hang together, he could turn around the mass exodus to eastern prep schools.

From a long, handwritten letter to Frances Bolton some verbatim excerpts tell a lot about the school and their relationship.

December 15, 1929

My dear Mrs. Bolton:

... the Christmas play is in rehearsal and the school is a busy group of stage carpenters, electricians, property men, printers, builders of Christmas toys, craftsmen in Pewter and Silver or copper, or etchers on linoleum for Christmas cards, to say nothing of collections of old clothes and toys for schools in Kentucky.

The Play is developing very well and the Little School is doing a good job with it.

A week ago on Wednesday, Thursday, and Friday I met the parents of the 10th, 9th, & 8th grades respectively. I set forth the relation of parents to the school in its earlier days when almost everyone had the interest of a founder. I pointed out, that should still be the relation, in short that they should first see the school as an idea & an ideal & then as a place for their boy's education to begin. I urged they see the school as a whole & not through their one child as a member. Some duties & obligations as such a member of the school was suggested & incidentally their duty to let others know of their faith in the thing we are trying to do. It was suggested that if each one did his or her job in this connection the school might well have a waiting list of long length & with the greater field of selection an even greater opportunity for finer work. I am placing in the hands of all these parents a list of boys from 5 to 7 yrs from which they may find many of their friends & have the school in mind when the right opportunity presents itself.

... This talk led into a discussion of the Eastern School or the Home plus Hawken.... they believe in the latter. They fear that other parents are sending their children away & do not wish to leave the son in what they term "a residue." I tried to point out that such reasoning created a vicious circle in which each was blaming the other & that it needed only for them to get together & say "My boy will stay" when the rest would follow, "and mine" and mine, etc.

One Dad has already phoned me that if the others of the group will keep their boys here he will. I have written other members of this group ... suggesting they give me advise [sic] on a procedure to answer the above

Dad & I hope for some good. If by some good fortune the 10th group can be kept intact it will have a powerful morale effect upon the younger group. Of course the proportion desiring to go east is about the same as usual, but these groups are also larger than usual & I simply cannot sit by & see these boys go, & do nothing about it....

Your sincere friend
Charles Stephens

The Faculty and Frances Bolton

Frances Bolton communicated with members of the faculty directly, and was concerned about them even after they left the staff. However, the following letter from Smeed to Frances Bolton is partly quoted not for its weight but because it shows the faculty's easy confidence that this woman of the world was interested in the smallest details at Hawken. Smeed, on December 12, 1929, is answering her letter about Jim Hawken:

> The only indication I had that Jim was at all "down" when he left here in November was a remark he made about not being needed or wanted at school. He knows better.... I need him very much and I need both of you. And Steve (Stephens) needs you both whether he thinks so or not and Jim must know it.

Smeed refers to a proposal that Hawken become the nucleus for WRU's Junior College. "Jim's paper argues quite definitely against the plan."

The letter shows that Smeed knew this busy woman was interested in even the slightest school business: "You cannot know what your flowers do for the little school. It would be difficult if we ever have to get along without them .... That was a great idea ... so was the one about the rugs but the rugs, sad to say, can't be revived like the flowers .... I hope you don't expect to find them as fresh as you left them."

Smeed tells about the new library furniture " ... anxious to have you see it. Will you ever be back before we are done with the house? ... The work is so good ... that it is difficult to make people believe the boys did it. As a matter of fact I'm afraid Sipple and Carter in their enthusiasm for perfection, have had too many of their own hands in the work. But the boys think it is all theirs and are wild about it. At present the Christmas play is in process of" ... etc.

ROBERTA'S OTHER SCHOOLS

It is interesting to add up the scope of community education innovations of Roberta Bole and Frances Bolton. We have seen Frances' work in bolstering nursing education and nurturing Hawken School. Roberta founded Hawken, then the Major Work Program for the Cleveland public schools. In the period 1925-31 she labored to establish still another distinguished teaching institution.

She lost her brother, Albert Holden, in 1913. His great dream had been to establish an arboretum on the Holden farm lands. He had often planned with Roberta a huge tract with the right environment to support the largest possible variety of trees and plants from all over the earth. It would have among other functions a primary education mission, a forest where people could see the world's plants on one tract, in so far as this climate and soil would allow. It was to be a center also for training students in botany and horticulture. This mission became Albert's driving purpose, which he constantly plotted with Roberta.

Albert controlled a substantial tract of Holden land. However, implementation of the whole plan depended heavily on persuading his mother to allow the land in her name to be rejoined with his land and Roberta's. This she adamantly refused.

When Albert was in his final illness, he practically gave up his dream. Roberta stuck by him, told him not to give up his idea. She urged him to change his will in such a way that his arboretum dream could be established.

When Albert died, Roberta took over her

brother's dream aggressively as though she had inherited a sacred mission. Working intensively with lawyers and national forestry and arboretum consultants, she put together the land tract necessary adjacent to the Bole farm. She then worked with contractors on restructuring the land, involving road relocation and other earth moving. She then persuaded the Cleveland Museum of Natural History to manage the facility. And the Holden Arboretum was born.

Later we will see her start still another school.

On Campus

In the year of the crash and for two years following, the famous Hawken circus rose as an important event. The enthusiasm of Thayer Horton, who served on the faculty twenty years, electrified these elaborate outdoor productions. Some circus events in the 1930s were: Douglas Craig as Mr. Os, the Ossified Man; Harry as the snake charmer; a parade ... a gorilla ... wrestling ... acrobats. The circus ran in 1931, '32, '33. In 1934 it was replaced by "A Day In Athens"; then returned in 1935 before being discontinued. One strong trustee objected to it as "non-educational."

The school plays also were taken very seriously by faculty and students, and student critic reviewers: "It was a good play for the third grade" (mimeographed fourth grade newspaper).

A student review of the fourth grade play, *Columbus,* was severe: "I didn't like the play. The fourth grade boys didn't act well. I didn't like the scenery either."

Class committee appointments were safety and health, library, museum, house, entertainment, athletic, and collection.

The collection committee was applauded for collecting five hundred dollars for the Red Feather. The boys were to earn the money themselves.

In May 1931, John McCarthy inaugurated the first Father's Day at Hawken. Fathers abandoned busy schedules to join their sons for a chapel service, followed by lunch, conversation and a father/son baseball game (usually won by the boys).

The sixth grade was making ship models: the *Santa Maria, Leviathan,* Viking ships, and clipper ships.

A French table established in the dining room for fifth and sixth grades. No English was permitted. The sixth grade put on a play entirely in French, *Un Voyage En France.*

REORGANIZATION RECOIL

During Carney's sabbatical absence (1929-30), the board acted on some of the recommendations in the Western Reserve survey which Carney himself had commissioned. These actions were not all to his advantage.

It was felt that the big boys too much dominated the smaller boys in the same facility. Therefore the board rented a house on Clubside Road for grades three through six, leaving grades one and two and the senior grades in the main buildings.

Next, they created two separate schools, each with its own head: grades one through six, the lower school; seven through twelve, the upper school.

The lower school would be headed by Mortimer Smeed, a teacher phenomenon who will be large in this history.

They called him "Toughy." Strange name because he was an easy going man. Hiram Haydn, Hawken teacher who later became editor of national publications, wrote about him in the June 1946 *Reader's Digest* as *The Most Unforgettable Character I've Met.*

> To new teachers, Toughy's influence over the pupils—was incomprehensible. We could not understand how he could control them by talks. He never seemed to have a disciplinary problem, while we had so far taught nothing but discipline.... At the end of the first three months I picked up bodily one fresh little boy and carried him into Toughy's office.
>
> "Take him," I said, "before I murder him." It was my intention to resign that eve-

ning. But a half-hour later this boy came back to class so quiet, so polite, so cooperative, that I changed my mind. When I asked Toughy what had happened he replied, his eyes twinkling, "We had a talk."

His authority was so quiet that we seldom had a chance to observe just how he got his results. But at last I asked him quite bluntly.

"The first rule," he said, "is not to allow a crisis to develop. It's much harder to control a situation satisfactorily if it has reached the stage that calls for punishment. Never put a boy in the position where he can challenge or defy your instructions, and where, if he says the wrong thing, you'll have to call his bluff. Never ask him if he's done something wrong when you feel sure he has, for you're tempting him to lie."

"But I still can't fathom," I said, "how you can always see trouble brewing."

"You have to know your boy," Toughy replied. "It's always there to see, long before it actually comes on.... With a small school, we have a real chance to know our boys."

Every noon some committee of boys met at lunch with Toughy or a teacher to plan programs or activities. One, called the Executive Committee, was really a cover name for Toughy's Trouble Shooters. No other award in school meant so much as membership on that committee. Once on it, you were on the inside; you were working with Toughy to see to it that every boy was getting the encouragement and opportunity he needed to find himself. No member of the committee ever broke the trust invested in him: to keep secret the problems discussed there.

Of course, Toughy was not "tough." On the contrary, he was the gentlest man I have ever known. But it was the sort of gentleness that comes from genuine strength. He made terrific demands on himself and on everyone else. For he expected everyone at the school to live up to his full capacity; he asked that you find your best self and keep constant pace with it.

Mort Smeed was short, trim, prematurely gray with a deep voice. Discharged from the army in 1919, he was returning from Rochester to art school in Chicago. He stopped in Cleveland to visit his uncle, James Hawken. Two of the four teachers were out of action. Hawken, doing the work of three men, was exhausted.

Mort saw that there was something arresting and exciting here. The students almost had to be forced to go home at the end of the day.

"You're tired out," Mort said to his uncle. "Let me take your classes this afternoon. They may not learn much geography, but I think we'll get along."

Then he stayed a little longer. He met Helen Gallagher, married her, and stayed for a full career.

Toughy's enthusiasm for the job was contagious; it spread through the faculty. We became restless when away from the school; we began to come back after supper, to plan and discuss. As a result, informal faculty meetings would be held night after night in which we discussed boys, methods, and projects.

Toughy had many tempting offers to head other schools at higher salaries. When I asked him why he had turned one such offer down, he looked embarrassed.

"Why, I can't leave here," he said. "This is where I belong."

So he did.

* * *

John Carney returned from sabbatical to be confronted by the new organization. Of course he had worked harmoniously side by side with Mort Smeed for over a decade, and had been Smeed's headmaster.

He returned to find Mort Smeed head of Lower School and himself head of Upper School, and serving both schools in a new executive position called director of education was a Dr. G. Carlton Robinson of Western Reserve University, the same man Carney had commissioned to head the survey of Hawken.

John Carney wrote a frank letter to Joel Hayden, president of the board. It is a long plaintive letter suggesting deep soul searching by the author and considerable backbone. Substantial excerpts are warranted.

> ... [W]e have a weak executive and a Board of Trustees no member of which has a boy enrolled in the school.
>
> It seems to me that patient, painstaking zealous intelligent effort on the part of people who know and believe in the school is necessary *now*. It is not enough to have outsiders, however skilled, working on our finances, citing figures to show that our idea, our foundation, is untenable. Such an effort is all right if it goes hand in hand with the efforts of those who, with faith in the idea, the essence of the school, are working constructively for it. We must not have destructive activity only.

Carney expands on that weakness theme, challenging the board, then he particularizes:

> ... I spoke of the Executive of the School as weak. Mr. Smeed and I are working happily and earnestly together—nominally as the principals of two separate schools, the Lower and the Upper. There is no Director—no Headmaster. Mr. Smeed has not been authorized to assume responsibility for the School as a whole. The recent letters of the Board of Trustees have removed that responsibility from me. In one way I am relieved to be free of this responsibility. I would like to be entirely freed of executive responsibility so that I could do my work for

the school as a classroom teacher. But this ultimate definite responsibility for the school—the unit—the one Hawken School—should be some place ... No school with weak executive is a strong school. . . . .

Moreover I personally feel that the Board of Trustees lacks confidence in me. I do not see our relations, those of strong frank mutual confidence and understanding. This adds weakness to weakness. And as I can work only in an atmosphere of confidence, I feel it is only fair to tell the Board that I am frequently visited by the thought that my resignation from my position would be acceptable to them. . . . .

Perhaps I am destructive and obstructionist and therefore no longer of use in the forwarding of the plans which the Board has for the School. In any case we must not attempt the fatal and ridiculous procedure of working together without mutual confidence, frankness and understanding.

Yours sincerely
John Carney

Abruptly in 1931 ... John Carney resigned.

* * *

The deepening Depression diminished enrollments. Two of the seasoned headmasters were gone. Park and other schools were picking up extra students because Hawken's small-class concept kept its tuition high.

Financial advisers told the trustees the small-class concept was a financially infeasible idyll and could not be sustained in these times.

6. Day by Day

THE LARGE PROBLEMS of the administration and trustees were not laid on the boys. The school stringently sustained its raison d'etre—the education of the individual boys, in small classes, with attention to discovering and nurturing individual strengths.

Brand New Ancient Traditions

In the first decade in the new building there seemed to be a hunger for quick aging. Brand new "ancient traditions" were founded every year ... such as the Christmas play, the Hawken Circus, the Washington's birthday dance and John Ciarlillo bawling out his ancient stalled Chevy, "Carpo de geech!"

One very nice new ancient tradition was the "passing of the classes." At a given point in the commencement, the headmaster would call for the "passing of the classes." Then, as the graduating class members gave up their places, the lower grades each moved forward in the benches. This was particularly moving in 1926 when graduating Stephens Chamberlin spoke for a handful of boys who were "early Ansel Road."

In the following year thirty-four young alumni returned for the alumni dinner. Jim Weir and Patterson Bole and Sherman Hayden, the returning pioneers, made the speeches. Hayden was elected president (later the first alumnus to serve as trustee). Alvah Drake made a motion which might seem a small thing, but it was a move toward making permanent what was then tentative; he proposed dues of two dollars per year. The following year, when Jim Weir was elected president, dues were raised to five dollars.

The Daily Log

The boys sustained also their traditional Hawken

nonchalant humor, witness their yearbook account of 1928. Their own words reveal the personality of the school.

Day by Day 1928

September 21—School started with traditional good weather. In the court one hundred and thirty boys greeted each other. In the chapel a nervous president struggled with the school assembly.

September 22—The first football practice was held today. The squads sweated, and loafed when possible.

September 23—George Stanley, fully clad, won the diving contest in the fish pond. He was entered by one Dudley Blossom. Students, pouring into the court before lunch, saw the conventional articles of clothing drying on the patio, attended by flies.

September 28—Nash, our exponent of "neck-tackling," tried his art on a certain Bauman. After a few minutes of wriggling and twisting, a bewildered Nash held in his hand a head-gear. Bauman continued goalward.

September 30—Hawken beat Roxboro, 32–0, in a game which had all the appearances of a marathon. "Spike-um" Bauman placed the ball over the goal three times; a lesser light twice. The spectators cheered.

October 3—A plague of white mice has hit the school. Kenyon Bolton is responsible of the invasion.

The new boys were allotted to their respective societies today. A volley of hand-clapping greeted each boy as he walked from one end of the gymnasium to the other to be congratulated by the officers of his society.

October 6—The upper school heard a talk by Dr. Bayard Dodge, head of a school in the Near East.

October 11—Nash made another of his classic neck-tackles today, this time with success, on Shepherd.

October 14—The Grays defeated the Reds 27–0 in football. Nash played well for the Grays. Mr. Stephens scintillated among the spectators.

October 17—Mr. Stephens and Joe Eaton are building places "to lose things in" behind the stage. The division of labor is notably fair: Joe does the grunting, Mr. Stephens the work.

October 18—The Executive Committee of the Assembly met today for a purpose known only to the President. Such an orderly crowd has not been gathered since the French stormed the Bastille.

October 19—Bauman crashed over the line twice to defeat Mayfield 12–0. Nash, God's gift to practicing physicians, disabled two opponents.

In the auditorium, Shepherd fought the assembly with Mr. Stephens the third man in the ring.

October 20—The Executive Committee met and decided "something" today.

October 21—The Grays beat the Reds 28–7 today. Mr. Bauman, of the Grays, ran hither and yon, scoring all the touchdowns, except one. At the end, the Reds gave nine rahs for George instead of for the Grays.

October 24—The entire school heard a talk by Dr. Covert, the father of our Mr. Covert of the seventh grade.

October 25—The Hawken lightweights lost to Onaway, 12–6, in a hard-fought game.

October 28—The fuel oil supply tank for the heating system is being dug up and replaced with a new one.

November 1—The Community Fund campaign was launched today. Robert Beatty, Mr. MacMahon, and Mr. Stephens spoke. A movie machine, which sounded like a Ford with a loose axle, showed pictures.

The first program of talks, by our noble seniors, was given today.

November 4—The Gray team beat the Red team 19–0 in football. Hubbard, a new backfield find, performed nobly for the Reds.

November 7—Mr. Paul Rea, father of John Rea, a Hawken Alumnus, talked to us about the Community Fund.

November 8—The members of the Lower School were put to work cleaning off the snow from the football field. The work was accomplished by means of an organized snowball fight.

November 9—The School team emerged victorious from the game with the Western Reserve Academy Lightweights by a score of 13–0. The field was lined with spectators and among them was "Char" Bolton.

November 11—A bench collapsed in the Glee Club rehearsal today. There are those who believe that it was not caused by the singing.

November 16—In accordance with their prerogative, the Seniors have collected most, if not all, of the erasers into their room. (Mr. Carney has not yet discovered the eraser shortage in other rooms, but when he does, he will probably substitute an activity for the Seniors that is a little more in accord with his own idea of a scholastic pursuit.)

November 21—The Lowers played their last game, and the Reds won, 19–6.

November 23—A fighting Red team beat a lackadaisical Gray team 12–6. The Grays scored early in the game and were ever afterwards on the defensive. In the preliminary game the middler Gray team beat the Reds 6–0 with Pelton and Humphrey starring.

George Bauman won the jersey awarded to the best-all-around football player. Letters were given to the first team.

November 28—Preparation for Christmas celebration was started today.

November 29—A good-natured, if nothing else, stage staff has been formed.

December 2—A swimming meet was held today in the pool at Daisy Hill Farm. The boys and members of the faculty who attended, were the guests of David Jenks.

December 6—The stage hands, to their great sorrow have knocked to pieces everything within range and so they must start on construction work soon. The Glee Club and Orchestra are hard at work.

December 12—Alas, alas! All the frivolity has disappeared now. Everyone goes about his work seriously and the stage hands remain after school to work.

December 16—Everything went off smoothly at the Christmas celebration. After the singing of the carols by the choir, the lights went out; the audience became silent; and the play began. At the final curtain the players were greeted with loud and sustained applause. After much hand-shaking the guests departed, leaving the faculty to nurse numb hands. Soon Johnny, the janitor, was left alone, whistling merrily as he began to take down the wreaths and other decorations.

January 2—Everybody came back to school somewhat the worse for the round of holiday parties. It is estimated that two weeks of school work will set most of the boys back on their feet.

The School team defeated the Alumni at basketball, 18–11.

January 6—We heard an interesting talk by Major Pechkoff, of the Foreign Legion, today.

January 9—The new winter schedule went into effect and Mr. Stephens, in the absence of Professor Einstein, was busy explaining it to both boys and masters.

January 19—"English Nine" presented a comedy, "The King's English," to the school and its guests. The play was very funny and Mr. Covert and his English class are to be congratulated.

January 23—The School basketball team won from Roxboro, 20–9.

January 27—The school was entertained by a group of players from the Mask and Wig Club of the University of Pennsylvania.

January 31—The School team lost in basketball to Mayfield, 28–7.

February 10—The Sixth Grade defeated the Seventh Grade, 18–9, in a game after school.

Most of the members of the Seventh Grade have been wearing their Scout uniforms this week.

February 21—The annual school dance for the boys of the upper school was held tonight. The committee on decorations evidently spat on its hands and went to work with a will. The Seniors and the ever-faithful Mr. Stephens are to be congratulated on the party.

February 28—The Grays beat the Reds in basketball, 37–11.

March 1—The school team defeated the faculty, 26–22.

The preparation of the set for "Wappin' Wharf" started under the direction of Mr.

Eisenstaat of the Playhouse.

March 2—The Grays beat the Reds in basketball, 67–10.

March 6—The faculty came back in its second game with the School team to win, 23–21.

March 13—The Rev. Joel B. Hayden returned to school today, after being away because of sickness. Faculty and boys were glad to see him.

March 16—The members of the faculty and their wives were the dinner guests of Mr. and Mrs. Benjamin Jenks, the parents of our David Jenks.

March 20—The Pastime, a new publication put out by the members of the Sixth Grade, appeared today. The forty-page paper was written, printed, bound, and sold here at school under the direction of Mr. Smeed, Head of the Lower School.

March 23—The Players' Club presented "Wappin' Wharf" to an enthusiastic audience made of boys, parents, and friends. Cyrus Eaton, of the Fourth Grade, played a flute solo between the acts.

The Year Book goes to press today, and tomorrow spring vacation begins.

Alumni Luncheon

The fourth annual dinner of the Hawken Club occurred on Friday, December twenty-third. This year, as last, the dinner was held at the school, in the gymnasium, which was especially decorated for the occasion with Red and Gray banners and the school colors. The office and faculty room were, by one o'clock, crowded with forty-two alumni, more than have ever before been gathered in one place, and a little later the association sat down around the long horseshoe table to a magnificent luncheon prepared by Mrs. Summerville. The dinner was shared by the alumni with Mr. Hawken, Mr. Carney, Mr. MacMahon and Mr. McCarthy, as well as five members of the Senior class.

Sherman Hayden, President of the Alumni Association, presided over the speeches and the business meeting which followed them. He opened the meeting with an announcement of the first Alumni Bulletin, which was successfully published during the fall. Mr. MacMahon, the second speaker, recounted several funny stories, which brought much laughter from those who used to delight in Mr. Mac's humor. Next Joseph Nutt, of Exeter Academy, suggested that a third officer be added to the two then in existence, who would edit the Bulletin. He also asked that since the Year Book had given the Alumni a section in it, the Alumni should reply by subscribing to the Year Book. Tom Grandin, of Andover, suggested that the Alumni dues should be raised to a height sufficient to cover the price of the Year Book, and that each member of the association should receive a copy as one of his privileges. Mr. Carney said his customary few words, with his notes on a piece of scratch paper, which created amusement among the old boys who were accustomed to the well-known chapel orations. Mr. Hawken, who, at the request of the President, spoke extemporaneously, talked a little about the School, and asked that, since he no longer had any official connection with it, he be made a regular member of the association.

The business meeting followed, with the annual elections, in which J. C. Weir, of Harvard, was elected President for the coming year; Stephens Chamberlin, of Yale, Secretary-Treasurer; and, in accordance with

Joe Nutt's suggestion, Edgar Taylor, of Amherst, Editor of the Alumni Bulletin. Mr. Hawken was voted a full member of the Alumni Association. The dues were raised to five dollars, to cover the Year Book and publications of the association. After this, the meeting was formally adjourned, but the boys lingered long in conversation and reminiscences about the School.

7. Crash!

AS ABRUPT AS walking from chapel directly into midweek scrimmage were the changes of 1932. Nearly simultaneous leadership changes in both trustees and administration brought on stage two men not impeded by excess reflection or hesitant self examination ... Liv Ireland and Carl Holmes.

"I think," speculates Jim Ireland, "Mrs. Bolton told the two new young trustees [Ireland and Tom White] it was time for them to take hold on the deficit."

Before the two new men signed on, there is merit in looking first at previous trustee action from its beginning.

Jim Hawken was on this board. At the second meeting, October 19, 1929, he reviewed Mrs. Bolton's offer to foot the deficit five more years if necessary and to add to any sums collected to bring the endowment to five-hundred-thousand dollars. Frances Bolton, then only forty, said that she had already provided for that in her will in case of accident.

The young school held to its original compass, picking its way carefully among many tempting diversions offered to it. For example, in that same meeting, Dr. Vinson proposed a possibility: because Western Reserve University was considering dropping freshman and sophomore years, might Hawken consider adding them?

Ten days after that meeting trustees and faculty stared at a four-inch-high block letter headline —

CRASH!

The 1930s came in like winter kill.

* * *

Beyond strategic planning, the board got down into operating detail, for example raising Miss Eck-

The Hawken Boy bust by Joseph Motto (1928)

On pony (above), Robert White, '36

Nelson Logan, '39; camel unknown

Bobby Crowell (left), '37, as Charlie Chaplin and Edwin H. Pierce, '35 as "The Shark"

Ed Godfrey, Mort Smeed, and Joe Motto (top photo) put finishing touches on performers. Only the first savage was identified: Melville Ireland, '39. It appears the audience (bottom photo) had as much fun as the performers.

Courtney Burton is the butler (1929)

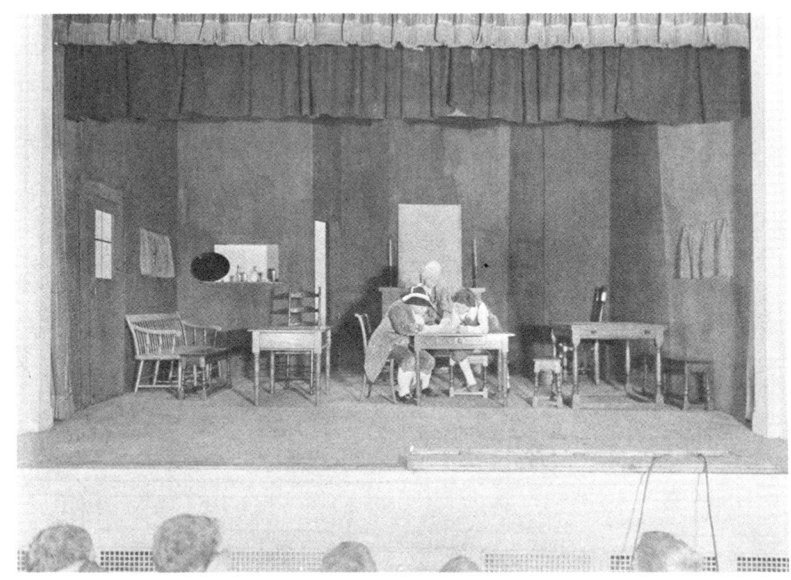

Treasure Island

1930 Yearbook staff (top photo): Al Conkey, Ben Taplin, and Adrian Foose (back row); John Calfee, Ben Schneider, and Francis Silver (front row)

Mr. Motto's art class attempting to replicate the Parthenon (bottom photo): John Nash, Joe Motto, Benton Mellinger, John Cashman, Harvey Brooks, Franklyn Judson, Frank Taplin, and Jack Collens.

Class of 1936 (This photo first appeared in the 1928 Red and Gray Book.) (back): Mrs. Adams, Scott Inkley, Dwight Morse, Henry G. Wischmeyer, Jr., Frederick Hills, John Sawyer, Arthur Bazely, Jeffrey Cuddy, and Miss Luehrs; (front): Dean Morse, Theodore T. Peck, Elton Hoyt III, Robert Y. White, Melville H. Ireland, Frank E. House, III, and Marshall Dyer

Bottom photo: At work

Lunch in the classroom

A Sport for Everyone and Everyone in a Sport

The 1920s

HAWKEN
1930

ert's salary to $175 a month for eleven months per year; refunding seven dollars and fifty cents to the parents of a boy who dropped out; more economical sourcing for groceries.

At the first 1931 meeting Frances Bolton commented on the delightful atmosphere, physical and otherwise, of the lower school, "preserving much of the feeling of Ansel Road."

She did warn, however, about the new costs and recommended moving the Lower School into the main building now.

At the sixth trustee meeting, Joel Hayden persuaded them that they should expand the field of those eligible to be trustees. They called a meeting of corporation members and added four additional names: Calfee, Webster, White, and Ireland. Consensus grew that the whole board should resign and re-elect. Hence the new board: Robert M. Calfee, Sherman Hayden, R. Livingston Ireland, Asa Shiverick, John T. Webster, and Thomas Holden White.

In December 1931, with Hawken absent, the trustees were informed that Hawken's attorney had drawn papers assigning to the corporation the contract Jim Hawken had with the endowment association and the lease between the association and Jim Hawken. However, actual implementation of this lagged, inhibiting board action.

Over many meetings the trustees were constantly debating whether the school should be nine grades, ten grades, or twelve. This would change several times.

As the Depression deepened, the trustees felt that the teachers should not suffer a pay cut in view of the extra work load caused by the hiring freeze.

Discussion about expanding the school beyond ten grades halted in May 1932 because the transfer papers from Jim Hawken had not come. The trustees were operating a school they did not yet legally own.

Later in 1932 the trustees decided that because of the growing deficit they must talk to the faculty about a salary reduction.

Liv Ireland recalled, "In 1931 Tom White and I

came on the board. In 1932 Joel Hayden surprised us by resigning as chairman to take over Hudson Academy [Western Reserve Academy] and I became chairman.

"Mrs. Bolton, who had been footing the deficits since the school moved to Lyndhurst, guaranteed that she would continue three more years while we tried to pull this school up by its bootstraps."

Ireland intended to do just that. "He ran the board," recalls Char Hickox, "like Mark Hanna bracing a caucus of politicians." Ireland was then vice president of Hanna Coal Company. A handsome, wavy-haired man with a sun-spalted face, he operated behind a bow tie and a roll-top desk with a phone on an extensor bracket.

Tom White located a strong headmaster candidate at Fessenden School of Newton, Massachusetts. White and Ireland visited this candidate at a summer camp he operated in New Hampshire. At the meeting on August 12, 1932 the trustees decided to ask Carl Holmes to come to Cleveland with a view to becoming headmaster.

Suddenly, however, some trustees pointed out that they were doing well with a head of lower school and a head for upper; and no overall head. Why spend an extra ten thousand dollars a year for a headmaster they did not need?

Frances Bolton said, "Don't worry. If you can't meet it, I'll pay it."

Carl Nestor Holmes

Any one who has been in business or education can well imagine the approach of a new man coming from the outside as headmaster of Hawken. If he is shrewd enough to be chosen headmaster, he is surely shrewd enough to have learned that the central corps of this faculty ... Smeed, Motto, Stephens, Russell, and now McCarthy and MacMahon, were a tight family, all of whom knew the founder and still corresponded with him. The second headmaster had been one of them. If he accepted, Holmes would be the first outside headmaster. This faculty had a proprie-

Carl N. Holmes

tary attitude and were accustomed to running the school. Hawken had taught them, "Every master a headmaster."

Holmes probably also knew that previous administrators managed with a light and collaborative touch. Could a strong-handed outsider succeed here?

Striding across the campus in 1932 was a young administrator with professorial, round, steel-rimmed glasses, but no Socratic questioning in the eyes about who he was, what he was doing, or where he was going. An athletic body the match of John McCarthy stretched the shoulder stitches of a staid business suit. Not a man with self-doubts, young Carl Holmes already had behind him a leadership career. Out of Dartmouth with varsity baseball and hockey letters, he had been acting headmaster of Governor Dummer Academy in Massachusetts. He earned his master's at Harvard and was owner of a boys' camp, Great East Lodge in New Hampshire.

Like seasoned administrators, he made his major changes early before cement could harden around his feet.

He stepped up the accent on sports.

He brought in a new kitchen team, Mac and Winnie McCarthy, who had worked with him at his camp and would become a Hawken institution.

Observing the various subject specialist teachers trudging to the various homerooms with armloads of books and teaching materials, he reversed the procedure. Make the teacher stationary; move the kids.

* * *

Jim Hawken's interests were signed over in the fall of 1932.

There were increasing overdue accounts receivable as parents struggled to pay the tuition. The trustees therefore ruled that all lunch and transportation costs must be paid in advance by parents. There would be a system of deposit accounts against which students could draw for supplies and books. Sons of faculty would be guaranteed free transportation and tuition, but in other respects masters would be subject to the same payment system as other parents.

First grade tuition was reduced from $375 to three hundred dollars, lunches optional. Transportation reduced from seventy-five dollars to seventy dollars.

A large economy had been made in transportation. The special red car attached to the regular inter-urban was replaced by purchase of two large yellow busses which gave more flexibility, bringing the boys right to the campus, eliminating a mile walk from the rail stop through snow, ice, and slush. Those busses were replaced by the "woodie fleet," four (later six) Ford Country Squire station wagons. The masters drove these, picking up the boys at their houses and bringing them direct to the campus.

The board, discovering that $2,814 in receivables had been charged off without any authority, tightened procedures.

In March 1933 the treasurer showed the trustees the impact of impounded funds in the Guardian Trust. They decided to review the situation monthly, but for the immediate emergency: pay all mercantile bills in full, but temporarily pay all employees half their salaries.

Some of the trustees had credit accounts at grocery stores. During the worst of the salary cutbacks, Elmer Sipple remembers, "They paid us partly in groceries."

Seeking to loosen the financial crunch, Carl Holmes proposed that they open the building for a fee to Cleveland College adult education programs and publish a school brochure to bring the school to the attention of a wider market. He also proposed some paid-space advertising.

The Depression bore down on every trustee meeting. By the time the Depression struck hardest, the plant had a decade of young tigers' wear and tear on it. Adding the expanding desires of faculty, the needs were new study halls, an expanded gymnasium, and general repairs in the corridors.

Accounts receivable were in such arrears the trustees decided to withhold diplomas until parents made some arrangement to pay the tuition.

The school built up a fund of just over one hundred dollars by a series of "Depression lunches."

Scholarships

The school had granted a few scholarships prior to 1932 for various reasons. In 1932 the administration and board realized that there was no consistent basis and no definition of how long scholarships were to last. In 1932-33 there were thirty-three scholarship boys in an enrollment of seventy-five. In 1934, '35 and '36 the scholarships rose to forty-five; they were more carefully distributed and annual renewal was required. The rationale for scholarships was to improve the enrollment figures and quality of students, thus attracting new full-paying boys. This worked. In 1937, helped of course by improving business conditions, there were thirty-nine scholarship boys out of 135.

About this time the school established its competitive prize scholarship plan to ensure intelligent choice of candidates, and to inform the community in a professional manner that Hawken believed in scholarships to needy boys of promise.

The headmaster, in a recently querulous mood, added that this would earn the good will of the average citizen, which "we certainly do not have today, and this is a major problem we must face."

Because the school plant had become crowded, there was a move gradually to limit the scholarships by a flexible limit of about two boys per group with each new first grade. The result downstream in 1941 was the fewest scholarship boys since 1932. In that year Holmes would recommend increasing the scholarship admittances. Holmes also felt the faculty had better leverage in choosing the kinds of boys they wanted in the case of scholarships than in paid admissions; and that they should enlarge the scholarship population with the express purpose of enhancing the student body.

Country Day Camp

Various summer camps were an important part of Hawken for the "lifers." In 1930, David Russell and Elmer Sipple started the Hawken country day camp. Fifty years later they collaborated in an article for the *Hawken Review:*

> In those early days the freedom to create, to innovate, and to implement new ideas in education at Hawken were great motivating factors for the faculty .... Because of generous encouragement many new programs were developed in the arts and crafts, dramatics, science and music such as Thayer Horton's annual school circus, the Day in Rome, the Hawken School Press and the founding of the Country Day Camp.

> The founders ... were Sip, whose arts and crafts shop was crowded with creativity all day long; Robin S. (Wally) Wallace, who taught physical education; and I, a classroom teacher in the Lower School (David Russell).

> The camp was in session four days a week at the campus. We counselors called for the young campers—and there were around 30 of them in that first year (1930)—in the school's station wagons and brought them to Clubside Road.

> With arts and crafts shops open all day and hikes and field trips and playground activities, the young campers were fully occupied and so were the camp directors. Alice Sipple helped Mrs. Bauer with the noon meals and Harriet Russell assisted in other ways.

> Two or three times a season there would be overnight camp outs ....

[At this point, Elmer Sipple took over the narration.]

> The entire decade of the thirties was a difficult time for most independent schools and camps. Carl Holmes, who was seriously

attempting to maintain the high scholastic standards, asked me to be on the lookout for qualified young boys for the school among the campers.

During the decades of the 1940s and 1950s, the camp matured. Its popularity with parents was based on their recognition of our talented and dedicated staff men. It so happened that each man on staff in the late 1950s held a master's degree in education. Several of them were also principals of public schools.

FACULTY FLASHES

At one low point in the Depression Holmes reported to the trustees how the faculty had accepted the pay cuts with understanding.

We met that faculty when they were young. What are they like when seasoned?

Even if biased, some impression of the faculty can be gained from the off-stage comments of the boys. For example, it says something about MacMahon that just before an exam one unprepared lad said to a group, "Well, I can do no worse than flunk." One in the crowd said, "Listen, optimist, with MacMahon you can do worse. You can get killed."

Of Stephens when acting headmaster it was said, "The guy has an uncanny ability to be at the wrong place at the wrong time. Webster was about to throw Lincoln out the window when he looks up to see the boss."

About John McCarthy, "He's founder of the STKOAS Society."

"What's that?"

"Society to kill off all sissies."

McCarthy felt the new generation was soft. When helping with the coaching of football, he was very physical. He occasionally physically assisted erring students out of the classroom.

Of big Coach Elmer Sipple, when he appeared in a new suit, they joked that his tailor was a tent maker.

They said that David Russell was so systematic and

neat that he lined up the chemistry beakers with a ruler.

They joked about humorless, conscientious Horace Aylard, treasurer, that he tried to collect twelve cents postage from the yearbook board.

They were keenly aware of Mona Eckert, secretary, as the keystone. "If she ever quits, absolutely everything will halt."

Smeed the students admired totally, but the real verdict was—so did the teachers working with him. Len Carey recounts, "Smeed's faculty meetings always began, 'I haven't the faintest idea what we ought to discuss.' But then his meetings always became exciting discussions. Unforgettable."

* * *

But what of Carl N. Holmes?

A headmaster with a strong faculty and a bright student body must be not an administrator, but a leader. He is on stage day and night. He must be totally sincere in his concern for all the people. No dissembling is successful in such a goldfish bowl. On the other hand, if he attempts to be loved by all, he will surely fail.

"More than a mere headmaster, Mr. Holmes is a friend ... has an infectious smile," one boy felt, "sets even the timid boys at ease. Strong personality."

To the contrary, one of the early graduates who headed the alumni association remembers Holmes as "a gross bully."

A former financial staff man holds up the photo of Hawken beside a photo of Holmes and states, "Anybody can see the difference."

T. Douglas Stenberg, current headmaster and a close student of the school's history, considers the Holmes years "the great watershed era."

8. The Echo

AS THE 1930s Depression crawled deeper into Hawken territory, one might wonder without being the least facetious, why would the trustees continue to battle the enormous problems? Some schools were giving up. Few trustees at this time had boys at Hawken. If the school can't fly after a dozen and a half years of subsidy, hasn't supply and demand spoken? Cut it loose.

One major reason they could not cut it loose was that now overwhelming proof of the power of this brand of education was echoing home. For example, Richard Inglis, in a class of one thousand at Harvard, received one of the four highest ratings in the class. He was one of eight to make Phi Beta Kappa. One of the other seven was Hawken's Sherman Hayden. Hawken boys were setting those kinds of records in the top handful of U. S. colleges. They were also making themselves felt at eastern preparatory schools as top scholars and as sports team captains.

Even more important was evidence of success on the original Hawken raison d'etre—development of character. Wealthy sons who could major in art appreciation and polo were instead studying engineering at Yale's Sheffield, medicine at Harvard and some, preparing themselves to be teachers, abjuring high income professions to follow their own stars.

At Harvard, Francis Silver was hailed by fellow Harvard student, Ben Schneider, who had news for him: "You just won the hundred-dollar Latin prize!" Francis used the money to buy McCarthy a new book bag. That, too, showed the impact of Hawken faculty.

The trustees also saw the classic tour de force of character demonstrated by Charles Bolton.

Frances and Chester Bolton had put their three boys into the Ansel Road school ... Oliver, Kenyon, and Charles. Charles, after a great leadership record at Hawken, went on to Milton Academy in Massachusetts. He was the kind of kid who thought the world was his responsibility. In the summer of 1927 he was counselor at a summer camp for underprivileged boys near Boston. Supervising the swimming one day he dove from the float and struck the water at an angle which broke his neck. Suddenly he was paralyzed. A painful surgical odyssey of scores of operations followed by months and years of self-disciplined therapy finally brought slight motion, then more, then wheelchair mobility, then crutches, then two canes. Then the story of Char Bolton's life of research at Western Reserve in dentistry and in Guernsey breeding began to become known—proof of the power of character to change the world.

Ultimately he would go on to a life of public service, helping a list of service and civic organizations which filled two single spaced pages. However, his greatest contribution of all would be the achievements he influenced in others who watched him counterattack calamity.

That was perhaps the most visible example, but everywhere faculty and trustees were seeing proof of the superior results of the Hawken concept.

Serious concession, however, did need to be made to the Depression; the school dropped grades eleven and twelve. Therefore in 1933 the faculty needed to shift preparation from college board to secondary college board requirements. This might sound simple but it required much extra work because of the scholastic backgrounds which had been given the students under the college board emphasis. A stiffening of standards of achievement in the lower grades began.

In sports, particularly football, the upper school, because of the small class concept, had trouble even fielding a full team. But athletic director Ed Godfrey, with muscular help from short, ruddy, Latin teacher McCarthy, instilled the football teams with such savvy and self esteem that when University School freshman team came to play, Hawken scored on the first two plays from scrimmage. Final score: 60-0.

Holmes, a former All-American hockey player,

followed closely all Hawken sports including the second teams of the Lower School's Cyclops and Vikings.

There was a second powerful encouragement for the trustees in these Depression battles. They were seeing, besides dramatic successes by their alumni, the first signs of built-in continuity. For example, in 1933 the first of their own alumni returned to take a place on the Hawken faculty, Richard Inglis, teaching French, math and seventh grade science. Additionally 1933 saw the first three alumni sons enroll.*

There was a third powerful reason that trustees, faculty, and involved parents labored to sustain this small school through hard times. Behind everything was a spirit, very present even when absent ... Frances Bolton. Where is the man who was going to look into those straight-on blue eyes and suggest anything but continuation?

In 1934 salary cuts were partially restored. In a faculty not accustomed to much turnover, some teachers now left. Mr. Adams went to head a school in Seattle, Dave Russell also left. Their replacements were Mr. Inglis and Mrs. McCabe.

However the central corps remained: Stephens, McCarthy, Smeed, Sipple, Hayden, Horton, and Miss Luehrs.

Holmes was emboldened to present the board a large want list: a second gym, an enlarged library, a study hall, an outdoor covered playing surface for rainy days, and a hockey rink.

In 1935 Jim Hawken returned to visit. Heading off all honors, receptions, and speeches, he just wanted to talk individually to the masters and the boys. Holmes reported that "because he remembered the order of events he carefully chose times when he would not be noticed."

Holmes regularly pushed the board for new buildings. He wanted a separate building for kinder-

*Benjamin Patterson Bole III, '50, grandson of Roberta Bole, who brought Jim Hawken to Cleveland; Joseph Randolphs Nutt III, '51; and James Urban, son of George Urban, '24. It should be noted that these sons were enrolled at birth.

garten through third grade. He wanted a projection booth in the chapel. "Someday," he predicted, "motion pictures will be a big part of education." Holmes proposed to make it also an art film theatre which would bring the public on campus and thus interest more parents in Hawken.

Carl Holmes reminded the trustees that some of the faculty were becoming very senior. He doubted they could have saved much money for retirement. He asked the trustees to consider the possibility of some kind of a retirement plan.

A sampling of 1935 salaries gives us a yardstick on the times: Miss Price (kindergarten), $350.00; Sipple, twenty-eight hundred dollars; Smeed, four thousand, and Holmes, ten thousand.

Twenty-Year Mark
Alumni and Faculty

At the two decade mark Charles R. Stephens, who had not yet missed one day of school, addressed an interesting summary to the young members of the Hawken alumni association (there were no old ones yet, not even middle aged). He reported that the largest number of Hawken boys had gone to the following colleges in descending order: Harvard, Yale, Amherst, Princeton, Williams, M.I.T., Dartmouth, and Cornell. In this particular year there were ten at Harvard and twelve at Yale.

Some of these men, the pioneering students and classmates in knickers on Ansel Road, were still classmates in college in 1935: At Harvard: Ed Lenihan (economics and rowing); Phil Morse (biology); Bob Webster (English); Bob Bishop (English and history); Lew Affelder (*The Crimson*), and Jack Danforth (engineering); in the medical school, Bill Weir, Graham Webster, David Weir, and Ben Schneider; at Yale: William Bauman (Sheffield scientific, two years for excellence); Char Hickox (psychology); Fred White; Fayette Brown (history); Henry Harvey, Lewis Baldwin, John Calfee, Henry Royal, Bill Brown, John Nash, and Harvey Brooks; at Princeton: Ben Taplin, John Cushman, and Frank Taplin.

Stephens reported that of the then 172 alumni, forty were already out in the work world and fifteen were married.

MERGER PROPOSAL

To stay afloat in the Depression private schools were merging to make double use of facilities and faculty and to fill classes.

There was a usually empty office at Hawken reserved for Frances Bolton's visits. After 1929, however, she was generally in Washington. Chester Bolton, following a family heritage of public service, ran for Congress in 1929 from Ohio's Twenty-Second District. He won, and then won repeated re-election. Frances therefore established a home for the family in Washington, D. C., where she quickly involved herself in many capital affairs. Despite her action on the national scene she wanted to hear every detail about Hawken School. She came to the campus whenever home, and sometimes addressed classes or the assembly. Sometimes she would merely walk into the school unannounced, look around, have a short meeting with Carl Holmes, and leave. She was, as Francis Silver remembers, "a presence, good-looking, beautifully groomed with a tendency toward tweeds."

Park School in Shaker Heights approached Hawken trustees with a three-way merger proposal: Park, Hawken, and the nursery school of Western Reserve University. After study, Frances Bolton was concerned about maintenance of Hawken ideals in such a merger. She felt there would be divergence of standards among the schools. Despite the desirability of substantial savings she wanted more time given to the study.

MR. HOLMES AT WORK

While the Depression relaxed enough by 1937 to let enrollment rise to 111 (vs. seventy-five in 1932), it did not let up enough to release fifty-eight hundred dollars of Hawken funds impounded in Guardian Bank. The trustees resolved that, when released, the money would go toward staff back pay.

By 1937 Headmaster Holmes knew every brick in the school. Firmly seated as head he walked the grounds and corridors keeping the property and staff levels up, followed by his large Labrador retriever.

A musical man, he liked to play the chapel organ. But, not comfortable with the religious aspects, he delegated that to Lori Robey.

Herb Furst, third-longest tenured teacher (1945–84), recalls his technique, "for bawling out a faculty member ... never in public ... he'd call you into the office, soften you up with some small talk and salted peanuts ... then get down to it."

He pushed for improvements faster than the Depression was receding ... new fire brick for the furnace, a new motor-generator set, sump pump, wrestling mats, track roller, painting and ceiling repairs, and raising the two chimneys to push the smoke farther above the open classroom windows in a west wind.

Holmes in turn was being pushed by Winnie McCarthy for a new, large refrigerator and other kitchen equipment. Mac and Winnie McCarthy, whom Holmes had brought from Massachusetts, had improved the dining room, the food and the service. But Winnie, a small, spunky woman, gave Holmes a long wish list, "Or we're going home to Massachusetts!" The couple ("Mac 'n Winnie") had quickly become a Hawken institution as rooted in the affection as the courtyard fountain and Pan.

Holmes succeeded with many of his requisitions. There were new classroom desks designed by Charles Stephens with a special compartment for storing the large book bags. There were new drawing tables designed by Mr. Pierson. There were boundary boards around the hockey rink.

Holmes developed a great respect and affection for the faculty. In 1937 he addressed the trustees on the subject. A condensation of his remarks is interesting for several reasons. One is to note the staff continuity, another to note that Carl Holmes valued the personnel and the ideology of the founding faculty. Another is to note his change of attitude three years later.

Holmes told the board, "Mr. Stephens continues to be the stalwart standby he has always been .... One of the best mathematics teachers, an even greater contribution is his steadiness, his dependability, his unfailing loyalty to the school."

MacMahon, who handed out tons of homework to the boys in high good humor for twenty years, was given a half year paid leave for the second half of 1937.

McCarthy, the old Roman, leaves on a sabbatical to Italy after thirteen years at Hawken. He enrolled in several summer courses in Italian universities.

Holmes characterized Bragdon as one of the world's free spirits, giving the boys inspiration by his personal life and his English classes. He coaches dramatics and sports. He is a wit, "a bear for work, and one of the busiest men at Hawken."

Graydon Hough, age thirty, came here from Rutgers Prep. He would take the place of Dick Inglis. Hough was a very accomplished young educator who was also "so personable" that Holmes planned on putting him into enrollment work, making at least one call per day.

Lanky Hamilton Eames, a Harvard and Cambridge man, was a scholar, a great tennis player and a very colorful human being who fascinated French classes with stories about life with the Arabs.

Holmes reported that "Mr. Smeed had another great year. Inspires his boys with a deep and genuine interest in history and geography. As head of the lower school, handles routine details in an unobtrusive but efficient manner. Don't know what Hawken would do without Mort Smeed. Hawken will always be Hawken as long as this man is with us."

Hiram Haydn inspired boys in and out of the classroom in athletics, dramatics, and English. Haydn was a very sensitive man, Holmes said, "sometimes apt to misinterpret a remark or a situation, but when he is receiving the encouragement he so richly deserves, he's top notch." He had been with the school nine years.

Holmes characterized Sipple as "one of the steadiest men. Disposition to be envied, and work that he is doing in shop is one of the highlights of the school." Sipple's big wholesome personality is popular with the boys and the men. He had been with the school twelve years.

Holmes feels Thayer Horton is not happy with his assigned position, for which Holmes partially takes the blame.

He cites as "comers" the two youngest teachers, Pierson and Conkey, '31-I, art and music, resourceful, innovative, and eager.

Ed Godfrey has made phys-ed important at Hawken. "A terrific worker, he is organized far into the future." (Meacham Hitchcock, '42, remembers "Ed Godfrey required all students to take 'posture pictures', front and side, clad in undershorts. After a series of fitness tests, he set up a physical fitness course for each student. We hated them!")

Miss Benning was hired to teach third grade. She is Hawken's first remedial reading specialist. At first she had some trouble adjusting her public school experience to Hawken's ways, "but now fits in beautifully. The third grade is better off with a woman teacher than it was with a man."

Eleanor Burditt of Boston "is extremely promising to replace Miss McCabe who is leaving to be a full-time homemaker."

"And now for the Grand Lady, Miss Luehrs. For 20 years she has been teaching Hawken first grade, and we hope she'll be with us for more; but she can't be.... It seems with each succeeding year it is necessary for her to take a little more time off because of illness."

Holmes uses this to bring up again the subject of "what to do for teachers who retire because of old age, after many years of service." He suggests the board offer assistance. This is one of a series of requests by Holmes to institute some kind of a retirement package.

Faculty Wives

Faculty spouses can be sand in the gears, but Jim Smeed, '43, remembers "at Hawken, they were very important. They filled in to help with scores of chores including driving the station wagons. Especially—they created, by their entertaining, a faculty social world which made for great unity and morale." Just on the spur of the moment, Jim could name Mary Hines, Marian McMinn, Polly McCarthy, Eleanor Roundy, Rachael Hayden, Ada Stephens, and Harriett Russell.

This tradition carried forward. Alice Zimmerman, an accountant in the office and backbone of the staff along with Millie Smith, remembers "these social affairs were so Hawken-intensive, some evenings we'd lay down a rule, Tonight, No Hawken Talkin'."

* * *

In a February 1938 board meeting trustees devised a plan to keep all ten grades in the main building, limiting enrollment in each of the first nine grades to thirteen boys. That would mean nine grades of thirteen, or 117 total; then establish a small tenth grade resulting in 120 boys, the estimated capacity of the school. Tuitions would total thirty-seven thousand dollars. An alternate plan was to move the first three grades into a separate building and increase grades four through nine to twenty boys in two sections of ten each.

However, in 1938 enrollment leaped to 135 boys.

This meeting also reviewed how much was received yearly from the endowment in the Depression years: for 1932-33, forty thousand dollars; for 1933-34, thirty-six thousand five hundred dollars; for 1934-35, forty-two thousand five hundred dollars; for 1935-36, forty-five thousand dollars; for 1936-37, forty-five thousand dollars.

The September 1938 meeting authorized construction of a new building.

Will Frances Run?

The years 1939 and 1940 had some downside news for the school. Congressman Chester Bolton, who had largely supervised construction of Lyndhurst and had continued quietly assisting school financial affairs, began to suffer heart trouble in 1939. He passed away on October 29, 1939 at age fifty-seven.

He had more than most men can boast. Besides his wife, Frances, who converted Washington, D. C., into their personal home town, he had three amazing sons. Char's heroic willpower we've described earlier. Kenyon was building a career in banking. Oliver had just graduated from Harvard and was heading for law and politics.

In Chester's death the school lost a powerful support. Additionally, it could also lose Frances. She was asked to run for election for Chester's unexpired term in a February special election.

If she decided to run and was elected, her time and interest would surely be consumed. What would be the effect on Hawken?

9. The Lady and the Tiger

IT WOULD AFFECT Hawken School that Frances Bolton finally decided that she would like to finish out Chester's term; she knew his position on certain issues and wanted to see his work completed his way.

Her natural graciousness camouflaged a healthy skepticism of the invitation to run for Congress in 1940. Republican leadership, she guessed, was not that enthusiastic about her holding the office, but felt the invitation a harmless gesture because, like all fill-in congresswomen except Edith Nourse Rogers and Mary Norton, she would probably drop out at the end of term, meanwhile having bolstered Republican party coffers.

Actually she thought she might do just that.

However, after winning the election, becoming Ohio's first woman in Congress, she found herself where perhaps she should have been all her life, exactly in the place where she could help the unheard people stuck in the cellar of America.

Cynical eyes in Congress watched her. Another token widow come to finish one term and leave? A Lady Bountiful playing great aunt to the unfortunate? And yet, face to face, they had to respect this very erect, tanned woman with the brilliant blue eyes.

Her initial shyness fell away as she discovered her capabilities on her first committee assignment (Indian affairs). She was soon known as one of the most conscientious, knowledgeable, and hard working legislators in the House. Her research was solid, her positions stolid.

However, word reached her that Ohio Republican men did not want her to run again. This had an opposite effect on her. She ran.

When the votes were counted in November she

scored a greater majority than Chester's best. Nobody wanted her but the voters.

The House had to take a new view of her. She was assigned to the House foreign affairs committee. Her long and dramatic career in the U. S. Congress is detailed in many other media, but relevant here is the following. Frances Bolton's routine constituent work load was heavier than other congressmen because her Twenty-Second Ohio District, nine hundred thousand people, was the largest. Her mail was an avalanche. Her offices in Washington and Cleveland earned reputation as the most efficient in all Congress. Would the school lose Mrs. Bolton to her increasingly demanding congressional assignments? It became difficult for her to get time in Cleveland; and when she did, hundreds of people demanded her attention.

There were other towering figures now involved in the school. And as for money, there were wealthy board members. For example, Liv Ireland, descended from the powerful Hanna family, represented combined fortunes. Why would Frances still be that important?

Roberta Bole brought James Hawken. Hawken brought certain pronounced concepts of education. Hawken passed the baton to Frances Bolton. Frances sustained those philosophical and didactic concepts, and carried on communication with the senior faculty. But during her intensive career in the world's largest legislative battleground, who would implement on the Hawken home front?

Liv

There developed a strange and magnificent partnership, not always smooth, but always forceful. Liv Ireland, as complex a man as ever straddled the worlds of rough and tumble industry and education, chaired the trustees. He wore authority as casually as the tattered Navy flight jacket he wore into the Union Club.

His colorfully profane manners were refined in the bituminous coal mines in Ohio, West Virginia, and Pennsylvania, and in toe-to-toe battles with John L. Lewis. His growl and shaggy bark hickory exterior shielded a hearts-of-celery streak which recognized the dedicated efforts of the least person on the Hawken staff. A little gray was coming into his leonine mane. His management method in coal mining was a roar when necessary, tempered with an amazing sensitivity to and awareness of good work being done by quiet people who didn't put themselves forward. Cavalier about breaking every rule in everybody's book, he studied peoples' characteristics with the precision of an engineer, which he was.

R. Livingston Ireland

He respected Frances Bolton. He would leave the philosophy to her while he would "handle the goddam problems."

It was found that the treasurer was in charge of purchasing, bookkeeping, and writing checks. Many purchases were made and paid without approval from any other quarter. Some approval should be provided. Next, for the convenience of some of the staff who had no checking accounts, personal bills were being paid with school checks, later reimbursed by payroll deduction. Despite the auditor's suggestion, Ireland voted to continue this small service to the staff.

He appointed a committee charged with finding out how other schools handled teacher retirement funds, and to frame a recommendation.

The committee came back with a plan called "the five-percent plan." Ireland discussed it with Frances Bolton; she favored the plan. However, the endowment association had no provision then for funds to cover such a plan.

When the alumni association met in 1939, they passed a motion that the officers meet with the agent of each class to discuss the feasibility of the alumni providing the school with a teachers' retirement fund. Remember these early classes were very small and the oldest alumnus still very young, hence any significant fund would need a high per capita contribution.

Alumni spirit that year was boosted by a football

game against University School in which Carl Holmes's son, Peter, '41, plunged across the U.S. goal behind a large guard, John Brewer, for a winning score. Carl Holmes and Brewer's father celebrated that night over strong waters.

By December 4, 1940, all classes had not yet reported, but the alumni of classes from 1924 through 1940 assembled a seed package of $1592, a retirement fund beginning.

Mood Change?

In the three years from 1937 to 1940 there seems to be a change in Holmes' mood or in his ideas.

At about the same time that he praised the faculty, he made an equally laudatory, rather excessive appraisal of the wonderful student body. "Heaven help any of us who may have to go to ... a large group education picture from Hawken. We are terribly spoiled ... by the cooperation we are getting from these lads ...." He said that the Hawken student "is normal, happy, confident, and has great possibilities ... and my only wish is that every worthy boy in the land could have its [Hawken's] advantages." He had also applauded what the school did for boys who needed special help in certain areas.

Suddenly then, in a 1940 board meeting, Carl Holmes's report leads off with a harsh appraisal and recommendation. He states that "about one third of our students have a good chance of becoming leaders, another third a questionable chance, and the last third no chance at all." He goes on to question the merit of accepting the bottom third. "Fine lads. They will be good citizens." But, "would not the upper two thirds be better served if there were no such lower third? May I whisper the fact that although these advantages of small group education accrue to the superior as well as the inferior student, they are much more fruitful with the superior lad, and should be even more so. Here we are spending much more money than we are receiving per boy, and yet allowing much of our time and effort to be expended on lads who ... will never be able to lead in any sense of the word."

After delivering that, Holmes moved on to the subject of faculty. For three years he had been telling the board that the superb faculty deserved a pension plan; yet at this 1940 meeting we find a querulous headmaster talking about teachers not quite good enough for Hawken, and most of those are those favorite old timers he "has just been protecting in the last three years. One cannot just thrust them out for younger and more energetic teachers, but the board must address policy. It may be that increasing the quality of the student body would decrease its size, and therefore the mix of the faculty, and the salary budget might be reduced. Then a temporary cut in salaries all along the line might be necessary. But whatever the financial effects, the idea is worth trying. Any sacrifices or any efforts would be very much in order. I hope this doesn't sound like crabbing. If it does, I'm sorry." Holmes offers a partial explanation, "Perhaps psychologically these eventful days have made me impatient with myself and my associates and my job."

With Hitler invading Europe one would think the headmaster would be anticipating loss of his younger faculty and glad of the older staff.

The trustees earmarked $2535 as a beginning of a participatory faculty pension fund. This came at a time when Stephens, Smeed and Luehrs each completed twenty-five years on faculty. The trustee pension fund and alumni pension fund would later be consolidated.

THE GREAT ROMAN

The big negative of 1940 was the sudden loss of John H. McCarthy. Scholar in the classroom, roughneck coach in scrimmage practice, a quick wit everywhere, John H. McCarthy had captured the boys. They came back to him for advice when they were men for a refresher on his constant admonition: *Mens sana in corpore sano.*

Charles R. Stephens, addressing the sad boys in assembly, said in part, "Not too well prepared you asked him a leading question to trend the discussion away from the lesson. Alas, too often failed, but when per chance you did succeed, you were taught a lesson more important than the one you escaped."

"Arsenal of Democracy"

In 1940 we were not in the war, but President Franklin D. Roosevelt's fireside chat told Americans that they must become the arsenal of democracy. Additionally, he announced plans to train fifty thousand airplane pilots.

Although the administration official line was that we would not send troops, experienced heads among the trustees and faculty knew better. Mobilization could strip the fine faculty again either by conscription or by the incentive of defense wages.

Joseph Arnett, a young teacher, tendered his resignation from the faculty, anticipating his call to the military.

10.   25th Anniversary: Where Are Our Boys?

AFTER A QUARTER century of a special kind of intense education, some may wonder what is happening to the boys out in the real world ... where are they, what are they doing?

The alumni notes which follow were published in the years 1937 and 1941. Scanning these unedited notes provides a rather good composite impression where Hawken education has taken these boys.

Alumni Notes (1937)

1924

A second daughter, Lorna, was born on November 13th to Mr. and Mrs. Sherman S. Hayden. Hayden received his M. A. from Columbia in the spring and is now doing graduate work there. His address is 22 Stratford Road, Scarsdale, N. Y.

William P. Palmer, Jr. is a special partner with Prescott-Biggar and Company in the Guardian Building.

Charles B. Perkins is now working with the Rhode Island Unemployment Compensation Board in Providence.

John E. Phillips is working with Werner G. Smith at 233 Broadway in New York City.

George Urban works at the Northern Ohio Food Terminal in Cleveland. He makes his home in South Euclid where he is active in politics, being President of the South Euclid Republican Club, Secretary of the Republican Precinct Committee Association, and a committeeman in Precinct A.

1925

Dr. Reginald W. Baker is now at the Norwood Hospital in Birmingham, Alabama.

Benjamin P. Bole, Jr., received his M. A. from Western Reserve University last June. He continues to work at the Cleveland Museum of Natural History and since last spring has been a member of Mayor Burton's Advisory Committee on Parks and Playgrounds. In May he arranged the Science program of the N. Y. A. Playground Institute here in Cleveland.

John C. Brayton is a partner in the Ruth Coulter Galleries on Carnegie Avenue. He specializes in fine book binding.

Stephens Chamberlin remains in the Credit Department of the Central National Bank in Cleveland. He has recently joined Troop A of the Ohio National Guard.

Alvah C. Drake, of Phipps, Durgin, and Cook of Boston, obtained a commission as Ensign in the Naval Reserve on August 1st. He has become a rabid amateur photographer and succeeded in getting one of his prints hung at the photographic exhibit in the Iowa State Fair last summer.

Thomas B. Grandin and his wife are somewhere in France.

John E. Kreps, Jr., is working with the Cleveland Tractor Company and has been transferred to Roanoke, Virginia.

Orville W. Prescott, Jr., lives with his wife and son, Peter, at 151 East 82rd Street in New York City. He works with the Cue Publishing Company.

James C. Weir was married on March 14th to Margaret Leland of Boston. They are living at 3686 Daleford Boulevard in Shaker Heights and Weir continues to be with the firm of Bulkley, Hauxhurst, Inglis, and Sharpe.

1926

Douglas C. R. Baker is Supply Buyer with the Higbee Company.

James C. Brooks, Jr., is back in the city after spending three years in Berlin, Germany, studying singing and Grand Opera. He has recently appeared in one of the opera productions at Severance Hall.

Ernest W. Lenihan is with Lenihan and Company.

Kirke P. Lincoln, Jr., is with the Carrier Transport Corporation in Cleveland.

John M. Rea is with the Metropolitan Life Insurance Company in New York City. On June 17th he became the father of a daughter, Mora.

Edgar A. Taylor, Jr., sends in the following: "After five years at DeVaux School, at Niagara Falls, I have come to Montclair Academy, Montclair, New Jersey, for wider experience, new habitat, and last but not least, a show or two in Manhattan.

1927

Charles B. Bolton after having liquidated a failing sheep business and published the Bulletin, is spending the winter in Florida.

Stevenson Burke is living in New York City where he is studying painting and sculpturing with Florence Lucius.

Morris Everett is now with the Otis Steel Corporation.

Clark Ford is a salesman in Cleveland for the International Harvester Company. He is a member of Troop B, Ohio National Guard.

John R. Nutt, Jr., is with the Chesapeake

and Ohio Railway Company. He is located in Cleveland and writes that his "vocation is soliciting freight and avocation, being beaten by the Democrats."

Justin G. Sholes, Jr., of the Ohio Chemical and Manufacturing Company, writes: "At present I'm on an extended business trip out to the coast by the north and back by the south. Sorry I couldn't be there for the gathering in December, but I thought of you boys with icicles in your beards."

C. Farrand Taplin, Jr., attorney at law with C. F. Taplin, is a member of Troop A, O. N. G., and was with them at the war maneuvers at Camp Knox during the summer.

Dr. Graham T. Webster is interning in Cleveland at Lakeside Hospital.

Dr. David R. Weir is an intern in Pathology at the Boston City Hospital. He is a member of the Harvard Clubs of Boston and Cleveland.

Dr. William C. Weir is now at Lakeside Hospital in Cleveland.

1928

George T. Bauman has been working since his graduation from college in 1934 as an aeronautical engineer with Great Lakes Aircraft, Sikorsky Aircraft, and the Chance-Vought Company. He is now working in Buffalo with the Curtiss-Wright Company and is living with his wife at 284 West Gerard Street, in Kenmore, N. Y.

Clarence L. Collens graduated from the Harvard Business School last June and is now working as Investment Counsel with Van Strum and Towne, Inc., of New York City.

Andrew Ford has become the proud father of a son born on September twenty-fifth. He and his family live in Hartsdale,

New York, and he is working with the advertising agency of Benton and Bowles of New York City.

Robert B. Grandin is now in Cleveland.

Henry C. Osborn, Jr., is now working with the newly organized Glascote Products, Inc.

Richard J. Shepherd is doing graduate work at Cornell University. He is studying philosophy and writes, "I would like to cooperate more with the Bulletin Questionnaire but am not newsworthy. For any further details, consult 'Who's Who 1950'."

1929

William C. Bauman is doing research work in Physical Chemistry in the Graduate School at Yale University.

Robert D. Beatty, Jr., is with the Eaton Manufacturing Company in Cleveland.

Dudley S. Blossom, Jr., is in the Graduate School at New Haven studying international relations. His engagement to Jean Vilas was recently announced.

Morris A. Bradley is working with the United States Coal Company in Cleveland.

William B. Chamberlin, Jr., is at the Harvard Medical School in the class of '38. He is a member of the Lancet Club.

Joseph Eaton, Jr., is working at the Eaton Manufacturing Company. He was married on the fourth of June to Margaret Hamilton and is living at 17322 Kinsman Boulevard.

Homer Everett has recently left the Addressograph Multigraph Corporation and is now working at the Glascote Products, Inc.

Richard Inglis, Jr., continues as a member of the faculty at Hawken.

William R. Nash is President and Treasurer of the Milan (Ohio) Brewing Corporation.

George A. Stanley, Jr., is working with the E. A. Pierce and Company of 51 East 42nd Street, in New York City.

1930

Guthrie Bicknell is working in the Terminal Tower with the R. C. Products Company.

Kenyon C. Bolton is working at the Cleveland Trust Company in the Tax Department. He has been a member of Troop A, Ohio National Guard, since last January and spent his summer vacation at Camp Knox during the war maneuvers in which the Troop participated.

Courtney Burton continues to be with the Ferro Machine and Foundry Company.

John W. Coulton is working in Cleveland with the Elwell-Parker Electric Company.

George E. Merryweather is with the Motch Merryweather Machinery Company.

A. Benedict Schneider, Jr., is in his second year at the Harvard Medical School.

Francis F. Silver is at the Western Reserve Medical School.

Dan T. Wellman is working with the Wellman Bronze and Aluminum Company. He and his wife are living at 1913 Staunton Road in Cleveland Heights.

Fred R. White, Jr., is working with the Oglebay Norton Company. He joined Troop A, O. N. G., last January and was with them on their summer war maneuvers.

1931—1

Alexander C. Brown, Jr., works with the Air Reduction Sales Company and is a member of Troop A, Ohio National Guard.

Fayette Brown, Jr., received his B. A. from Yale in June and is now studying law at the University of California.

Albert B. Conkey, Jr., is now on the faculty at Hawken School in the Music Department. He graduated from Chicago University with a B. A. degree in June.

John P. Danforth is at the Harvard Graduate School. He is studying Engineering.

Adrian F. Foose, Jr., a former Editor of the Bulletin, is working in Los Angeles with the Multigraph Sales Agency. His address there is 509 South Virgil Avenue.

Charles Hickox is a senior at Yale University. He is a member of Beta Theta Pi.

William Pelton is with the J. C. Penney Company in Mansfield. He writes, "The J. C. Penney Co. is a chain of 1497 department stores. It started out west and spread all over the country in the smaller towns and cities and is now entering the larger cities as a first class store. I feel sure this company has a better future than any other in its field."

Harry C. Royal, Jr., was married on July 15th, to Marna Willetts Brower. They are living at 1801 Spring Drive in Louisville, Kentucky, where Royal works with the Standard Oil Company of Kentucky.

Frederic H. Swetland was married to Nathalie Penrose of Hartford in Seattle on May 15th. He is teaching at the Lakeside School in Seattle.

Benjamin H. Taplin graduated A. B. from Princeton in June and is now working for Pickands Mather and Company in Cleveland.

1931—2

David C. Bole, Jr., a senior at Amherst and treasurer of the Alpha Delta Phi, a member of the College Christian Association and the Sphinx, and a member of the baseball team, writes, "I had the best two weeks vacation imaginable from the monotony of eight weeks with the Cleveland Trust Co. this past summer—place Lake Temagami. I strongly recommend this as a guaranteed remedy for tired minds and bodies."

Jonathan L. Collens is a junior at Yale University.

Albert C. Fonda spent last July and August traveling in Mexico. He is a junior at Western Reserve University and is doing N. Y. A. work translating French legal documents. He also is tutoring a University School student in three subjects.

Jonathan Ford is working with E. J. Quirk, a builder of small homes.

Sheldon Grubb writes, "took 8000 mile auto trip last summer all over the west—Sandiego to Spokane. Visited 11 national parks and didn't get a ticket or touch another car." Grubb is on the Dean's list at Amherst where he is a senior, a member of the Pre-medical Club, and belongs to the Phi Kappa Psi Fraternity.

Franklyn S. Judson is a junior at Adelbert College, Western Reserve University. He spent the summer working nights at a Standard Oil Gas Station.

Frank E. Taplin, Jr., Princeton '37, is vice-president and conductor of the Triangle Club. He writes, "This year's show played Cleveland on January 1st. Composed music and orchestrated score for this and hope to graduate in June if I survive my fourth Triangle trip." Taplin is a member of Tiger Inn, was elected Phi Beta Kappa junior year, and has recently been awarded a Rhodes Scholarship.

1932—1

Lewis J. Affelder graduated with honors

from Harvard University in June and is now with the Wolf Envelope Company in Cleveland.

Charles K. Arter, Jr., graduated Cum Laude from Amherst in June with honors in history. He was married in August to Lora Hansen and is now living in Wellesley, Massachusetts, where he is in the class of '37 at the Babson Institute. He is a member of D. K. E.

Lewis W. Baldwin graduated from Yale in June and is now at the Harvard Law School.

Peter Bellamy is cub reporting with the Des Moines Register Tribune in Des Moines, Iowa.

Harvey Brooks, class of '37 at Yale, rows on the crew and is a member of the Elizabethan Club, Political Union, Sigma Xi, and Phi Beta Kappa.

William W. Brown, Yale '38, is a member of the D. K. E. and rows on the crew.

G. Armour Craig is a senior at Amherst. He is a member of the Alpha Delta Phi.

Willard J. Crawford, III, is working in Cleveland with the Y. and O. Coal Company.

Henry C. Harvey received his B. A. degree from Yale in June and is now at the Yale Law School.

Emory G. Hukill, Jr., is in the class of 1937 at Case School and is active in the honorary chemical society, Alpha Chi Sigma.

James D. Ireland is off on a bumming expedition around the world, probably ending up in many and sundry jails. He has recently finished hitch-hiking around Europe and recommends Munich for beer and jails.

Tracy K. Osborn is doing special work at the Case School of Applied Science.

William Osborne lives with his wife at One Union Street in Willoughby. He works with the Lake Shore Lumber & Coal Company.

Hermon B. Peck is a senior at Williams. He is on the baseball squad, is assistant business manager of the Gulielmensian, and is a member of the Model League, the W. C. A., and is Chairman of the Trails and Cabin Committee of the W. O. C.

Everett S. Sholes is at the University of Arizona. He is spending this winter studying Mexican and Central American Archaeology and in making trips to these countries. He will probably spend most of the coming spring in Mexico City.

1932—2

Robert H. Bishop, III, a junior at Harvard, is a member of the Mountaineering Club and a Business Associate of the Harvard Advocate. Last summer he took a trip to Moose Factory in James Bay via the Opasatika and Messanabi Rivers.

Oliver P. Bolton won the sophomore competition for football manager at Harvard and will automatically be varsity manager in 1938. He is Chairman of the Freshman Committee of Phillips Brooks House and is a member of the Hasty Pudding Club and the Delphic Club. He goes out for tennis in the spring.

William Calfee is in the class of 1939 at Harvard University.

James H. Hoyt, II, is a member of the class of '39 at Yale where he plays football and is a member of the D. K. E. Fraternity.

Gilbert W. Humphrey is a sophomore at Yale. He is a D. K. E. member and plays varsity football and hockey. His two well placed dropkicks were recently responsible for Yale's victory over Harvard.

Edward F. Lenihan, Jr., is a junior at

Harvard. He was in the Leverett House Christmas play.

Hubbard Little is working with the Universal Drafting Machine Company in Cleveland. He is taking a year out to work and is then going to M. I. T. where he is a member of the Phi Delta Theta fraternity.

Henry B. Matthes is in the class of '39 at Lehigh. He was on the freshman wrestling team and a member of the American Olympic wrestling squad.

Maxwell Matthes, Jr., is a junior at Lehigh. He played freshman football and ran on the freshman track team.

Malcolm R. McBride is on the Glee Club and goes out for tennis at the University of Minnesota where he is a sophomore.

Phillip W. Morse is in the junior class at Harvard. He rooms in Lowell House.

Claude J. Peck, Jr., is a sophomore at Yale. He is on the soccer squad and a member of the Zeta Psi Fraternity.

David Swetland is a junior at Williams. During the summer he visited his brother Fred and wife in Seattle for a short time before he "plutocrated it back home and to college." He also was at the Hawken Camp and "tried to be efficient and look as if working." At college he is a member of Phi Gamma Delta, dabbles in the Sketch, is a member of the Liberal Club, and was elected this fall to the Hopkins Log.

Robert C. Webster is a junior at Harvard. He plays inter-house baseball, track, and football and rooms in Lowell House.

Alumni Notes

1924

Charles Perkins, a lieutenant in the U.S. Coast Guard, has been in active service since May, 1941.

George Urban continues as Market Master and Superintendent of the Northern Ohio Food Terminal. He is a Republican Precinct Committeeman, and was elected to the City of South Euclid Council for a second term on November 4, 1941.

1925

Dr. Reginald Baker is practicing medicine in Dora, Alabama. He writes: "Greetings to all. Regret that I cannot attend Alumni Luncheon. Will always have a warm spot in my heart for old Hawken."

Pat Bole continues his activities at the Cleveland Museum of Natural History. He is Vice President of the Hawken School Board of Trustees. His elder son, Benjamin Patterson Bole III, is now in the first grade at Hawken, under the tutelage of Miss Luehrs.

John Brayton writes: "I tell you I have two daughters and you ask me my activities!!"

Edward Maeder writes: "This business of defense priorities has knocked my contracting business to glory—so I am taking a job which is good enough to take me to the Southwest. Future address unknown at time of writing."

1927

Joe Nutt is with the 107th Cavalry at Camp Forrest, Tennessee, having been inducted into Federal Service March 5, 1941.

1928

Andrew Ford has returned to Cleveland. On October 1, 1941 he was transferred from the Chevrolet Motor Division of the General Motors Corporation in North Tarrytown, New York, to the Cleveland Diesel Engine Division. He is married and has a son and a daughter.

1929

Bill Nash has been in active service since March 5, 1941. He is a "Corporal in the 107th Cavalry (King's Three Ring Circus)" at Camp Forrest, Tennessee. His second child, Cornelia Nash, is now ten months old.

Ted Robinson Jr. is in New York, where he is doing writing and departmental editing on *Time* magazine, and occasional free-lance writing. He says, "I joined the staff of *Time* last May, after a year of writing Notes and Comment for the *New Yorker*. Had a short story published in *Harper's Bazaar* last July or August."

1930

Kenyon Bolton, a first lieutenant in Troop D, 107th Cavalry, has been in active service since December 12, 1940, and is at Camp Forrest, Tennessee.

Courtney Burton has been appointed Executive Director for the Ohio State Council of Defense, and is now in Columbus much of the time. His second daughter, Marguerite Rankin Burton, is two months old.

Dr. Francis Silver, a first lieutenant in the Medical Corps of the Army, has been in active service since July, 1941. He spent two months at Camp Blanding in Florida, and is now with the United States Forces at Trinidad in the British West Indies.

1931—I

Alexander Brown has been in active service since March 15, 1941, and is with the 107th Cavalry at Camp Forrest, Tennessee. His first child, Alexander C. Brown III, is three months old.

Jack Danforth was married September 6, 1941. He is working in the Marine Department of the Babcock and Wilcox Company in New York. His company, a manufacturer of marine boilers, is extremely busy with Maritime Commission and Navy Contract work.

Bill Pelton has been in active service since June 21, 1940. He is a first lieutenant in the Air Corps, and is serving as operations and supply officer at the Victoria Pursuit School, Victoria, Texas. He has been married for a year.

Ben Taplin has been in active service since October 1, 1940, and is with Troop D, 107th Cavalry, at Camp Forrest, Tennessee.

1931—II

Frank Taplin, this year's president of the Hawken Alumni Association, is with the United States Naval Intelligence Service in Tutuila, Samoa.

1932—I

Harvey Brooks took his Ph.D. in Physics at Harvard last year, and is now a Junior Fellow of the Society of Fellows, doing research and teaching at Harvard.

Bill Brown graduated from Yale Law School this year, and is associated with Day,

Cockley and Davis of Cleveland. He is at present on leave of absence, having begun service as a flying cadet at Maxwell Field, Montgomery, Alabama, on November 19, 1941. His enlistment is for three years.

Armour Craig is an instructor in English at Amherst College. His first child, James Ball Craig, was born in September.

1932—II

Oliver Bolton has been in active service since March 5, 1941, and is a second lieutenant with the 107th Cavalry, Troop D, at Camp Forrest, Tennessee.

Bill Calfee has been in active service since March, 1941. He is a second lieutenant in the General Staff Crops at Washington.

Philip Morse was married June 21, 1941. He is working in the advertising department of the Cleveland Plain Dealer.

1933

Robert Morse is doing special work in the Production Control Department of the Pratt and Whitney Aircraft Plant in Hartford, Connecticut. He writes: "My only comment is that I am tremendously happy and busy in my present employment ... Even when the work is apparently dull and repetitive, it actually is not because of the feeling of accomplishment.... But the beautiful thing as far as my job is concerned is that the horizon of work that has to be done always retreats."

Malcolm Vilas is a corporal in Troop D, 107th Cavalry, at Camp Forrest, Tennessee. He writes: "In Troop D (formerly Troop A) it seems that Tennessee, Arkansas, Louisiana and Carolina maneuvers take up most of my time. Rumor has it that we are off to Michigan, next."

1934

Kenneth Baker is at Howard College where he holds an athletic scholarship. He is participating in football and basketball, and is a member of the Student Publication Board.

Winchell Keller is at the University of Arizona. He writes: "I am a Junior in the School of Business Administration. Returned to school last year after working for Bendix Aviation, Ltd., in Burbank, California ... I frequently see Marshall Dyer ... who is in the engineering school here. And I occasionally see two other alums: Hubert Merryweather and Everett Sholes, both of whom are ranchers. This school feels deeply the loss of Bill Bishop. He certainly was well liked down here ..."

David Nutt has been in active naval service since May, 1941, and is at present stationed near Boston.

1935

Roger Clapp received his A.B. from Harvard last June, magna cum laude with Highest Honors in Physics. He is a graduate student in Physics at Harvard. He holds a Parker Fellowship and a National Scholarship. His main outside interest is rock-climbing.

Tim Ireland is a Senior at Yale, where he is Crew Manager. He is on the Dean's List this year. He is taking a Civilian Pilot's Training Course under the C. A. A.

Tom Taplin is a Senior at Princeton, where he is active in the Triangle Club.

1936—I

John Price is President of the Sock and Buskin at Western Reserve University where he is a Senior.

1936—II

Frank House is a Junior at Yale, where he is majoring in English, is chief aide to the Master of Berkeley College, participates in 150 pound rowing and sings in the Glee Club.

Richard McBride is also a Junior at Yale, where he participates in Pierson College athletics and in the activities of the dramatic society.

John Newman is in his third year at Cornell. He has been on the Dean's List for two years. His activities include: "Ass. Manager Frosh Crew, Red Key, Majura, Retort & Beaker."

Ted Peck is a Senior at Amherst. His activities include *Touchstone* (college magazine), Aristian Association, and Flick Club.

Willard Walker is majoring in Industrial Administration at Yale, and is taking Naval Reserve training.

1937

Robert Crowell is "in the service of the U. S. Army Ordnance Dept., Cleveland District War Dept...."

Calvin Dalton is at Case School of Applied Science: Cum Laude, Tuition Scholarships, Band, Orchestra, Cheerleader, Phi Delta Theta Fraternity, and Cal Dalton and His Orchestra.

1938

Charles Bradford graduated from University School this spring, and is in his first year at Cornell where he is a student in Administrative Engineering.

John Parker graduated from Exeter and is a Freshman at Yale, where he belongs to the Glee Club and the Outing Club.

The Annual Luncheon and Meeting

The Annual Luncheon and Meeting of the Hawken School Alumni Association was held on Saturday, January second, 1937, at one-thirty o'clock in the Commons Room of the School.

There were forty-three Alumni present and also seven teachers and a former master: Messrs. Holmes, Stephens, McMahon, Sipplc, Bragdon, Godfrey, Aylard, and Adams.

The President of the Association for 1936, Dr. Graham Webster, was in the chair.

After all the food in sight had been consumed, the business of the meeting got under way. Stephens Chamberlin read the Treasurer's report for the year which showed about $200.00 in the bank with the Luncheon and the Bulletin still to be paid for. There being no other business the elections for the officers for 1937 were opened. James C. Weir and John Calfee were nominated for President and Weir was elected. John Calfee and Albert Conkey were nominated for the two year term of Treasurer and Calfee was elected. Albert Conkey was unanimously elected Editor of the Bulletin. Fred R. White, Jr., continues as Secretary for one more year.

Mr. Holmes then spoke. He mentioned

the higher grade of work being done by the boys in the School and of the fact that there are fewer problem pupils. He commented on the fact that Albert Conkey has joined the faculty as music instructor and had stimulated the interest of the boys in this field. He also told us of the new type of desk that Mr. Stephens "is about to patent," of the use of the 16mm. moving projector machine, of the equipping of the west end of the Commons Room as a Library Lounge, and of the fine work of each individual teacher in his field. Mr. Holmes concluded by urging all Alumni to use the School freely and to be seen more often on the Badminton Court.

There being no further business, the meeting was adjourned.

(Signed) Fred R. White, Jr.
Secretary.

New Members

This year the Association has increased thirteen in number. We are all glad to welcome the following boys into our group:

Scott R. Inkley	Willard F. Walker, Jr.
Robert Y. White	Douglas S. Craig
William Devitt	Theodore T. Peck
John Price	Herbert A. Spring

Melville H. Ireland
Robert B. Woodward
William Garrett
D. Mills Boffey
William Wareing

11. AWOL for the Christmas Alumni Lunch 1941

LIV IRELAND, remembering the eagerness of his handful of Yale classmates to drop out of college to form the Yale unit of the Navy fliers, warned the trustees to expect to lose young faculty.

Frances Bolton was struggling with her conflicting opinions about America entering the war, and she felt a terrible responsibility.

"Day That Will Live in Infamy"

When we entered the war, the school did lose young faculty and it also lost some boys because parents were moving. Carl Holmes suggested that four private schools in joint venture operate a pre-school and kindergarten through third grade to offset faculty and enrollment problems. He also proposed some advertising because "there may be some people out there who are making new money from war work and could send their children to private school if they knew about them and understood that they aren't country-clubbish." Many years later the four schools did form an association which advertises at this writing, but in World War II Hawken experimented alone with advertising.

During a strike of waitresses, the older boys took over the job and did it well, suggesting to Holmes that perhaps they could also do some painting, scrubbing and sweeping. Football is better for developing a boy, he said, "but everybody likes a change." The work would have to be real work, he said, "because one cannot fool boys."

Roberta's War Farm

The Bole family, beyond being founders of

Hawken, would be deeply involved to the present writing. Roberta continued to influence friends in raising funds for the school. Her son, Benjamin Patterson Bole, would be the first of three generations of twelve Bole children to attend Hawken.

However, two weeks before Pearl Harbor, Roberta's husband died of Lou Gehrig's Disease. Together they had had a farm where they spent summers. He raised horses (and she was a good horsewoman); she raised Guernsey cows and flowers.

The marriage was considered a storybook romance. Benjamin Bole supported heartily Roberta's many activities which expanded to horticulture, genealogy, large family gatherings, Italian Renaissance painters, Dunham Tavern restoration, Cleveland Museum of Art, and Yucatan excavations. She wrote two cookbooks and loved to travel. However, since Ben Bole would not travel, she held her trips down to two weeks.

When Ben Bole died she closed up the farm, the center of their greatest happiness, and vowed never to go back. However, she later decided the best thing she could do for the war effort would be to raise food. She opened the farm and organized the Farmerettes.

Living on the farm, about nineteen teen-age girls and grown women, with Roberta as instructor, raised oats, corn, alfalfa, tomatoes, and potatoes. Rising at six-fifteen in the morning they churned milk into butter and canned applesauce and fell into bed exhausted shortly after sundown.

* * *

For publication in the *Alumni Bulletin,* Dave Bole, secretary of the alumni association, wrote on December 9, 1941 from Davis-Monthan air field in Arizona, in part: "Since the War declaration yesterday ... the probable effect on Christmas furloughs ... I'll have to depend on your mail for my part of the Christmas luncheon and of Hawken generally. Remember me to Carl Holmes and all who attend the Luncheon—and others too, if they have good excuses for being absent. Kindest regards, Dave Bole."

As the war moved into 1943, the board discontinued the tenth grade. Guardian Bank returned $1409 which was distributed to faculty. The war continued to raid the faculty making it a period of constant substitutions.

The original corps faculty was aging but continued its high level of performance. For example the headmaster reports to the board, "Mr. Smeed has been heading up the Lower school in his inimitable fashion. Although tired at times I cannot recall him missing a single day, and I am sure he is in better health than last year. This in spite of the fact that he has taken on the duties of bus driver and the art classes left uncovered by Mr. White's induction into the army."

The headmaster is scrambling to keep the school staffed. Turnover is very high because of the war; competition for teachers over 38 years of age is rugged.

He suggests to the board the possibility of making some lower grades co-ed to fill enrollment.

The war struck home hardest not when the lists of Hawken wounded came in, but when the lists of the Hawken killed in action began building up. Those men were: Kenneth D. Baker, '34; William Bishop, '34; Edward D. Brown, '32-II; Stephens Chamberlin, '25; Roderick A. Gillis, Jr., '38; James L. Greene, '38; Daniel R. Hanna, III, '37; Edward F. Lenihan, Jr., '32-II; John E. Putnam, Jr., '36; Theodore Silver, '32-II; George A. Stanley, Jr., '29; Willard F. Walker, '36.

12. Postwar Roll Call

VJ-DAY UNLEASHED a fast-paced race to repair, recruit, and replace; a race between capacity and enrollment (144 in 1945).

Woodies wearing out ... tires, hoses, fan belts. Wartime shortages still on. Main building, twenty-three years old. Laundry list of repairs generally approved except replacement of hot water pipes with copper, "unless leaks get a lot worse." More urgent in postwar labor boom is weekly raise for maintenance staff from forty-two dollars to fifty. New primary building needed. Recommendation: defer until deficit eliminated.

To correct tardiness at board meetings, Liv Ireland decreed, "Last man here pays for the drinks." He suddenly announces an anonymous gift of fifty thousand dollars for a new primary building. Trustees accept. Architects engaged. Completion target, 1947.

Sometime previous to this Carl Holmes decided Hawken could no longer survive as a small school. He obtained approval to double the size gradually by adding a second first grade section each year for eight years.

Letter from Frances

Frances Bolton was deeply involved in the postwar national issues and politics. Her stature had risen enormously; she was the second woman in history to address the full Republican national convention. Her hair was now white. She was working for increased opportunity for black medical students, loans for undeveloped countries and she was opposing the hydrogen bomb development. She was now becoming a champion of women's interests. She was deeply concerned about holding onto South Korea. In the middle of her busiest years, and despite her stature, analysts were saying she would lose the next election to a young lawyer, Chat Patterson. She campaigned hard and buried him under a ninety thousand vote majority.

Her work in the House was solid. Eleanor Roosevelt called her a congressman's congressman. Her opponent on the foreign affairs committee, James Richards, said, "When she makes up her mind to get something done, you might as well give up."

In the midst of all this, Hawken School was on her mind.

Liv Ireland read to the trustees a letter from her recommending that at this time the endowment association be merged with Hawken School trustees: "It would be to the general benefit of the school to have the trustees who are running the school also responsible for its future financing."

If the two bodies adopt her suggestion, "I shall be glad to carry whatever deficit may occur up to twenty thousand dollars per year for the next five years so as to relieve the consolidated board of current problems and leave them free to plan for the future." She went on to say, "This seems a good time to inform you of my intent in the matter of a final gift ... barring cataclysms ... $200,000 contingent upon the rest of the money to carry annual operating deficit being raised."

There were still not many alumni out in the world, but they were doing well and had an esprit de corps. Jim Ireland had not attended many meetings, but at one meeting he attended which reported sixty-five hundred dollars in alumni gifts, Jim injudiciously commented, "You ought to be able to do better than that." So naturally they made him treasurer. He then started the "Thousand Dollar Giving" plan. Meacham Hitchcock, associate headmaster for development at this writing, called it the start of organized alumni giving.

A friend to all – John Ciarlillo (with John "Rusty" Chandler, '49)

Mr. Dimpsey's 1947 football team

Track and field

Hawken's athletes of the 1950s are pictured in the following four photographs.

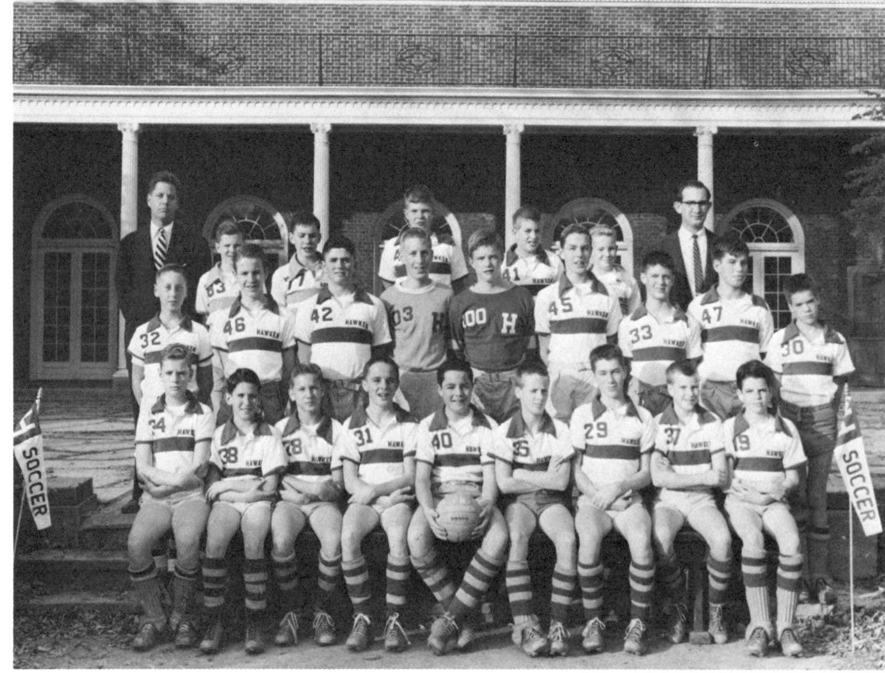
SOCCER
SOCCER

THE CLASS OF 1957:
Much was happening in 1957 . . . President Eisenhower was sworn in for his second term in office. Princess Caroline was born in Monaco . . . Joseph McCarthy died. The American Heart Association publicly announced smoking promotes cancer. The Edsel hit the streets and troops were sent into the school of Little Rock. In October — Sputnik. An the faces of Hawken . . .

HAWKEN
LYNDHURST OHIO
GRADE 2
MRS DANIELS
& MRS MC CABE
MAY 21 1957
OHIO SCHOOL PICTURES

HAWKEN
LYNDHURST OHIO
GRADE 3
MRS EWERS
& MISS CRAWFORD
MAY 21 1957
OHIO SCHOOL PICTURES

HAWKEN
LYNDHURST OHIO
GRADE 4
MRS VOGEL
& MRS BOGATAY
MAY 21 1957
OHIO SCHOOL PICTURES

HAWKEN
LYNDHURST OHIO
GRADE 5
MR LINDBLADE
& MR SIPPLE
MAY 21 1957
OHIO SCHOOL PICTURES

HAWKEN
LYNDHURST OHIO
GRADE 6
MR FURST
& MR SMEED
MAY 21 1957
OHIO SCHOOL PICTURES

HAWKEN
LYNDHURST OHIO
GRADE 7
MR HENRY
& MR GARFIELD
MAY 21 1957
OHIO SCHOOL PICTURES

HAWKEN
LYNDHURST OHIO
GRADE 8
MR HINES
& MR ARMINGTON
MAY 21 1957
OHIO SCHOOL PICTURES

HAWKEN
LYNDHURST OHIO
GRADE 9
MR ROBEY
& MR STEPHENS
MAY 21 1957

The famous barn at Gates Mills

Mr. Stephens in class

HAWKEN GROWS TO GATES MILLS

The next eight photographs depict Hawken's growth to Gates Mills.

Mr. Smeed with Marshall Rose

The Kirtland Camps

Ben Bole and Frank Dimpsey of the phys-ed department started the camps in Kirtland next to the the Arboretum. They began with six boys in 1946. When Dimpsey left in 1963 there were sixty-five boys in the Red Barn Camp, thirty-five boys in the Red Oak Camp and thirty girls in their own camp.

The Teachers Are Hawken

Except for the fact that Charles R. Stephens had not yet missed one day of school since he started, the postwar decade brought staff surprises.

The Hawken community was accustomed to teachers staying a long time; Hazel Benning taught third grade twenty-five years.

Many an alumnus suddenly became aware of his own age when he heard the news in 1946. Miss Luehrs had recovered from pneumonia, but would be unable to return to classes.

In 1949 the alumni were stunned again: Ross MacMahon and his huge beetling eyebrows and Captain Dingle were leaving. The school had already lost McCarthy and Carney and Hawken.

Changes were not only on the faculty; Everett M. Baker resigned as a trustee to become dean of men at M. I. T. But not before he had sparked the formation of the Fathers' Club on May 10, 1946.

Would Hawken ever be the same again?

Can legends be replicated?

What most alumni had little chance to know was that, just after the war, a young David Armington signed on. Holmes described him to trustees as "a jewel in the crown."

In 1946 there graduated from Hawken Chuck Stephens, son of Charles R. Stephens. Few knew at the time that he would be back a few years later to join the cadre of young new teachers.

Onto the Hawken staff came a young Harvard graduate with a severe Massachusetts twang and the outdoors all over him. When he put on a suit and tie for faculty photos you could hardly recognize him.

Charles Poutasse. He had been the Massachusetts state entomologist and he had worked at Holmes' summer camp. Holmes had observed about him something that thousands of others would experience. He had magic with animals and children.

The eyes studied you straight on, interested, not judging. He had a knack of letting people be who they naturally were. He taught that what you are is probably all right. Trust it. Every boy is not a quarterback.

He did not come to teach an academic subject. Shop was his assignment (for in-service training he and his wife, Betsy, built their own house). His shop assignment would soon change. Generations of corporate executives would tell you today that what he taught was life. And he still calls them Jimmy and Freddie when they meet him at Hawken alumni functions today. They hope he still thinks they're all right. If they're not, he'll probably tell them. He's blunt with adults.

By the most unlikely strategy for success in a sophisticated world, Poutasse would become a powerful influence; he helped people.

Meanwhile, in the first semester of 1948, with one hundred eighty boys in school, twenty-six of these in the new building, Carl Holmes, the longest tenured headmaster after fifteen years on the job, left on sabbatical leave. He spent it traveling the country studying various schools. Charles R. Stephens in his thirty-third year, still without a day's absence, still the loudest singing voice in the chapel, stood in for Carl Holmes during the latter's sabbatical.

* * *

In the chapel is a handsome board on which were engraved the names of annual "Head Boy." This board was filled by the last half of 1948. Carl Holmes recommended to the trustees that the practice of electing a head boy be discontinued. "It is too much to be put upon a fifteen-year-old boy, and not a sound procedure."

There was considerable discussion on the subject.

Sitting through it with alarm but without comment, was trustee Char Bolton. The trustees, however, agreed to dispense with the Head Boy custom.

Char Bolton left the room at the close of the meeting in deep and troubled thought. Apparently he was the only one who felt as he did, so he could be wrong. But his thoughts smoldered several days. He finally asked Carl Holmes to circulate a letter to trustees, faculty, and parents, signed by Bolton, making the case for the continuation of Head Boy.

After opening courtesies, and Char Bolton was a courteous man, he wrote, "Bluntly, my position is that a great mistake has been made in eliminating this honor. I note that in the bulletin you say: 'After due consideration'. This leads me to believe that you have left the way open to reinstate the custom. . . . I frankly hope this is true.

"If, by the time a boy graduates from Hawken he is not ready for such an honor as head boy, in my opinion the school is failing dismally in its efforts on behalf of young manhood. I don't believe the argument that harm may be done to the recipient . . . . Suggest the faculty reconsider this whole problem . . . and bring it up again at the next trustees' meeting."

FINANCIAL TEAM

In 1948 Trustee Tom White, treasurer and member of the investment committee, reported the endowment portfolio comprised: American Snuff, Standard Oil (N.J.), Eaton, Time, Inc., Chrysler, B.F. Goodrich, National Biscuit, Cleveland Skating Club, and U. S. Treasury Bonds.

By 1950, he reported the endowment fund at $326,243.74 invested sixty-four percent in common stocks; eleven percent in preferred; twenty-five percent in cash and bonds to produce $16,781. The pension and retirement fund stood at $16,397.

In February 1951, at the urging of White and other trustees, Morris Everett came onto the board and the investment committee. In October of the same year Tom White was killed in an airplane accident near Washington, D. C. Everett picked up the financial baton. Few knew then he would serve the board three and a half decades, earning the Carl Holmes Award. He became over the years the financial watchdog with a quiet bark but a sharp eye.

Anybody's list of the twenty most devoted Hawken servants names Morris Everett. His son, Morrie, carries on the Everett tradition.

While finance usually topped the trustees' agenda as they labored to lift the school from Frances Bolton's support, 1951's agenda was especially financial. There were small and large items.

Carl Holmes regularly pressed for teacher raises. Ballooning postwar industrial salaries were diverting teachers from classrooms. Some young teachers were subject to military draft or recall for new wars. To sustain Hawken quality education Holmes said, "We need to be able to make a teacher an offer he can't refuse."

The trustees rejected some small requisitions like replacing oil-fired boilers with gas (four thousand dollars). Yet in the same meeting Ireland polled the board on approving two hundred thousand dollars for possible construction of a new building. The ayes were unanimous.

ROBERTA BOLE

The June 16, 1951 trustees' meeting formally memorialized Roberta Bole, who died in 1950. It was as if the trustees wanted to leave a very unequivocal statement on the record. The resolution stated in part, *"In truth Mrs. Bole was the founder of Hawken School.*

"It was she who found in James A. Hawken the essence of her ideals for a teacher for her son at a time in the history of Cleveland, when, in the opinion of many, private education was not living up to its reason for being."

The statement spelled out her role in founding the school "modestly but with assurance" in cooperation with Mrs. Weir, Mrs. Teagle, and Mrs. Hayden.

STAFF MATTERS

In 1954 Carl Holmes briefed the board on the whole teaching staff. He pointed out that the few remaining veterans were approaching sixty-five. He wanted some to retire but wanted to keep on three of the founding teachers including thirty-nine-year-veteran Stephens (who still had not missed a day).

But he presented the progress of a remarkable young cadre. He was already moving Charles Poutasse from shop to two fourth grade classes and science, "shifting him to duties where he will shine, rather than glow." Young David Armington "is another one of our hopefuls. Keep him in mind for a future head of one of the Hawken schools." He even compares him with the legendary Smeed.

Holmes described Byron Williams, who handled both upper and lower school science. "He's tough, but good. He is a workhorse ... everything done thoroughly and well. Students howl and squeal to their parents, but end up singing his praises." He speaks of Lorimer Robey as "our most promising star, the only real scholar and a truly great teacher."

Then he speaks of the class to graduate in 1954. Charles R. Stephens wrote a poem to that class which has been reprinted often:

> I am like an old tree, standing by a
> stream
> Round whose feet the river bends,
> eddying at my feet.
> Here within the shade I shed, it swirls
> as in a dream,
> Pausing briefly on its way, never to
> retreat.
> Class by class you face me briefly,
> 'ere you're gone
> To take my shade, but quench my thirst
> all the while you stay.
> Then gaily rushing on into another eddy
> drawn,
> There beneath another tree you pause
> upon your way.

> On flows the stream and on as class by
>   class you come
> To linger for a little time here within
>   my room.
> Expectantly you rush away, glad the
>   stay is done.
> Regretfully I see you go, and sense a
>   moment's gloom.

HEADMASTER

All savvy leaders understand the ineffectiveness of a lame duck position. Carl Holmes had kept a close secret for years. Only slight signals were available to his closest associates, whom Peter Holmes believes were McCarthy, Eames, Muriel Bell and Mac and Winnie. One of these signals was noticed by some and then dismissed. In 1953, Carl proposed that a board be mounted in the chapel giving the names of faculty who had twenty-five years of service to Hawken. At the end of his proposal he grinned, "I can propose this without embarrassment as I do not expect to last out twenty-five years at Hawken."

Carl's son, Peter, traditionally raced his father in the hundred, and traditionally lost. But he remembers the year he won. He also knew that since 1943 his father carried in his left hand trouser pocket a small brown vial.

As Carl Holmes walked the campus with his great Chesapeake Bay retriever, Cap, few knew that he had twice been mustard gassed in World War I. They blamed his constant cough on his chain smoking unfiltered Lucky Strikes. Frank "Jack" Dimpsey in the athletic department admired Holmes, so it concerned him that Holmes "wore heavy clothes in hot weather. Maybe circulatory problems."

Muriel Bell, assistant treasurer and secretary to the headmaster, was a devoted admirer of Carl Holmes's deep involvement in the school. "He knew every single boy and every parent." She probably knew Carl Holmes' better than anyone on staff.

Carl Holmes' management way was to be always in motion around the school, on the grounds and in the classes. Therefore, his office and desk top wore the clutter of an aggressive administrator. He would leave it that way when he rushed off to fill in for a suddenly absent teacher. He relished substituting, no matter the subject.

Muriel Bell's view is informative, not only about Carl Holmes, but the school.

She was secretary to headmasters from 1942 to 1968 and became assistant treasurer when Horace Aylard left. That hardly tells it. She was bus driver, drama rehearsal director, liaison to parents and trustees, general pinch hitter, and, especially, confidant to the boys in a largely male school home. Char Bolton called her Ma Bell and Mother Superior.

In 1942 she was forty, childless, and taking a business course at Spencerian College when Carl Holmes called.

Her view of Holmes may be biased but her view of the school coincides with the majority of those alumni and faculty interviewed by the authors. "If there was ever a place that was a family, it was Hawken School. We had no rules. Boys who went to other schools could not understand this. When you have a family there are certain things that are expected without a book of rules. There was no vandalism because no one was going to hurt his own property.

"Everyone knew the board members, and we were close to the parents, too. The people who had three or four boys at Hawken were part of the school for twelve years or so .... When Bruce Rankin was born, instead of sending the mother a congratulations card, I sent her an application blank signed with references of all the people she knew at Hawken."

Muriel Bell had a unique quality—when a boy's morale was low he would come to talk to Mrs. Bell. She took a lot of her work home to make time for these long talks with the boys. She asked Carl Holmes, "How much do I have to tell you about these confidences?"

"Only what would help the school or the boy."

And so to this day she still has secrets with some

alumni.

She helped new teachers find places to live, then brought them home for supper.

At one point Carl Holmes got the idea that he was going to discipline boys by dictating a letter to their parents in the boys' presence. But Muriel, taking the dictation, would have tears running down her cheeks, so Holmes quit that.

One of his methods which she did approve, and which harks back to Jim Hawken's founding principles, was accenting the positive rather than beating on the negatives, "The school did not discourage a boy because he couldn't read, but encouraged him because he could paint."

Holmes, according to Muriel Bell, was sensitive to teachers' moods. When a teacher would seem to be down, Holmes would detect that; at lunch time he would take the teacher out of the dining room and say, "You go down in the kitchen and have lunch today." That would get the teacher some relief from the boys, and more important, expose him to McCarthy's therapeutic jokes.

Muriel Bell recalls, "In the commons room at Christmas we always had a beautiful tree which Mr. MacMahon always decorated. And the Christmas play was one of the best traditions. The mothers helped with the costumes. The music teacher, Jack Raish, and Mr. Stephens did the sets (and he was a perfectionist), and everybody had a part. I helped with the directing. I could take a boy out of any class and help him with his part. It made the whole school come together. One new teacher said to me, 'No boy is coming out of my class to do that.' I heard that for about two minutes, then I had him helping me as a part of the whole thing. Dave Armington wrote some of the plays."

Muriel Bell explained, "Near the end Carl was getting sick. He knew it and I knew it, but nobody else knew it. He'd go out and run around and be the big shot and talk to everybody, and then he would come back to the office and wilt.

"He said, 'When I retire I want you to stay for one

year and help the new man.'"

Charles Stephens noticed in the spring of 1955 that the clutter was diminishing in Carl's office in general. And in early May he noticed the desktop almost totally bare ... "as if Carl were preparing ... to leave things wrapped up neatly behind him."

On May 16th, 1955 Carl Holmes died.

It was two years short of a quarter of a century of Holmes' headmastership of Hawken School.

Charles Stephens had been considering retirement. But he was asked to stand in for Carl for 1955-56.

Book II
The Builders

13. Changing the Watch

RICHARD W. DAY memorized the eye chart to pass the test for the U. S. Marine paratroops. In 1956 he memorized Hawken School carefully on an extended campus visit and later explained to the trustee search committee, which included interim headmaster Charles R. Stephens, how he would intend to function if made headmaster. Over forty other candidates, he passed that test.

In the fall of 1956, the boys saw a tall square-jawed former Marine striding the corridors.

"He was a Marine paratrooper," explains trustee Jim Ireland, "and everything he did, he jumped in with both feet."

Richard W. Day

Richard Day, with specialities in Greek and history, did his undergraduate work at Yale and earned his Ph. D. at Harvard.

Having worked for Marine generals, Day faced any gods with his hat on. He was comfortable with the board, and early introduced his recommendations. One might expect from a Marine recommendations emphasizing sports, construction, discipline, and hardware. To the contrary, Day's focus was the academic side. His house, provided by Hawken, had to have the library room shored up to handle the weight of his personal books. The spectacles seemed out of place, but the Hawken community soon discovered Day was not only keenly interested in the subjects to be taught, but all techniques for teaching those subjects. He imported distinguished visiting educators to counsel with faculty and, to keep Hawken academically ahead, he would encourage experimenting with new methods.

If one of Dick Day's innovative programs fizzled, he dropped it. If it showed promise he nurtured it.

Some of these impacted education far beyond Hawken campuses. Elizabeth Kelly used in-class dramatizations to teach certain complex points in history and English classes, even math. Day, impressed with the clarity and impact of lessons taught this way, encouraged her to expand the technique and to show the other teachers.

Elizabeth Kelly's reputation for these classroom demonstrations spread off campus and she was stolen away by another private school. She went on from there, and today, nearly four decades later, she is in demand as consultant to schools, demonstrating her method of teaching by dramatization.

Day's initial recommendations to the trustees were bold:

• build up the library which he considered only moderate;

• establish a kindergarten;

• put K-3 all under one roof;

• although teacher salaries had just improved at the recommendation of Stephens, Day alerted trustees he would request another revision;

• increase Mac and Winnie's food budget by $120 per month so that faculty could come for coffee and confer with each other in the kitchen; something about coffee in the kitchen improves collegiality;

• make the school financially self-sufficient by 1961 ("Times are good. Isn't it a good time to help our donors improve their tax deductible standing with the IRS?").

Day was also astute. He asked for appointment of Stephens as assistant headmaster. Stephens planned on retiring at the end of the following year; but Day asked him to stay another year. Stephens was also pleased.

Stephens received a letter from Jim Hawken which we partially reproduce, not so much in tribute to Stephens, but for its revelations of school history.

> I wish you could know how often I thought of you and how affectionately ....
> And when I think of the school of today I think of you and Mort, each in his own de-

voted way, carrying on the inspiration that was the school's humble beginning.

What faith and courage you had when you peeped in the windows of that shabby house on Ansel Road and discovered ... a puny plant that gave not the slightest promise of growth. And I know quite well that the poor little scrub had withered and died if you and John Carney, Fannie Luehrs and later on Mort, had not come along to give it your loving and expert care. This is very often my thought when I'm tempted to dig up and throw away a poor, rickety seedling that shows no sign of ever getting its roots down .... Well, you didn't turn your back on the seedling and now the ol gardener (meaning you) has a plant that he can proudly exhibit at any garden show.... I wish I had that satisfaction.

And yet had I remained at the school's head the school would have perished. There's one chapter in the life of the school that will never be published in its history. So be it.

I am so pleased to know that you like Day. I feel that the school is now under the man who will understand it. I never felt this about Carl Holmes. And I am happy to know that his first years can be blessed by your wise tutelage.

The price of the school's existence was a compromise. We can only trust that that was wise. I think it was. And now perhaps in Mr. Day the compromise is bearing fruit ... worthy of its first inspiration.

Is John Chiarillo still working at the school? When you see him tell him I often think of him and love him very much. Jim.

Day pressed the board aggressively for his programs. In his second year he asked for the teacher raises. He also requested a headmaster discretionary fund. He aggressively recommended expansion to twelve grades. Intermittently, the trustees had studied this. Under Day's persuasion, they now re-examined it.

Trustee Jim Ireland remembers, "We had hard soul searching. Would we need a separate building from lower and middle school? Did we have enough land? Would enough parents stop sending their boys east?"

There should be thirty boys per grade in two sections. The trustees acquired an estimate on construction—one million dollars. They surveyed the community demand for twelve grades and debated the idea into 1958. Char Bolton, then a trustee, said the Boltons would make land available for the building.

That year, for the first time in its history, following a nine-thousand-dollar-deficit year, the school showed a fifteen-hundred-dollar profit.

In that year Day had four experimental programs in action. One was to determine whether the fourth grade or seventh was the better year to start French. A second brought in a Miss Crane to run a teacher training program. The third program eliminated remedial reading by using a kinesthetic approach taught by Miss Gillingham. The fourth allowed upper school boys to elect art, music or shop in lieu of athletics.

In 1959, trustees approved the kindergarten for twenty children; and completed for $342,000 the separate primary building proposed by Day.

Hamilton Eames took over as head of the upper school, and since the great Elmer Sipple would retire this year as head of summer camp, Lee Henry, a new teacher, was appointed assistant head. Henry would later become language department head and would become one of the lifetime Hawken teachers.

The trustees in those days ran basically one-man committees, sparse of speech, especially to families. The introduction of the Leicestershire Method in primary school was an example. It involved integrating grades one and two, and three and four. While the concept had merit, it did not succeed with the parents for lack of communication.

Another program introduced by Day which bedeviled parents was mathematics to other than base ten. Trying to help their boys, parents were tied up for hours.

Since the trustees had enormous fiscal issues constantly before them as well as small ones (constant attempts to stop flooding in the basement kitchen), one might expect the board concentrated on the logistics, plant and finance. To the contrary the trustees always recognized these as side issues to the raison d'etre ... superior education. For example, when Liv Ireland made a mailing to parents and friends of Hawken, he seldom talked about facilities; he featured academics and elimination of human xerography in school. In 1959, for example, he explains, "Our faculty of forty maintain a pupil-teacher ratio of nine to one."

Ireland knew the academic programs, "In mathematics we have also adopted a new technique ... in Grade I through VI. Cuisenaire rods developed by a Belgian ... to convey a grasp of basic mathematical concepts ... in much the same way that our spelling curriculum conveys the basic concepts ... of our written language.... Hawken has always been known for the quality of its mathematics."

Ireland explained the teacher training work in connection with Western Reserve University.

In an ensuing letter he explains, "Our alphabetic method, now in its second year, is more than justifying our decision to adopt it. In last year's first grade every boy learned to read and spell with confidence .... News spread to neighboring schools ... which have sent representatives to observe."

He describes the reading and math ungraded school (kindergarten through six), in which boys can move up at their own pace. A fourth grade boy can do sixth grade math, without losing the security of staying with his own class.

Incidentally, experimentation was partly the cause of Hawken's sometime reputation as "too liberal." In education gossip there was a saying that when Hawken experimented, University School would watch. If the new technique succeeded, U.S. would adopt it. If it flopped, they would not.

While Ireland does press the fund drives, the excitement in his letters is about acquisition of superior teachers and superior academic achievement: "In the recent National Merit Scholar examinations, 40% of the senior class were selected as semi-finalists or received certificates of accomplishment."

Ireland's superior business acumen was veiled in these letters touting academic accomplishments; but shone through particularly in 1975 with the creative "Ireland Plan"—donors were permitted to defer payment of the principal of their pledges, annually paying the interest which the pledge would have provided.

The Balanced Board

The three top alumni association members sat on the board ex-officio, with voice but without vote. Meacham Hitchcock, '42, president of alumni, sat on the board this way. In a way Hitchcock has been associated with Hawken for life. He lost his father when he was four, hence the men on the faculty meant a lot to him and spent a lot of non-academic time with him. He went on to a career in industry but remained very active in the alumni association, becoming an association board member, then president. After his term as alumni president, Dixon Morgan asked him to consider becoming a regular trustee. Morgan was a worker—a lawyer by trade and legal counsel, secretary and for years a one-man budget committee for Hawken. Hitchcock demurred.

Pressing the matter, Morgan said, "You would enjoy the work because we have a very balanced board: Dick Day on one side and all the rest of us on the other!"

While Dick Day and the "balanced board" were busy moving Hawken School into the new era that was to be the sixties, changes were also taking place in the student body and their attitudes and activities—evidenced by the *Affirmative No,* the student newspaper born of this period.

Marjorie Johnson (fondly known as *la grande dame* of the school), who succeeded Lee Henry as language department head, also became faculty adviser to this upper school newspaper. She recalled it was named as a grin at what students considered the administration's sometimes wishy-washy attitude. The paper has won many interscholastic competition awards. Its bold, sassy, thoughtful and factual pages comprehensively report upper school activities.

Mrs. Johnson characterized its life in three eras. In the first, it was staffed by the cream of the student crop who had no intentions for journalism careers. The second era drew journalism aspirants who went on to journalistic success. The recent era, she feels, is staffed by students seeking good extracurricular credits for college applications.

The *Affirmative No* remains alive and well in the 1990s but many wonder about the unusual title.

In 1964 there was some discussion about changing the name and the editors responded in their December 11th issue with an editorial "What's In The Name?":

> ... the assumption that cynical pessimism is synonymous with affirmative no appears to be false.
>
> If properly understood affirmative no applies not only to the faculty's wall-of-jello type response to student appeals but also to a philosophy of evaluation and selection inherent in the Hawken system. (Perhaps) a positive idea to forestall hasty decisions while searching for better solutions.
>
> *Affirmative No*—this title has striking character. Better to ponder, denounce or applaud a name ... than ignore it.
>
> Affirmative no suggests compromise ... implies freedom of discussion and the belief that that which is worthy will survive critical evaluation.

The Old Tree

Mile-post events crowded this decade 1955-65. The retirement of Elmer Sipple was one. Then in 1959, after forty-three years, Charles R. Stephens missed his first day of school. The old tree retired. Hundreds of Hawken alumni and parents recognized the departure of the last of the pioneer faculty.

The Stephens imprint on hundreds of alumni still exists. Meacham Hitchcock called him "the greatest faculty influence on me. He had a steely eye, but you knew he loved you."

It seems almost like fiction that the very next year there was a Charles Stephens on the faculty, Charles L., son of Charles R., returned to Hawken as a teacher. He had graduated from Hawken in 1946, attended Rochester University, taught at Worcester Academy, and returned to Hawken in September 1960 to teach history and English in the eighth and ninth grades. He later became middle school chairman.

As the last of the original corps retired, new distinguished young teachers came aboard in larger numbers.

Rising up also was a young middle generation of teachers brought in by Carl Holmes, particularly Poutasse, Armington, and Eames. They were firmly seated before Day's arrival, and had enthusiastic constituencies of their own. They would test his leadership for they were opinionated, confident, and "every master a headmaster."

Day, also with strong opinions on educating, would get crosswise with some faculty. No academic leader of consequence can be universally loved. Day kept some faculty irritated and off balance by opening nearly every meeting with a new idea, new system, new technique; more new plans than many felt could be properly assimilated. The atmosphere often became highly charged, some suspecting Day liked change for change's sake, a bull who brought his own china shop, never consolidating before moving on to something more exciting.

On the other hand some would follow him anywhere. One veteran faculty explained, "He encouraged a teacher to innovate. He wanted you to stand up to him about your ideas. If you did so successfully he'd back you one hundred percent. If you didn't, of course, he tended to run over you. So it's understandable that some didn't like him."

Chuck Stephens, son of a great headmaster, ranked Day "the best in the business."

Day would drop in on any class any time and observe. Although he was skilled at acquiring and maintaining the hardware, and although very athletic himself, his big interest was in the didactic processes. He constantly introduced for trial new methods, and dropped them if they disappointed.

Day was aloof from students and not clubbish with faculty. While the demeanor does not win the jolly-good-fellow chant, it does have some merit. It avoids some of the quarrels entangling the fraternal-type leader. There was no ambiguity about who was in charge of what.

The faculty, however, was very much a club socially. They enjoyed each other's company after hours. Frank Hines, the English teacher who had a special arrangement allowing him to attend the Kentucky Derby annually, took with him the faculty wagers to place at the track.

"You Seem To Be the Man To See"

Headmaster Day wanted his teachers to have top academic degrees, but he chose his executives wherever he found the talent. One was in the basement.

Latin and math are important, of course, but in a school of boys rising an average of three and a half inches a year, lunch is high priority.

On the gym floor at a quarter till noon, three dining tables are hastily folded down from two walls. Two more folding tables are set up in the middle.

Boys in suit coats and ties charge in to sit at the eight tables. They hold back until the teacher has said grace. They hold back until the teacher lifts his fork. Then—release.

They watch as dessert comes up from the basement on the dumbwaiter, hoping it is covered with Winnie McCarthy's chocolate or butterscotch sauce, and that it is not "fish eyes and glue" today.

Down in the basement things are not so calm. Mac and Winnie McCarthy are in charge of the kitchen. Mac is in a white T-shirt, white trousers and a clean apron at the insistence of fuss-budget Winnie.

To know Hawken School, a reader needs to know about Mr. and Mrs. Francis McCarthy.

When Winnie McCarthy first arrived back in 1933 and saw the kitchen next to the boiler room in the cellar (Winnie's nomenclature), she nearly quit. Food deliveries were daily because there was no ice box. The meals had to be sent by dumbwaiter up to the gymnasium dining room. That was in the bottom of the Depression. Three women in green dresses and white aprons worked with Winnie, serving the meals, a dollar a day. They came by streetcar, twenty cents round trip.

The kitchen was entered by descending stone steps, slippery in winter. The milk, delivered at nine-thirty in the morning was often frozen.

After a year, "We yelled at Carl Holmes," Winnie remembers. "We can't get out a decent meal under these conditions. We're going back to Boston!"

Carl Holmes arranged for some small improvements including a dishwasher. But Winnie continued campaigning.

Mrs. Bolton would come down to the basement occasionally for a friendly visit. She would make no comment, but after she left some improvements would materialize.

Achieving a better dining facility made more work for the McCarthys as the board decided to hold some dinner meetings there.

Money was tight. A board member called Winnie, "Don't serve that sherry at tomorrow's board meeting. We can't afford that."

"Oh. All right. I'll tell the trustee not to send over

any more."

"Oh? It was a gift? Then that's okay."

Char Bolton knew how close the McCarthys were to Carl Holmes. Therefore, when Carl Holmes passed away, Bolton came to the McCarthys to ask if they would stay on. Under the emergency, they reluctantly agreed.

However, the next headmaster, Dick Day, had a responsive ear to the dining facility problem. He would drop by the kitchen for a cup of coffee and some conversation.

Winnie McCarthy, who approached all people at eye level, stood up to Day one day after she had slid down the snow-covered outside cellar stairs, "This is our last year. We can't take this. We're going back to Boston."

Day knew when to command and when to listen. What was needed?

Winnie told him and he told the board: A large kitchen right next to the dining room; two freezers, a milk house so that the milk wouldn't freeze.

Winnie managed a very efficient operation. Mac did much of the cooking.

One thing Dick Day especially noticed, however, was that Mac kept excellent cost records and controlled costs well. One day when the McCarthys were visiting the Days, Dick asked, "Mac, would you consider taking over the business manager job?"

Mac demurred, "I've not had any formal education."

"I know, but let's just take it one step at a time, and work it out together."

There was a long narrow room used for costume changes for the theatrical productions. They made that Mac's office. He shed the kitchen whites and put on a necktie. They gave him a small desk and a chair and a subtle suggestion that it was no longer so appropriate for him to be seen washing down the school busses.

However, Mac was smart enough not to let his new white collar interfere with his close camaraderie with John Dremen, the inside maintenance man, and

John Ciarlillo, outside.

Mac knew that business managing a school meant largely keeping the plant operating. One of his first problems was keeping the Ford station wagons running. The three wagons had grown to eight and you had to have a supply of spare parts and know what to do with them. Many a winter day Mac was under the hood.

He started a program of adjusting the transportation charges to parents to cover replacing the vehicles and he worked at selling off the oldest ones for the best dollar. Later he moved to leasing. The fleet ulti-

14. Gates Mills

AS EARLY AS 1956, a strong sentiment developed for creating a high school on the Lyndhurst campus.

The eastern boarding school migration was less compulsive. Some families disliked their boys leaving home so early. Others wanted an alternative high school to University School. The cost of sending boys east fueled some of the drive for twelve grades at Hawken.

There was also strong opposition. The influential voice of Charles R. Stephens, for example, had come down vigorously opposed, "We are doing a great job at the present size. Don't spoil it by over-reaching."

Jim Ireland, classmate and good friend of Char Hickox, Willard Brown, and Fayette Brown, came on the board in 1959 in the middle of the debate. (Meacham Hitchcock, in doing some research, calculated that Jim Ireland has given 169 years of service on various civic boards.) Courtly Jim Ireland, sitting erect in his office, remembers, "Dick Day pushed very hard to add grades nine through twelve."

But this gave the board another time of hard soul searching. As Ireland remembers, "It would mean a lot of adjustment. Tremendous new costs. New staffing. But above all, did we have enough land? It did not seem to many of us as if we did."

One Sunday morning early, Jim Ireland got a call from Dick, "Can I come over and have coffee ... strong?"

"Come ahead."

Day arrived, super-charged, and told the following story. He had been at a dance last night when on the floor he heard a young woman behind him speaking to her partner in agitated tones and loud, "That damned University School turned us down!

Wouldn't accept our farm!"

Ireland remembers, "By the description, I knew immediately that had to be Annie Stockton."

The farm in question was a twenty-five-acre fraction of the beautiful Walter C. White Circle W Farm in Gates Mills, including a pillared mansion which looked across a long sweep of green to a very large polo horse barn. Gates Mills was a compellingly beautiful little world of wooded hills, valleys, and streams which in 1826 drove the sawmills of Holsey Gates and his two brothers.

Jim Ireland recalled, "Hawken people immediately contacted Ann Stockton. The farm could be available to Hawken School." The arrangement also initially included the option to buy additional acres of the three-hundred-acre farm, receiving one acre as a gift for each acre purchased.

That led to intense trustee debate. Could we manage a split campus? Would we be practically doubling costs for adding only four more grades? "One powerful rationale was that the split campus would be like life itself; a small boy could grow up on a small campus through Grade 8, then advance ... as in life ... to a larger world, the upper campus."

Skipping the drawn out decision-making, the final verdict on March 7, 1960 was—go.

The terms of the gift were complex but basically provided that Hawken School could purchase additional acres and be gifted one acre for each purchased, up to a certain limit.

The powerful call to expand any institution or business never comes at a comfortable time. The trustees had just spent three hundred forty-two thousand dollars for an addition to the primary school. They were fast approaching the 1961 target date for becoming financially self-sufficient. The board raised the tuition seventy-five dollars, but acquiring this property would surely lock them into deficit operations.

Taking over the Circle W farm was tremendously intricate. Trustees had to pursue availability of water, utilities, and zoning approval, state and local, for operating a school on this property.

They organized a building fund drive, then proceeded to untangle the legalities of acquiring approximately sixty-five acres of the estate of Mrs. Walter White with option to acquire adjacent property, not to exceed 250 acres.

With an architectural firm engaged, (Little & Dalton) for the arts and communication building, they hoped to open classes in the fall of 1961. The large polo pony stable would be used for athletics and shop. The main house would be for dining and administration. A large classroom building would be built, the R. Livingston Ireland Building.

The fund-drive goal for the new high school was two million, one hundred seventy-five thousand dollars, half for bricks and mortar, half for faculty salaries and endowment. Trustee Alfred M. Rankin reported in June 1959 on the status of the fund raising for this Gates Mills campus. Special gifts had reached one million dollars; regular pledges, six hundred sixty-five thousand; firm promises, one hundred eighty-six thousand. "Very reasonable expectations," four hundred thirty thousand, and "hopes," four hundred eighty-two thousand dollars.

Compounding the financial challenge in June 1959 was Day's announcement of twenty-six thousand dollars uncollectable tuition and the establishment of a medical benefit program for faculty.

Suddenly a fire broke out in the beautiful horse barn. Trustee Jim Ireland elbowed Day, "I know you set that fire, Dick, to get the insurance money to build the gym."

Costs for phase I of the new Upper School were estimated at six hundred fifty-five thousand dollars; phase II two hundred twenty-seven thousand dollars. Lyndhurst's new building, parking lot, driveway, and remodeling of the main building, three hundred seventy-three thousand.

Tuition for the new high school was one thousand dollars.

Hawken East

On September 10, 1961, 134 boys traveled the long, up-hill drive circling a magnificent slope of Circle W pasture. The breeze was flavored with new cut grass. This was the Hawken east campus.

Although unfinished in construction, it was staffed to compete with the best schools in the nation in preparing boys for college. The erudite Hamilton Eames, who amazed boys by writing in Arabic, headed a largely new and brilliant faculty. Charles L. Stephens, for history and English; Gerald Wilson for mathematics; Tucker Fox for French and development fund work; Katherine Dunlop, librarian.

Hamilton Eames, noted for the quality and elegance of his language, addressed the parents on the aims of the upper school. No perfunctory placebo, his talk was memorable. Before "excellence" became a diluted buzz word, he said, "We ... are directing toward the single goal of excellence .... We begin with the 'word' ... seed of all cultural life." He reminded the audience of Francis Bacon's summary, "Reading makes the full man, talking the ready man, writing the exact man."

Eames said, "Verbal discipline is our first concern." And he concluded with Santayana's definition of intellect, "the faculty of seeing things as they are."

* * *

In the midst of the tremendous administrative and construction overload, Liv Ireland and the trustees still keep their eye on the academic target. Ireland's letter to parents and alumni does not feature the bricks. He spells out the four new divisions of the school: kindergarten through third grade, fourth through sixth grades, seventh and eighth grades, and ninth through twelfth grades.

Each division has a chairman responsible to keep in close touch with each boy's progress and maintain liaison with parents. Elton Knutsen, science, has general supervision of Lyndhurst; Hamilton Eames for the Circle W campus.

He explains that in the past summer "six faculty

members worked a month developing new teaching materials in English, math and history."

He details the graduate work pursued by faculty in the summer.

He details some methods used by some teachers; Molburg, chemistry and physics, "uses the chemical bond approach techniques;" Ferris, French department, "is a firm believer in the direct approach, using only French in the classroom."

PRIORITY "A" LIST

In October of 1962 the trustees made a Priority "A" list which needed to be accomplished before opening the 1963 school year—finishing locker rooms, dining room tables, sports uniforms and equipment, teaching aids, books purchased for the library, repair of a faculty cottage at Circle W, work on the ditches on County Line Road, make decisions on a proposed swimming pool and skating rink.

The board increased the number of trustees and took aboard in 1963 Raymond Q. Armington and Willis B. Boyer.

... AND EVERYTHING ELSE

In the middle of the thus-far largest expansion (1962—540 boys, forty-one faculty) other profound challenges struck.

15. The Builder Meets the Founder

A HEADMASTER, like a major league coach, plays every day to a stadium of fans and critics. The cheers will switch to jeers and back every quarter. If in the crowd roar he is to control the game, he must know who he is and why he chose his game plan.

Richard W. Day, with the body of a rangy wide receiver, was an intellectual; his majors, history and Greek. He approached educating as life's important cause, as had James Hawken. He had joyous respect for the teacher with subject expertise. He studied teaching method continuously. What was not of educational value on the schedule he dismissed summarily; but if a staff member made a case for any activity, he listened with a truly wide open mind. If the case was made, he approved quickly.

If the case was not made, he turned away abruptly. According to one long-time faculty member, "Day killed the gymnastics program. I loved Hawken. Day took the delight out of it for me. When I was out sick he sent McCarthy to my house to see if the sick day was justified."

Muriel Bell, from her central position, said that Day "tightened up things that may have gotten a little loose when Mr. Holmes got sick." Muriel would never say a bad word about anyone, but suddenly she noticed the boys were not coming to talk to her. By the grapevine she heard that Day made her office off-limits to the boys.

She resigned. "That spoiled it for me. The boys were the whole thing."

One teacher said, "He kept a very sloppy desk, often leaving important papers exposed. One teacher pulled a salary list from Day's trash and spread it through the faculty. It showed who got the big raises."

Another emeritus faculty member described Day as "the greatest headmaster I ever had." John Calfee's estimate: "Dick was a real leader, straight forward ... and out front all the way."

Len Carey, former fifth grade homeroom teacher, knew Day quite well. He summarized him as an educator. "Dick wanted to make the school better. He believed in no hierarchy in education—'leaders are also the servants.' He demanded a complete education. Brought in educators from all over the country for seminars both for the faculty as well as the students. Anna Gillingham—alphabetic/phonetic approach to teaching reading; Cuisenaire rods for teaching numbers and number combinations and enhancing approaches to learning addition, subtraction, multiplication and division of numbers; ITA— the Initial Teaching Alphabet, a British method of teaching reading and writing. These were a few of the new ideas.

"Dick had a real hands-on approach," according to Carey. "Came into the classrooms frequently. Always unannounced. Sometimes would take over the class. He worked hard at everything he did—stirred up thinking. Wasn't always the most tactful person, frequently even a disruption to the educational process. But everything he did was for the good of the school. He was always educating himself as well as others. Some faculty objected to this, many—but not all. Dick had the pulse of the school and knew what was going on throughout the school. Lunched with students in his office with great frequency."

Faculty members seem to remember Day most for his deep respect for teacher expertise in the disciplines; his efforts to improve teachers; his surprisingly strong feeling for the arts and artistic creativity; his emphasis on clear, concise thinking and speaking; and his encouragement of student involvement in the complete Hawken educational scene.

Richard Davies came aboard as a math teacher in 1963. He had not had much contact with the by-now quite formidable headmaster, but he had been here long enough to hear about Day's directness. So he was somewhat thrown off balance when Day walked into his classroom session one day, right up to the front of the class where he folded his length into a student chair and listened intently. As Davies continued to teach, Day joined in the discussion, questioning both students and Davies.

Davies's boss, Ramon Steinen, soon heard about the visit and questioned Davies—what had Day said to him when he left the class.

He said, "Thank you very much. Can I come back tomorrow?"

Steinen broke out a grin, "Congratulations!"

"Why?"

"You passed the test. Otherwise he would have said, 'May I see you in my office at your earliest convenience.'" Davies went on to become head of the lower school (1970-81).

There was some sentiment that in the growing faculty there was poor opportunity for the new teachers to meet the veterans. Dick Day tried to correct this. For example, he staged a weekend picnic for new faculty to meet the veteran faculty. This failed miserably. Of the veteran faculty, only Poutasse and one other showed up.

Interesting to watch, because it typifies an ageless dichotomy in education, was the guarded respect between two men—lanky Dick Day and five-foot-eight-inch Charlie Poutasse. Every school has these two.

Poutasse, as chairman of primary, was in a strangely influential position (which it never occurred to him to realize). Parents turned over their small ones to him at their most tender age; and he had the responsibility of the child's entire intellectual beginning, the most determinative years. His manner was parental, and often absently he was addressed, "Dad."

Day loved system in academics, identifiable techniques, lesson plans, use of textbooks—methods, with labels, things on which a teacher could be evaluated neatly.

Poutasse, though he actually had a very precise and original system, didn't recognize it as such. Hated system. And few watching him in action would detect a system. Certainly few could define it. He rejected working from a textbook and wearing a jacket and tie. Instead of being in his office where Dick Day felt chairmen ought to be at opening of school, Poutasse was out on the apron in the snow, receiving the kids with a greeting, "Hi!," and getting any special information from parents. "I want to know if a child had a bad night (and a lot of these kids do). And I want to know who's picking him up after school. And I want to relay that special information to the teachers."

Instead of applying for a substitute when a teacher was absent, Charlie took the class. In his own classes, he didn't use the book. He asked each child to bring something scientific from home, a leaf, an egg, a plant. The lesson would take off from that. "These kids need a chance to be on stage. A chance to talk. At home they don't get it." Often Poutasse would bring his own mystery show-and-tell in a bag, each child to reach in and feel it and decide what it was—a rock, a shell, a frog.

Then, after school, it bothered Day that Poutasse would be out front again. "I wanted to make sure," Poutasse said, "that each child was going home with the right party. We had custody cases where the mother planned to pick up the child, but the father came earlier and did so. And other worse things. I need the parents to tell me home problems, so I can understand what the child is facing."

He also wanted to tell the parents a few things. For example, he told one woman, "Now Helen, every night when he gets home this particular week, you need to take twenty minutes and just devote them exclusively to him. Ask what he did, who he played with. He needs that this week."

"Oh Charlie, we can't. It's cocktail hour."

"Cancel cocktails."

And what Charlie said, they did.

If Jimmy threw up on the floor, Poutasse didn't

send for maintenance, he cleaned it up. "Why make the kid think he caused a ruckus?" If a child couldn't get his boots on fast enough, Charlie did it. Most amazing to onlookers was a nearly mystic phenomenon. An unattended roomful of helling kids could be on the verge of destroying the real estate. Poutasse would enter, and the room would fall to a deafening silence.

These methods drove Dick Day up a wall. But a man like Poutasse, who gets results, and worse, who never in his life worried about being fired ... is a problem.

And so the two men faced each other with a grin. About not using the book, "Well, Dick, you can tell the evaluators I use the book. I'll have it open on the desk."

About the no coat and tie, "Well, I have a bad neck. Injured. Necktie is bad for it." The fact is Charles Poutasse has had a constant headache ever since he was injured in the army.

"Okay, Charlie."

And on Poutasse's part, he backed up some of Day's optional programs which others boycotted. A genial truce between two strong men.

ADMISSIONS

Day early recognized that integrating the school without admissions interference from the board was vital to the health and strength of the school in a 1960s world. He pressed the board aggressively on the integration subject.

The trustees had just taken on huge financial commitments and their top priority was fund raising. They would have liked a chance to concentrate on that before tackling this new subject.

The faculty, however, in close touch with the education picture of the 1960s, pressed for immediate integration so aggressively, Charles Stephens, the younger, remembers that when asked if they favored it, some faculty said that unless integration occurred promptly, "we will resign." Much of this new faculty was young and very much in tune with the movements of the 1960s.

The head of the primary department said, "If we initiate, it has credibility. If we're mandated, it doesn't."

This board was not against integration. What they did fear, Hitchcock recalls, was that once such an admissions policy started, minorities might "flood the school with applications, qualified or not," along with some percentage quota, taking academic quality control away from the school.

This was no idle concern in an era when students were commandeering college administrative offices, torching dormitories, and demanding trendy ethnic curricula of questionable long-term value.

However, Hawken became the first private school in the Cleveland area to recruit black students. The pioneer was Charles Jordan.

For a year the board screened black student applications. Hitchcock remembers how that ended. A newly appointed trustee, Willis Boyer, president of Republic Steel, asked why the board was getting into applications, "After all, that's out of the board's usual charge." He asked if the school had admitted any black students yet and was surprised to be told they had several. The new trustee explained that his son in the school had never even mentioned this; apparently had not found it noteworthy.

The board then decided that if the minority presence was not even noteworthy for students, why should the board get involved in the administrative job?

Day appointed Tucker Fox, French teacher and development office staffer, to a new post of director of admissions.

Tucker Fox died suddenly of a heart attack. Day called Janet Hoerr just before New Year's Eve 1962. Would she be admissions director part time? She demurred. Her experience was thirty years as housewife and mother of five. But she had chaired two mothers committees. She became interested in Hawken when she visited to see if the school was right for her son, Stanley.

Janet Hoerr reluctantly accepted the job. Her first rule for herself was a medical saying, *Primum Non Nocere*—first, do no harm.

Some policies which she instituted endure today: she felt teachers should have a voice in admissions, so she formed faculty admission committees for primary, lower, middle, and upper and she invited applicants to visit class.

The admissions responsibility is pivotal because long term it determines the very make-up of the school population and later the alumni population. In the collision between the Hawken traditional make-up and the 1960s national reach for pluralism, the admissions decisions could never be totally popular.

The job became a full-time venture. But since it was a boys school, Janet Hoerr thought the director should be a man; and eventually told a future headmaster that if he could find one she would resign. He found Vin Fiordalis, '57, but persuaded her to stay for primary. The next director was Robert Tupta. A later widely acclaimed director of admissions was math department head and football coach Frank Brandt. For many Hawken alumni he was the first faculty they met, and is still number one in their memories of the school.

In establishing admissions policies, trustees had to be concerned about numbers of admissions *per grade* to sustain class sizes progressing up the grades. In the 1960s this quota-per-grade consideration was complicated by the recurring proposal of possible merger.

David Weir, trustee and former board president, leaned back with a filtered hundred and recalled the sequential merger negotiations: "The grand plan for several years had been to make a loose coalition of four schools, Hawken, University School, Laurel, and Hathaway Brown. These talks went on intermittently for several years, particularly between Hawken and Laurel."

Each school had a merger committee. Also there was a joint merger committee. Negotiation stretched over years and several hundred pounds of studies, surveys and hearings. The problems were enormous. "There was a feeling," Weir recalls, "that the Laurel faculty opposed it, fearing they might be submerged or diminished. And I dare say they were right."

There were many meetings and debates, separate and joint. "Finally it broke down when in a joint meeting Ted deConingh of the Laurel board got up and said ... you understand this was all done in a friendly, civil manner ... but he said, 'I guess it gets down to ... we just really don't want to do this. We're getting along very well.'"

STRANGE PARTNERSHIP

Charles L. Stephens, interviewing a former staff executive, heard this description of Day as headmaster: "Innovative, great courage of his convictions but open to challenge and discussion of those ideas. Bucked the status quo to get what he wanted for the school. He was a visionary—took quantum leaps, frequently leaving his average colleagues far behind. He could be very upsetting to various groups, especially the trustees. Dick lifted Hawken well above the other three independent schools—he was looking into the twenty-first century."

With a picture like that of Day—aggressive, determined, obdurate, sometimes abrasive—the reader might be startled by the close collegiality which developed between Day and the gentle James A. Hawken. In reconnoitering his new school, Day went to Pasadena, California, for the purpose of talking to Hawken. A close professional relationship then developed by telephone and by mail:

December 8, 1959

Dear Dick Day,

I wrote you earlier to tell you my thanks for your note, read what I wrote and then destroyed the letter. It was just too sloppy. I'll try again and try to be more simple.

I wish I could make you understand what your acknowledgment means to me. All that Mort, Steve and some of the old boys and parents have told me about you assures me that my wishes and hopes for the school are being fulfilled in you. Before your coming to the school I hadn't been so happy. I knew it was growing materially and being successful from the world's sense of values and as it never could have been under its original direction. But I feared this was at the cost of a quality which we first caretakers certainly didn't create but which we reverenced and tried to serve. Of course dead, faithful Mort and Steve were keenly alive to that quality and gave it their very able and unreserved devotion. But they needed a leader, a leader with the same vision, the same dedication but with credentials acceptable to Cleveland men of affairs—and their wives.

You are that leader. I thank God for you. And I thank you for the fellowship you offer me. I know that I've been living in the hearts of most and Steve, Fanny Luehrs, some few boys and parents but I've been so long out of the school itself. You have generously reestablished me. Thank you and God bless you.

Sincerely, Jim

P.S. What you say in your bulletin makes me feel quite at home and the news in Liv Ireland's letter is thrilling.

An Announcement

At the April 10, 1963 meeting of the board, Dick Day requested that the trustees appoint a fiftieth anniversary committee to make preparations for an appropriate founder recognition two years hence. Dick Day was not one to run on in booster speeches, as some do, about his feeling for the school. But suddenly his devotion flashed clear as lightning by one act in which he put Hawken ahead of his career.

On June 9, 1963 Liv Ireland called a special meeting of the trustees to make a startling announcement. "Mr. Day has been offered the headmastership of Phillips Exeter Academy." Many consider that the top job in the preparatory school business. "He has accepted the offer, but on condition that they let him stay here one more year to supervise the graduation of the first twelfth grade class on the new campus." Dave Weir said, "That took a lot of guts on Dick's part. They could turn him down."

Ireland said, "They have accepted his condition."

16. "To Summarize ...
We're Running Like Hell
for Broke!"

A PRIME CRITERION in seeking a new head-master was—find one who would consolidate the gains and reduce the frantic pace Day had set.

The board contacted seventy candidates, all rec-ommended by trusted friends in education. They refined this to twenty-two headmasters of other schools and asked five of these to come and spend time on campus. Of these they offered the position of headmaster to young, athletically built Edward R. Kast, headmaster of Short Hills Country Day School, Short Hills, New Jersey.

Ed Kast would take over at the school's highest yet enrollment—560 boys.

This (1964) would also be the first year since 1932 that Liv Ireland would not be board president. Char Bolton became president October 28, 1964.

The board desired to hang Liv Ireland's picture in the corridor at Circle W campus. Ireland said, "If such a picture of me should ever be hung in the school, I will resign immediately from the board." He added that such pictures should be of headmas-ters, faculty, and loyal employees.

Kast reported on a study of the school which showed that boys who have the best standings in their grades in the upper school came to Hawken before the sixth grade. Boys who came in the ninth fell at the bottom of the chart.

New method fads sweep through education as they do through industry. And every headmaster has his pet didactic theories. Kast urged the faculty to "shift from telling to asking." The idea was that the

Edward R. Kast

164

student brain should not be viewed as a locker to be stuffed with facts, but an intricate mechanism for reasoning. The teacher's mission was not so much to deliver facts, but to develop the student's reasoning power.

This was not a Kast original, nor did he so present it. Socrates had seized the high ground on this, but it was going around at the time.

* * *

In the late 1960s Hawken experimented amid controversy with the Leicestershire integrated day program in elementary education advocated by the National Association of Independent Schools. This was one of the several innovations which gave Hawken the reputation among its friends as a risk-taker, and among its critics as an unstructured maverick.

This program at least *appeared* to be unstructured to the point of chaos. The visitor saw students all engaged in separate activities at any given moment. Not seated at their desks, but located randomly around the room where various education resources were located—books, art materials, exhibits, science materials. Advocates argued that it was the epitome of structure if one really believed that the object was to develop the *individual* according to his individual characteristics.

The negotiations about buying additional parts of the White estate continued over many months, complicated by the possibility of the White heirs drilling for oil and gas on the property. However, the board did exercise the option to buy an additional thirty acres immediately.

A very quiet gift of fifty-five thousand dollars from four families constructed the Lyndhurst pool, to be named in honor of long time physical education instructor, Edward B. Godfrey.

Kast's Wish List

Like all new headmasters, Ed Kast soon came up with his long-range assessment of school needs to keep up with the school's destiny. Lyndhurst enrollment again has exceeded capacity and needs major expansion. Both campuses are overtaxed. Gates Mills needs room to house books, art, music, and audio visual facilities, an auditorium and a stage, wood working and mechanics shops and a language lab. Both campuses need more classrooms, faculty lounges, and offices. The greenhouse behind the White House should be restored for the science department. They need tennis courts, additional locker rooms and phys-ed facilities.

"And What the Hell Are We Going To Do about It?"

Although no longer president of the board, Liv Ireland was still a powerful trustee voice, and loud. On October 13, 1965 he briefed the trustees on what they had committed to and what they needed in the future and pointed out in addition they were facing an immediate annual deficit of fifty-four thousand dollars.

"To summarize, we are running like hell for broke! And what the hell are we going to do about it?"

The youthful headmaster brought mature answers to the table. Not to be lecturing men who were themselves financial masters, he cast his remarks as experience of educators in general. "Unlike every successful business, every successful educational institution, *because of that success*, has great need for funds." He explained that, unlike a business, an educational institution did not produce any retained earnings to be used for expansion.

"Tuition increases over the years are not the answer. Nor will annual giving close the gap between income and expenses. Endowment is the true solution. The major effort in the next five years should be to increase endowment from $1,500,000 to $5,000,000. That would raise the income from investments from $58,000 to approximately $200,000 a year."

This meeting crystallized thoughts already forming.

STUDENT BODY

The 1966-67 year opened with 599 boys. Losses to boarding school were only six boys. Of the graduating class of fifty, forty-seven were headed for college. Faculty stood at seventy.

Academically, Hawken was a pressure school. It was difficult to be admitted, and, once admitted, students found the program rigorous. Statistics give some idea. For the 1966–67 year, fifty applied for admission to kindergarten; thirty-six were accepted. For all other grades, two hundred fifty-four applied for six openings. Forty-six students left, thirty of these at the request of the school for inability to keep up.

Partial or full scholarships were awarded to ten percent of the boys.

The on-campus summer camps for both boys and girls brought in good revenue, contributing about one hundred and fifty thousand dollars. The Hawken day camps in fact continue to be very successful under skillful direction for the last two decades by Tom Bryan, director of athletics at Gates Mills.

The year 1967 saw 615 boys enrolled. Kast said he needed help with his job and requested that they hire, as his assistant, a genial young teacher from Cranbrook School near Detroit, James Young. The board approved this hire, and at a very good salary for those times.

Kast then moved his primary office from Lyndhurst to Circle W. For the first time the headmaster would not be headquartered at Lyndhurst which had the larger enrollment.

The true leader and head of the upper school at this time was a man who inspired a powerful student, if not parent, devotion, the remarkable Peter Relic. In the memories of many alumni he *was* the institution.

We have seen veteran faculty leaving. The same was happening on the board. We have not noted all the board members who left, but there is reason to note the death of trustee Charles Farrand Taplin, Jr., who represents a certain type of board member who completed a Hawken circle.

Taplin was one of the pioneering Hawken students who graduated to Princeton, then Harvard, then through a business life of achievement, then back into Hawken as trustee, sending three sons to the school—a Hawken syndrome. Further, as a typical Hawken trustee, Taplin served on the boards of governors of Western Reserve University and the Bolton School of Nursing and on the board of University Hospitals, among other civic activities.

Citing Taplin's other work is not to recognize him in particular, but as typical of nearly every Hawken trustee, carrying a dozen or so major civic responsibilities. While this is not unique to Hawken trustees, the point bears making because it may be seriously overlooked by various of the school's constituencies.

Senior faculty also became entrenched in civic service. For example, Charles Poutasse spent fifteen years as volunteer fire chief in Munson Township. His wife, Betsy, served on the Chardon school board and with organizations protecting battered women. The English teacher, Zoann Dusenbury, famous and loved throughout the entire Hawken community, was active in Alzheimer's support work and was also involved in Betsy Poutasse's work with abused women.

Implementing part of Kast's expansion plan to raise capacity of Gates Mills to three hundred boys cost $549,611.26. To complete the rest of the plans for both Lyndhurst and Gates Mills, trustees estimated a need for three million seven hundred fifty thousand dollars more—without even getting to building endowment.

The need for the largest-yet Hawken capital campaign drive was clear. They hired Harry August as director of development and laid comprehensive plans for a very thorough and very major campaign. Char Bolton set himself an objective of raising two million dollars from the trustees alone.

The campaign committee listed 192 possible major givers, and appointed a team of fifty solicitors so that no one would have more than four people to contact. They provided for smaller givers who might want to furnish just one classroom and they kicked off this campaign in the grand ballroom of the Sheraton on April 22, 1969. Enthusiasm was high.

The campaigners then had no idea that just two months from that date, a certain event would blast the campaign apart.

*   *   *

Ed Kast, easy-going, low-key, known to the faculty as Bud, had a hands off approach toward his administrators. Not particularly an innovator, he impressed most of the faculty as a very able administrator.

"Kast emphasized integrity in teaching," Len Carey remembers. "'It's not what you do in front of my eyes that counts, but what you do behind my back,' he'd say."

With his wife, Angela, he was committed to the arts. He developed "Art Days" at Hawken, and brought in artists for a week at a time, including artists in music, drama, and graphics.

Well regarded nationally, he was elected to several offices in the Country Day School Headmasters Association of the United States.

Ten-Year Plan

In the winter of 1967 a new and valuable publication appeared, *The Hawken Alumni Review.* Edited by Charles L. Stephens, this publication was a powerful force in binding alumni to the school, important in view of the plans to build up the endowment. A Hawken alumnus would typically have allegiances to a boarding school, to an undergraduate college and to a graduate school. It was important for Hawken not to be left out of this group.

Ed Kast appointed a long-range planning committee of faculty who met frequently over a year-and-a-half span. From this came the Ten Year Projection Report. It had much to do with architecture and admissions and staffing. But especially, it involved education plans. A few examples of the didactic conclusions are interesting:

- increasing emphasis on independent, self-directed study, and increasing reliance on source material rather than text books;
- more team teaching;
- flexibility within a grade and within a class so that students may progress at their natural pace;
- greater opportunity in the arts;
- emphasis on independent laboratory projects
- emphasis on service to others; and
- emphasis on how to use source material.

Implementation began in the spring of 1968 when trustee Meacham Hitchcock began working to bring computer classes to campus. He persuaded four fathers to fund a pilot project to determine the value of a computer course on campus as opposed to a course then being conducted at a Hawken father's office. By 1970 the program was well underway; participating with a consortium of four schools.

About the same time, a voluntary program called the Senior Project involved students (and a sponsor in the chosen field) in business, government, social service, or professional worlds for three week periods. The object was exposure to the "real world." The first group of seniors reported enthusiastically that the program was an eye opener.

The ten year projection was further implemented in l969 with establishment of an ethics course under James Bresnicky.

While the *Hawken Review* brought good news to the alumni, it also brought the bad. One of the best-loved figures on campus for many classes was the towering six-foot-five-inch, gentle Latin teacher, Lorimer Robey, considered by many to be the brightest intellectual genius on the all-time Hawken faculty. He died in 1969.

BACK TO THE RAISON D'ETRE

The trustees prepared very carefully for the large development fund drive they were mounting. In one session they made a breakdown of priorities, deciding in what sequence the major projects would get funding as their financial drive brought in money.

The interesting part is that as the criteria for the allocations, they restated, as they saw it, the educational principles of the school which they listed as:

- emphasis to the individual boy and his needs;
- in teaching at all levels: truth, honesty and trust in your fellow man;
- love of learning for learning's sake;
- encourage critical thinking; study the past critically so that intelligent choices are made for the future.

* * *

In late 1969, Edward Kast announced that he had accepted the post of headmaster of Germantown Academy.

17. Person to Person

IN 1968 FRANCES BOLTON, having served in Congress nearly three decades in leadership posts, including senior member of the foreign affairs committee—lost the election. At eighty-three the face lines mapped human misery which she had studied first-hand in Africa and Asia.

Despite this world-wide experience and awareness of massive needs in the world, Frances was no less interested in two small patches of Ohio at Lyndhurst and Gates Mills. On a visit she would say, "Where is that chair I gave you?"

The trustees named the main Lyndhurst building Bolton Hall. Liv Ireland recalled how in 1932 she had twisted his arm to become a trustee. "As an ex-Navy flier and a coal digger ... I didn't see where the devil education would fit into my scheme of things." He finally accepted and "talked Tom White into it also .... We didn't know at the time the chairman of the board, Joel Hayden, was about to retire."

Ireland, suddenly chairman, explained the first three-year struggle to increase enrollment and cut down the deficit; then "we went back to Mrs. Bolton and reported our progress. We were willing to continue if she was willing to support us. But we still had deficits to be met. Well, she was enthusiastic .... Mrs. Bolton had great imagination. She was always anxious to have us try something new. We didn't always like her ideas in the way of innovations, so we had to come up with some innovation each year ourselves to get the drop on her and sell her on our idea before she had a chance to spring something else on us. And it worked out very well."

He explained the piece by piece additions from 1947 to 1959. The second grade building; a kindergarten, then third grade classrooms and a building to house the fourth through sixth grades.

"In this process we obviously didn't have the funds to build buildings and we weren't well-enough established in the community to start a big campaign so we went to our fairy godmother and said tactfully, 'Gee, if only we could do so and so and so.'

"'Well, what exactly did you have in mind?'

"'Well, it just happens I've got some plans in my pocket.'

"And she would say, 'Well, I'll underwrite that—provided you can continue to decrease deficits and get this institution in the black.'"

Ireland summarized, "We all got to be very, very thankful to Mrs. Bolton for getting Hawken School really going as a real honest-to-goodness institution because she was our fairy godmother in those days and gave us the greatest cooperation, believe me!"

* * *

Except for one or two years, the deficit never left. It grew. The ambitions of the school also grew until in 1969 the trustees launched a capital drive for three million seven hundred fifty thousand dollars, knowing that even beyond that they will need another drive for endowment. Therefore—during the years 1968, '69, and '70, one sees a board of trustees with the patience of Job; and a board which kept its eye on education objectives throughout a period of financial and social pandemonium and some mutiny.

The Speech

As the trustees were mobilizing all their strengths and asking friends of Hawken to extend themselves as never before, the student commencement speeches of 1969 were being prepared. The decade of the '60s, with its free-wheeling challenge by youth to all institutions of business and education, had produced some good results, causing people to see the errors of raw materialism, environmental damage, corruption in government, and the viciousness of war.

However, some of the enthusiasts carried challenge to the point where it was fashionable to insult all institutions.

Two of the upcoming graduation speakers were upset because of the dismissal earlier of some friends. They submitted their commencement speech scripts to the faculty for review very late, leaving as little time as possible for review. In script form, the speeches were insulting to Hawken School; but in the spirit of free speech, the faculty approved them. However, the style of actual delivery magnified the bite of the scripts to a stunned audience. Richard Davies described the main speaker, John Kennedy, as having "venom dripping from both sides of his mouth."

The audience, mindful that they were being asked for really major gifts for the capital fund, sat startled to hear:

"I cannot deny that my time here has been wasted—only two members of the faculty made any effort to understand me ... the school was truly a bad thing for me ... I am sick of institutionalized education ... manipulation which I find obscene. Most of my time spent at Hawken was devoid of thought and filled with trivia. I cannot bear the thought that I have wasted my entire youth."

There was ten minutes in that vein. The other senior speaker presented almost equally soothing thoughts: "We have learned gutless compromise. We curse the stupidity of the system, but rarely fail to play along when that grade or college admission or social status is laid on the line.

"That we have learned to live this way is not solely the school's fault, but the school is responsible, and so are we, and so are you."

Richard Davies recognized it as "a low point in the school's history."

Soon after this, Meacham Hitchcock was writing to fellow trustees, "The ripples following the graduation speeches have become a tidal wave."

Alumni reaction blasted in like the rainlash after the hurricane.

The capital fund drive ground to a halt.

* * *

The once-submerged merger planning with Laurel resurfaced and intensive coed committee study resumed and continued for several years.

The enormous capital campaign promised to become even larger. If the merger transpired or if Hawken decided to go into coeducation alone, trustees foresaw possible need for a ten million dollar campaign at the very time that the damaging commencement speeches of 1969 had grounded their campaign.

Ed Kast left to become headmaster of Germantown Academy. Trustees appointed a new search committee.

If that were not enough, there bubbled to a head at this time a large faculty unrest which had been brewing some years. Faculty felt estranged from the trustees.

Some faculty members say that trustees Liv Ireland and Meacham Hitchcock spent a lot of time at the school, but that they seldom saw the others. The younger faculty probably had little concept of the tight schedule of the typical board member who usually managed a large business and served on several other boards.

However, at faculty request, the trustees set up a series of joint meetings.

It is doubtful the faculty inspired much good will by these meetings. It would require considerable restraint on the part of a trustee saddled with raising several million dollars for the school, to sit through the speech made to them April 22, 1970 by the Upper School chairman, John K. Pickering, in part:

> It is our purpose to identify and to try to understand the nature of any divisiveness that may exist.... [W]e must, after having tried to understand its nature, attempt to eliminate it. In the event we fail we will at least have had a stab at understanding one another.
>
> ... I hope that no one will be singularly sensitive to what I say. But I have reached the point in my career at Hawken that I want most earnestly to call things as I see them. Most of us here have been on the

wheel of fire the past year and some perhaps much longer. It is time, I believe, that
we either get off the wheel or put the fire
out.

A few minutes ago I said that I was
proud of the curriculum of Hawken School.
And that is true. But all this, the curriculum,
is just so much rhetoric. A course of study is
good only in direct proportion to the talents
of the faculty.

Pickering cited turn-over in faculty as a sign of
Hawken instability. "At the Upper School only two
teachers, one who is part-time, have been here continuously since the school's inception just nine years
ago. There has been instability and, I am afraid, it
does not promise to lessen. It behooves us to analyze
why."

He cited two teacher applicants whom he considered to be outstanding, who withdrew their applications

because they had heard that some faculty
members, including administrators, were
leaving Hawken and that some others were
considering leaving, and because the selection of the headmaster was still uncertain,
they decided not to come. I consider their
decision a serious loss to us ...

Most people, trustees, alumni, teachers,
who remember Hawken fondly, do so, in
part, I believe, because there were educators
here who regarded teaching at Hawken
School a proud and rewarding career. Because of them there was a stability, an identity. This, I believe no longer exists to the
degree that it should. It can or could but it
will come only after all elements associated
with the school come to an agreement of
what they want the school to be. Until then,
I very much fear, the gas station image aptly
suits Hawken School—a convenient spot
where educators drop in for fuel en route
to a more desirable destination.

> As the school exists today the ambiguity has become very difficult to live with—for some, impossible .... A major problem of the school is to eliminate this ambiguity. Otherwise, parents, trustees, students, headmasters, and teachers will pull out. Let me give you a case in point. My own. I came to Hawken eight years ago. The Upper School was one year old. ... I found a school which, to my mind, having come from a tight, highly structured, high-powered academic school, was loose and relatively directionless insofar as standards, both academic and social, were concerned.

He said it took him a while to adopt the Hawken philosophy that the individual student did not exist to foster the institution, the institution existed to foster and enhance the student's individualism. "Imagine my bewilderment and surprise then when the first time the philosophy was publicly tested [The Speech] the establishment's outrage over freedom of expression indicated that the philosophy was merely paper and that freedom of expression was fine so long as what was expressed was pleasing.

"I would pinpoint lack of trust as the major problem ... in the relationship between trustees and faculty.... If people cannot or will not communicate, then there is no trust."

He stated that, "people need to know that their efforts and successes are understood and appreciated by other people with whom they are in compact. I, for instance, have little sense of well-being. I spend, it seems to me, an inordinate amount of time and effort thinking about Hawken School and trying to make it work, and yet, and this is a sad thing to say, I feel alienated from it.

"I won't catalogue the causes of alienation." However he does. In part:

> • the hurt and anger of teachers in being offered a pay raise that is not commensurate with the rise in the cost of living;
>
> • the teachers' sense of being had, that

they give much and little is given;

• the trustees, burdened by budgetary problems, thinking that they give much under the circumstances but that perhaps not much is given;

• the sense of a precarious career on the part of the teachers because of instability;

• the shock of trustees in having to listen at commencement that all education, including that at Hawken, is obscene;

• the sense on the part of the teachers that the trustees may not approve of the results of their labors;

• the disappointment and irritation on the part of the trustees in being rebuffed when they seek donations.

And so on.

It is time we started talking turkey to one another. Let's find out about one another.

* * *

In December of 1970 some trustees must have had occasion to think back on that speech when they heard about the death of Jim Hawken (December 22, 1970).

To be sure of representation at the funeral by the old corps, Frances Bolton sent Mort Smeed's son, Jim, airline tickets to California. There was one other Hawken person present at the funeral on a hillside in Pasadena—Justin Sholes, former Hawken student, '27.

Jim Hawken had a privilege denied many founders. He saw his school of nineteen boys become a nationally distinguished school still operating on his founding principles.

* * *

The headmaster selection committee of trustees studied a list of fifty-nine candidates. It was laborious work. The man they chose could not begin in time for the 1970-71 school year. Therefore, they appointed Ed Kast's chief assistant, James Young, acting head with Mr. Davies, head of the Lower School, as assistant headmaster.

The board hired a consultant to continue the headmaster search. However, in November 1970, David Weir urged nomination of James D. Young for full headmaster effective immediately. This carried, making Young the sixth, and youngest, headmaster in Hawken history.

Young, a graduate of University School and Dartmouth College, with a master's degree from Wesleyan University, came to Hawken via Cranbrook School in Michigan and Woodstock Country Day School in Vermont. His upbeat, genial demeanor and personable style would make him a popular administrator. But his first proposal to the board, that faculty be included in budget preparation decisions, was hardly popular. The trustees rejected this, but did invite two non-voting faculty to budget meetings.

James B. Young

Jim Young's style, Len Carey remembers, "allowed faculty plenty of elbow room. He was an innovator."

* * *

With those vitriolic graduation speeches still damping the big capital fund drive, the turmoil of coeducation debate, the truculent faculty complaints, and Ed Kast quitting, the trustees showed fortitude and generosity of spirit in holding course.

Addressing a combined student faculty audience May 22, 1970, Liv Ireland, who had been president of the board from 1932 to 1964, said, "Just so I know who I'm talking to, will all faculty raise their hands so I get an idea where the hell they are. Thanks."

He then referenced Ed Kast's departure to take another job. He explained how many other faculty and administration had left, then he said, "But ... in all my business career, I've always felt honored whenever somebody from outside wants to pick someone from my team because they think my team is good and therefore ... they get somebody who ... will be the cat's whiskers for the job they want done. Sorry to see him go, but feel very complimented that they chose to rob us of Kast because we did a good job on him when he was here."

18. Coeducation?

AS THE COEDUCATION movement at Hawken heated up in 1971, the trustees interrupted the debate to stand in silence in honor of James A. Hawken, who passed away the previous December.

The coed advocates pushed aggressively in 1971 and an ad hoc committee was formed within the Board of Trustees to study the idea. David Weir examined other coed private schools and met some of their headmasters. The committee collected and studied endless reports, for example, from Exeter, Lawrenceville, and Lakeside, Washington, which were considering coeducation or had already made their decision. The committee explored a study by the National Association of Independent Schools which stated there was "a definite trend toward coeducation and it was favored by the parents, students and faculty of the majority of American independent schools."

The Fathers Club sent questionnaires to Hawken parents. Forty percent were returned, fifty-seven-and-a-half percent in favor of coeducation. A poll of students and faculty showed seventy-five percent in favor.

A very extensive report of the trustees' research on coeducation feasibility gets down to detailing multiple choices of physical plant arrangements. Merger with a girls' school was still an option. Despite strong preparation to go it alone, talks continued with the girls schools, Laurel and Hathaway Brown.

An architectural firm estimated construction costs for coeducation at one million four hundred thousand dollars but warned that building costs were rising ten percent per year.

Amid coeducation-merger negotiations, trustee elections came up. Prior to the vote, chairman Char

Bolton announced that his health would not permit him to give enough time to serve as chairman. However, they re-elected him anyway.

The trustees agreed in 1972 that the election of a "qualified woman trustee would be a wise move at this time." Mrs. Frank T. (Suzanne M.) Murray came on the board in the vacancy of Ellery Sedgewick, Jr. in 1973 and was appointed to the education committee. Suzanne Murray would be followed swiftly by other mothers. The chairwoman of the mothers' club would soon become a trustee. Governance of the school was expanding to a wider community. More key administrators and heads of education departments were regularly invited to board meetings.

In 1972 the development committee outlined a program calling for ten million dollars over the next ten years.

We've seen the coeducation idea rising for years, beginning mildly with John Carney's hints, then pressed by Carl Holmes, and aggressively favored by Dick Day. Young was for it. As it came to the front burner in the early 1970s, Char Bolton at first opposed it. Jim Ireland was vigorously against it as were many others. The opposition often had the benevolent desire not to damage the girls' schools in the area. Many Hawken parents, alumni, and board members had ties to both Laurel and Hathaway Brown.

Some parents felt the boys would be distracted from studies. Grades would fall.

What about faculty opinions? One seventh-grade teacher said, "When the girls come, I go." (Today he teaches at Laurel).

But in the primary department where it was supposed coeducation would begin—if it began—department head Charles Poutasse registered as strong an opinion as he did on all subjects which concerned his primary children, "I want coeducation for two basic reasons. One ... we're missing out on a lot of fine children because half the children are girls. Second, we have a lot of little sisters who think the school their brother goes to is the only school in the world. They want to come because brother goes here. They come with mother to pick him up. But they can't go here. Why not?"

They put him on a committee to worry about coed architecture. "That's not a problem. When a boy goes in the bathroom he'll turn the sign to 'boy'. That's a problem?"

Poutasse did not favor faculty meetings, "mostly orations," but he used that forum for his thoughts. He was surprised that some women teachers violently opposed coeducation. Some teachers said, "If girls come in we'll lose our football team."

David Weir explains, "I wanted coeducation because boys and girls have got to get along sometime. Better earlier. People with coed experience are better off."

Amidst studies of coeducation and talks of merger, several programs were instituted to test the waters. One such experiment was an exchange program for Senior Projects.

The June 19, 1971 issue of the *Affirmative No* reported that three Laurel seniors had just completed four weeks of intensive work in pottery for their senior art projects under the supervision of George Roby in the upper school art department. Two Hawken seniors taught a course at Laurel on "Alternatives in Education."

The next school year would introduce the Four-School Cross Registration Program (Hawken, HB, Laurel, and University). The September 9th issue of the *Affirmative No* announced that twelve girls from Laurel and Hathaway Brown would be studying art at the upper school under the auspices of this new program. The students reported, "Cross registration gives Hawken School the opportunity to experience a year-long coeducational atmosphere." The acting head of the Upper School, Ronald Robinson, was quick to add "while such a program shows the school's acceptance of the idea of coeducation, it still 'has no implication of decisions that the school might make.'"

The debates within many groups—students, faculty, staff and the board—were intense and prolonged during David Weir's presidency of the board. The board seldom voted on an issue because they did everything by consensus; however, on coeducation they would vote.

Just before the final vote, Liv Ireland harrumphed, "I'm a little old for this job and certainly out of it as far as coeducation is concerned, but I will back the board's decision 100 percent regardless of which way you go."

Despite the affirmative vote, David Weir explains, "Finally, we installed coeducation over the dead bodies of several trustees."

The trustees always attempted to present a united front to the world. The May 23, 1972 issue of the *Affirmative No* ran the headline above the masthead "*Unanimous Approval!* Trustees Support Co-Education."

The story read, "At a February 22 meeting, the trustees gave unanimous approval to the Ad Hoc Coeducation Committee recommendation that Hawken School undertake coeducation when feasible." Headmaster Jim Young stated the recommendation was made in the interest of better education and service to the community as there were no existing nonsectarian, coeducational, independent schools in the eastern Cleveland area. Young also reiterated the recommendation was not a result of financial losses due to sagging enrollment.

In the fall of 1973, six girls toddled onto the Lyndhurst campus and entered kindergarten.

The ice being broken, it was time for the heavy work to begin.

To accommodate coeducation on the grand scale several additions to the academic and athletic facilities would have to be made on the upper campus. Additions and alterations would include an arts and communication building, a wrestling room, remodeling of the existing academic building, and expansion to the parking lot.

Although all these facilities would not be ready for the opening of the 1974-75 school year, eighty-six girls would enter the ranks of the upper school (bringing the enrollment total to 340) along with thirteen additional faculty members.

The original meeting to discuss curriculum changes was interesting. The board president stressed the importance of this to the chairman of the education committee. Expecting a lengthy process, Chairman Hitchcock assembled a broad committee of faculty and parents. At the first and last meeting, however, the changes concluded upon were only three: a woman physical education instructor, modern dance and possibly gymnastics.

Even at that early date the long term gender ratio goal was set at fifty/fifty; short term forty/sixty.

Since half the nation is female, Hawken had doubled its potential market.

Having both male and female students added new perspective to discussions. Arguments such as "Is God a man or a woman?" arose and led to debates not probable the year before. Larry Nelson of the English department noted, "girls have added varied opinions in class which have sparked lively discussions." Mr. McCahon in the math department remarked, "the addition of girls has made no difference in class ability. Academically, girls are an asset to the school." This opinion seems reinforced by the fact that Hawken's excellent college acceptance record did not miss a beat during or after the transition.

Coeducation brought increased interest in existing school groups: Red Key, debate, yearbook, Senate, and choir groups grew in size and ability. There was more participation in team sports, and all teams were well supported.

Strangely enough, there was initially very little dating. It seemed more a brother-sister relationship.

19. Salary: $1.00

THE YEAR 1974 stormed in. David Weir briefed trustees on the three confronting priorities: implement upper school coeducation successfully; ensure completion by September 1 of the arts and communications building (running six weeks behind); and, build the capital fund.

* * *

In the school year 1974-75, the newly established Upper School Senate, an organization of faculty and students, bit into a red pepper. The senate passed a resolution that a final failing grade would be recorded on the school's own records, but *not* on transcripts to the outside world. The transcript would carry a notation "failing grades not reported by Hawken."

When this came up to the trustees for ratification, Jack Sherwin, '53, vigorously dissented. The subject would be debated at several levels for several weeks.

* * *

Hawken was not immune from the normal problems. Two upper school boys were suspended for behavior at a rock concert. Drug use was discovered involving fourteen upper school boys. And after the SAT tests there was a large unscheduled student celebration with very strong waters.

In 1974, trustee Ralph T. King reported for the development committee: "Pledged or paid to date one million seven hundred thousand dollars by three hundred forty people." William Cummings, director of development, reported the fund campaign, "in doldrums during the summer, is gaining momentum in the fall. Over one thousand solid prospects have yet to be contacted. A gift from each, half the size of the five-thousand-dollar average of the three hundred forty contributors, would put us over the top."

He added, "We are very close to the point during our last campaign when 'that graduation speech' stopped us."

The recession of 1973-74 concentrated the board's attention on finance during this period, interrupted briefly by the question of student beards and lagging construction from ground water and strikes.

The 1974-75 budget shows a deficit after annual giving of one hundred seventy-five thousand dollars despite a twenty-seven-percent rise in tuitions. Endowment income was down by seventy-six percent. Without new gifts, the endowment would drop from two million six hundred thousand dollars to six hundred thousand dollars. There were a significant number of delinquent tuitions.

By November 1974, Morris Everett, Sr., reported the market value of the endowment portfolio at $1,043,400, producing annually about seventy thousand dollars. The board explored many avenues for new funding, including reclassifying those who left Hawken after seventh and eighth grades as full alumni, and sending them the full alumni material.

Amid these problems came another. David Weir called a special trustee meeting January 31, 1975 which he opened by asking William C. McCoy, '38, to read aloud two letters from the headmaster, Jim Young, one addressed to the board, one to David Weir. The letters requested that he be relieved of responsibility as headmaster because of "a series of events in his personal life."

Weir then asked Ralph King, a trustee, to retire from the room. He then told the board what had transpired in discussions among the executive committee on how to fill the headmastership overnight.

The board wanted a strong educator for headmaster. Ralph King remembers, "I made no pretense of being an educator, but I knew we would not find a top educator in twenty-four hours." King recalled the tactical situation, "We had just gone coed and needed to present a conservative, well-managed face to the world."

Therefore, King told the executive committee that he would be willing to serve as headmaster for one year, giving the search committee time to find the best headmaster.

With King out of the room, Weir said he considered this offer "most fortuitous." The faculty especially trusted King. Weir recommended the board take King's offer very seriously.

They appointed Ralph King interim headmaster, effective immediately; annual salary, one dollar.

Ralph T. King

Search

The school mounted perhaps its most thoroughly organized headmaster search to date with very specific goals: proven administrative experience preferably in a big school, and a man with strong academic focus. They found a man they considered ideal, Thomas Read. However, he withdrew as a candidate to accept the headmastership of St. John's School in Texas. Trustee McCoy saw something between the lines. He used that event to query Read on whether there was something about Hawken which would deter a good man from accepting. Read said, "Yes—it will be very hard on an incoming headmaster to start off with a budget deficit. It forces him to begin with unpopular decisions such as limiting teacher raises and increasing loads."

The search committee hired a professional search man and ultimately selected Edward Read of Greenhill Schools, as one-year interim Hawken headmaster for 1975-76.

In 1976, Ralph King suffered a heart attack and underwent open-heart surgery. With Read's full knowledge and understanding the search for a regular headmaster continued. Edward Read did a good job in his caretaker role which was not easy. He faced some large issues of budget and enrollment.

The November 1975 board meeting was an emphatic turning point. The board adopted some very strong statements ... "imperative to the future of the school that it operate within its income and adopt budgets accordingly." In that vein, they stressed that any future building projects would be undertaken only *after* funds were in hand or pledged.

They also unanimously agreed to undertake a major drive to have the endowment reach six million dollars within five years.

Read also faced some lighter issues ... the alma mater song needed some coedification of lines such as "proud sons we'll ever be." Hawken boys found themselves being suddenly excluded from social events in the other three other private schools. Why? For several years Hawken had been dissatisfied with the value of being a member of the CCIS, a consortium of four local private schools, Hathaway Brown, Laurel and University School. Membership dues were a significant expense; Hawken finally withdrew. It was from that time Hawken boys noticed few invitations to the social affairs of the other schools. Ed Read increased informal contact with the other headmasters, ameliorating this situation.

The search committee intensively scanned the nation for a headmaster.

Ed Read's agreement was for one year. The school had now had three short term headmasters, Jim Young, Ralph King, and Ed Read.

In its sixtieth year, was Hawken drifting? Unstable, as Pickering accused?

Edward M. Read

Book III
The Momentum

20. A Third Era

> Any event younger than two decades should not be written as *history*. The event needs 20 years curing in perspective before rumor, rancor and admiration dry out and the patina of truth begins to harden around the edges. Until then, let the straight news accounts stand.
>
> J. J. Garth

HEEDING that caveat, these pages now record news as reported. The cast now multiplies and changes too rapidly for close-ups of even key individuals. However, since the events now fall well within the memory of the majority of alumni, the news items will be memory trigger enough for readers to fill out the picture in conversation among contemporaries.

Many distinguished teachers joined the faculty and dedicated trustees served. Each issue of *The Hawken Review* covers faculty action broadly and by name, and in addition usually profiles one or two teachers in detail. Thus the 168 issues of the *Review* from 1975 to 1990 taken together form a comprehensive history of personnel, including the activity of Hawken parents and faculty spouses.

* * *

At the sixty-year mark in 1975, despite certain problems, the school benefited by a six-decade build-up of momentum. Bright, ambitious teachers applied for positions, wanting Hawken on their resumés. The records set by Hawken alumni in colleges compounded the excellent acceptance rate for Hawken seniors.

* * *

The autumn of 1976 opened a new Hawken era. Coeducation, though only three years old, was quite smoothly in place. "Physical education," following the smashing all-teams victories of 1965, had evolved into rather big time "sports" to the pleasure of many and the alarm of some. Every Hawken boy or girl could still be on an intramural team. But varsity teams were making spectacular interscholastic records. The school joined Division A of the Ohio High School Athletic Association in 1976 (Division AA in 1985 when the school would field eighteen varsity teams). When coeducation arrived, Coach Tom Bryan punctiliously enforced a policy of new uniforms on an equal basis to boys' and girls' teams. He operated a no-cut policy which enabled sixty-five to seventy percent of students to participate.

Enrollment of African-American, Hispanic, and Asian students was firmly established.

A strong national academic reputation was firmly established, and its foundation classic.

The Hawken Review
Spring 1976

The Better Self

The course of study K-8 is based on those twin essentials of all learning, English and Mathematics. As a student's knowledge of his language expands he is increasingly able to absorb and define more complex ideas.

The mathematics program, also individualized according to the student's ability, stresses understanding of mathematical concepts. Here again, language plays a part since no problem can be solved until it is understood.

Foreign languages which give enlightenment to our own language are represented by the discipline and clarity of French and Spanish.

The science program is laboratory oriented, stressing investigation, observation, data collection and drawing of conclusions.

Art and music are required in K-8 since there can be no intellectual strength without cultural breadth.

* * *

A handsome, careful young man, who thought before he spoke, stepped into the headmaster's office with a premature dignity as if he had been there ten years.

T. Douglas Stenberg

T. Douglas Stenberg came to Hawken as headmaster in July 1976 from the Seven Hills Schools in Cincinnati. At that time Seven Hills was an eight-hundred-and-fifty student coeducational independent school on three campuses, pre-school to twelve. Stenberg was instrumental in the merger between the College Preparatory School and the Hillsdale-Lotspeich School which formed Seven Hills in 1974.

The Hawken trustees selected him from more than sixty candidates following a seven-month search. Salient in the choice of Stenberg was his experience as an established headmaster of independent secondary schools of Hawken's size.

Graduated from Bowdoin College in 1956 as a James Bowdoin and Alumni Fund Scholar with an A.B. in government, he held a master's in education research and measurement from Boston University, and a Ph.D. in education from the University of Minnesota.

In addition to being a headmaster, Stenberg had worked with admissions and college placement and had held teaching positions in mathematics and psychology.

When being interviewed for the job, he asked to interview the chairman of each trustee standing committee, "a rather unsettling experience," one former chairman remembers, "because each of us had to think about and express just what we were doing and why."

William McCoy, chairman of the search committee, stated, … "The selection of Doug Stenberg … should bring on a new, positive era for Hawken."

Why did Stenberg select Hawken? Students Eric

Biel and Barron Lerner published their phone interview with Douglas Stenberg in the October 14, 1975 *Affirmative No,* excerpted here: "Hawken's academic rigor, the attention given to experimental opportunities, differentiation between the physical education and athletic programs. Hawken's focus on the individual and its concern for the fine arts also impressed me."

Douglas Stenberg, an organized mind, has reflected long and deeply about the profession. Those thoughts are especially interesting because they may apply to leadership characteristics in other professions as well. Shortly after arrival he detected what had not been obvious to him during his previous visits: that this faculty felt very powerfully enfranchised. "Every master a headmaster."

Hence his challenge: how to preserve the strength of that strong proprietary attitude while deflecting the chaos of a hundred chiefs.

Second he realized much of this new young faculty had been attracted to Hawken by the novelty— new coeducation and new second campus and the reputation for liberalism (for example, no compulsory study hall for the ninth grade). How to harness this enthusiasm for the new yet retain the power of tradition?

To accomplish these aims, Douglas Stenberg organized faculty committee work, including budget planning, to capitalize the vigor and cool the chaos.

Stenberg's asbestos temperament handles academic kitchen heat. He identifies and explains three interesting abilities required to be a good headmaster. One—the ability to tolerate ambiguity. "The educated man sees both sides." Two—the ability to be comfortable with unfinished tasks. Three—ability to manage disappointment. "You've got to carve out four or five major concepts you believe in and go to the mat for them."

* * *

The Affirmative No
October 1976

STENBERG JOINS STAFF
Education Goals Defined
In New Document

On the suggestion of headmaster T. Douglas Stenberg a committee of faculty, students and trustees has drawn up a statement of purpose and goals. The document, approved by the Board of Trustees October 18, begins with the school's motto.

Although the board entered this somewhat patronizingly as an exercise in mere words, one former trustee recently reflected, "Looking back, those words have become a *most* valuable part of the school."

The document was long, and reaffirmed development of the individual in all facets. But Stenberg's purpose in the exercise was to remind, clarify, and unite faculty, trustees, and students behind unified goals.

He planned to use the refurbished statement of purpose in resolving certain problems which greeted his arrival. For only one example, he would use the purpose statement to help untie the very delicate issue of admissions to the Lower School, previously knotted with conflicting practices, policies, and opinions. The sensitive admissions policy on legacies was compounded by another difficult challenge: Hawken's policy of pluralism in admissions had made it the school of choice by superbly qualified minorities who found Hawken not only excellent scholastically, but also inclusively hospitable as opposed to exclusively hostile. Thus Hawken suddenly faced the possibility of severe reverse imbalance. The new written policy mandated that admissions mirror community make-up.

Still another test of the goals statement and of the new headmaster would rise swiftly.

The Affirmative No
November 8, 1976

Class Size, Teaching Loads
Questioned In Ad Hoc Study

The issue of increasing class sizes and teaching loads is being discussed by the Senate because of concern by teachers.

The Senate formed a committee to study class size. Their report, after comprehensive polling, favored keeping the enrollment of the Upper School to 375 and classes small. The issue would continue for some time. One of Stenberg's goals was to erase deficit operations. Small classes are high cost operations.

* * *

The Affirmative No
November 16, 1976

Senate Considers New
Class Ranking Change

A special Senate Meeting was held concerning the modification of the class rank system.

Some students in the Senate believed it would be more beneficial to the students if their exact numerical rank in class was reported to colleges as opposed to merely percentile ratings.

The resolution the Senate finally passed was—give each student his choice how he would be reported. Faculty Senator Keith Warner was among those opposing the resolution, "I'm opposed to the competitive aspect of the whole thing." He added, "I'm upset that we even play this game."

This Hawken Senate was then itself unique. It comprised students and faculty, the headmaster having veto power, sparsely used. Very fundamental school policies were proposed, argued, and established in this Upper School legislative body.

Many alumni have felt that this early legislative experience made them effective later in life's key meetings, conferences, committees and the quasi-political negotiations in business and civic affairs. The experience accrued not only to the seated senators but to the off-floor discussions, committees, and witnesses as well. That experience, coupled with Hawken's traditional emphasis on articulation, beginning with chapel talks, created effective graduates.

The subjects legislated in the Senate were fundamental, usually the province of administrators and trustees.

* * *

The Affirmative No
December 8, 1976

White House Listed
In National Historic Register

The 23 room colonial mansion was the residence of Walter C. White, head of White Motor Company, now included in the National Register of Historic Places.

White was killed in an automobile accident in 1929, but his wife, Virginia, continued to serve as hostess at the mansion for glamorous functions until her death in 1959.

* * *

Robinson Proposes
Curriculum Changes

"A drift toward mediocrity in the academic goals of our graduates," and the possibility of graduates not being exposed to certain arts, sciences, literature and history, are what prompted Upper School Head Ronald Robinson's curriculum proposal to re-evaluate required courses.

Robinson objected to some students graduating with no exposure to philosophy, the sonata form, drama, physical sciences, art, and history other than

American. He stated that the requirements had become too lax. "Students often take easy courses and avoid important courses, and they also try to specialize."

The new curriculum proposal passed the Senate. It included large changes in Upper School history, English, science, and math. The new curriculum would ensure a chronological study of fundamental world literature, dropping the Shakespeare requirement. A year-long course in European history would be required, followed by a year of United States history and one trimester of economics. All students would take one year of biology and one year of chemistry or physics. The two trimesters of algebra would expand to one year.

In 1977, the school learned of the death of two former headmasters ... Charles R. Stephens, "the Boss"; and Dick Day, who died at age sixty-one.

* * *

Following the death of Charles R. Stephens, *The Hawken Review* reprinted many letters received by Mrs. Ada Stephens and Charles L. Stephens. They are all earnest. But parts of three of them will have meaning to most readers.

"I was not shocked but just saddened to hear about 'the boss'. He was a real part of my life. What he gave me and my brothers and our sons just cannot be equaled. I was one of his boys. Willie Weir."

"Yes—one can weep a bit, but not in sorrow. And to you, my very dear Steve—deep, deep gratitude for the rare contribution you have made to the school. Frances" (Written to the son).

"I thought he was indestructible. I'm happy to learn he died of a heart attack rather than a lingering illness which would have driven him nuts. Liv."

* * *

The Affirmative No
January 26, 1977

Snow, Cold Snap Lines,
Sap Upper School Spirits

The Upper School shut down operations for an unprecedented five days in the wake of a record regional cold wave and sub-zero temperatures and damages to the phys-ed and science wings.

The Affirmative No
April 22, 1977

FRANCES BOLTON DIES
HAWKEN CO-FOUNDER

Frances Payne Bolton, 91, a member of Congress for over 28 years, a loyal and trusted friend of Hawken School, died March 9 at her home in Lyndhurst. Congressman Bolton (she insisted on the *man*) served on such governing bodies as the House Committee on Foreign Affairs, chaired a subcommittee of the War Emergency Committee in World War I [Ed. note. To student editors the two wars probably blurred. Frances was not in Congress in World War I.], the Indian Affairs Committee and the Eighth General Assembly of the United Nations in 1953. She authored several books on foreign affairs, founded the school of nursing at Case Western Reserve and was active nationally in the Republican party.

In the general cynicism about politicians the citizens of the 22nd District somehow realized that in Frances (That's what constituents called her among themselves. At home she was FPB.) they had the exception, a person who had no motive but to do the job of representing—a person whose office was organized and instructed to listen to constituents of all stations, and particularly those earnest voices unrepresented by lobbyists, lawyers, and high-level friends; this despite the fact that her district was at one time the largest in the United States (nine hundred thousand constituents).

Six hundred people came to her funeral in the Old Stone Church. That figure becomes thousands when we realize that many of these attended as *representatives* of organizations and African nations.

In addition to those, the crowd was sprinkled with national figures, friends from Washington.

At Hawken, those who knew the school history knew that despite the pivotal work of such as Roberta Bole, Jim Hawken, Henry Sheffield, Liv Ireland, and other giants, there would have been no Hawken School without Frances Bolton.

* * *

The Affirmative No
November 9, 1977

Lovell, Carr Clash
Over Course Weight

Lovell is concerned about the absence of special weights for students who take honors courses and have large class loads. He wants such students to receive larger credits on their college transcripts.

History teacher Bruce Carr is opposed, "There is no way a completely fair system could be devised."

While this last statement is true of education, and the world as well, there would seem no objection to more fairness, even if incomplete.

* * *

The Affirmative No
April 22, 1977

Multi-Million Dollar Barn
Gutted In Flash Fire

Ohio's largest non-commercial barn burned to the ground April 13. All that remained of the 55 year old landmark were two silos and the foundation. Catching fire at approximately 1:30 p.m. the barn was ashes in an hour.

Seven fire departments responded and students helped prevent the fire from spreading across the grass, beating the flames with wet towels and shoveling mud and hauling water from the marshy acres and cutting down smoldering trees.

The maintenance chief, Paul Taylor, discovered the fire and informed Robinson who called in the alarm. Then Robinson, Taylor, and two other staff men rushed to the barn, hooked up the garden hose, trying to hold down the fire. Marsee saved the cattle but a twenty-five-mile-an-hour wind whipped the fire out of control.

When the firemen arrived they issued equipment to students and showed them how to quell the brush fires, pour water on roofs of nearby houses, and remove valuables from the houses.

This was the third major fire in this barn, the second since owned by Hawken.

To alumni who loved this barn, the charred ruins tugged the heart.

This was not *just* a barn ... *The Affirmative No* for April 22, 1977 carried front page the story of Frances Payne Bolton's death but the inside center, double-page spread was filled with the fire and the history of this Hawken "treasure."

The fire chief of Gates Mills called it "the area's largest fire in history." Flames were visible from Interstate 271 and from five miles away in Mayfield

Heights; the smoke could be seen from the buildings on Cleveland's Public Square.

Professional firefighters numbered up to seventy-five. Still they enlisted students to help douse the blaze, which not only destroyed the barn but threatened faculty housing and adjoining property with spreading brush fires. Firefighters reported the situation would have been much worse without the outstanding efforts of students and faculty. Headmaster Stenberg rushed from Lyndhurst to see Peter Scott fighting flames on the roof of the Warner's house.

For many, the barn was a symbol of Hawken School. For others, it was even more; evidenced by the editorial in the same *Affirmative No:* "[The barn] was a subconscious unifying factor among the school's population. The fate of the barn and the fate of the institution's attitudes about itself were closely tied to each other. This loss is deeply felt." So much, in fact, that for a time there were rumblings of rebuilding this Hawken landmark.

21. Week by Week

THE STUDENTS and faculty continued studying their new headmaster. So did trustee Liv Ireland, who told him, "Dick Day was the paratrooper, Bud Kast was the movie star, you ... I haven't figured out yet."

This scrutiny didn't slow Stenberg down.

The Affirmative No
September 7, 1977

CAMPUS UNDERGOES PHYSICAL RENOVATIONS

Headmaster T. Douglas Stenberg has deemed Hawken's renovated structure the biggest physical change since the construction of the Arts-Communications Building.

The new Student Center is the most vital of the structural alterations at the Upper Campus this fall.

Not only did the two Hawken campuses differ in topography, they differed in spirit. Lyndhurst was the original, its corridors grooved with tradition and annual coats of shellac. The new Gates Mills campus to the contrary, naked of history, attracted young faculty eager to be part of the novelty.

Douglas Stenberg, therefore, was headmaster of two very different academies which he wanted to synchronize without undermining uniqueness.

* * *

The year 1977 saw Hawken athletics' spectacular rise continue. Track coach David Coad's team had a 7-1 record. The tennis team was dominating opponents with scores like 5-0. The girls' softball team was winning.

Faculty turnover was not great, yet new staff had to be added as some of the great teachers were shanghaied to head other schools, for example Byronesque Robert Wheeler, who had innovated so many Hawken programs, was drafted to head Park Upper School, Brookline, Massachusetts. In his fourteen years at Hawken as teacher, coach, and admissions director, he had charge of several extra-curricular projects including *The Affirmative No.* He started the Red Key, worked on the inner-city program, PACE; he put Hawken into the ABC (A Better Chance) Scholarship Program. He pioneered the Senior Project Program with Ed Kast; he coached soccer and freshman baseball. John Krotinger, '72, former editor of *The Affirmative No* summed up the man in a word ... "concerned."

The Affirmative No
September 7, 1977

STENBERG CITES FUTURE PLANS

Doug Stenberg took the students of the Upper School right into the school problems as adult citizens. At the opening of the 1977 school year he explained in *The Affirmative No* the school financial challenges.

While it was desirable to keep enrollment small, there was critical correlation between size and income. Tuition needed to be raised but still held within the ability of parents. Even with tuition raises it appeared the school must increase non-tuition income. This would be a problem because already seventy-six percent of Hawken parents and forty-five percent of alumni were contributing non-tuition income. Substantial increases in giving were hardly expectable. Increasing endowment was seen as the best route, but competition for endowment money was intense.

Coeducation is working (above photo); the chapel today (below)

HAWKEN IN THE 1970s
AND 1980s

Earth Day 1981 (above photo); Pioneer Day 1981 (below)

Fall Family Fair 1981 (top photo); Relaxing at the Student Center (middle photo); and Grandparents' Day (bottom)

WASIL

The 1975 team relishes their 33-7 victory over U.S. — their first ever.

Ken Anderson, former quarterback for the Cincinnati Bengals

Competition persists

1920s

Circa 1930

Circa 1943

First grade 1962-63

Herb Furst's sixth-grade homeroom, 1963-64, (bottom): Trip Ayers, John Hill, John Land, Dick Chapman, and Dick Lacey; (top): Pete Steck, Jim Weir, David Uible, Tony Taylor, and Mike Lutton

1990s

The Affirmative No
September 7, 1977

McCahon Sheds 55 Pounds

Math teacher David McCahon was ordered by two doctors to lose weight before returning to Hawken this fall. McCahon followed the drinking man's diet and dropped 55 pounds.

* * *

The tremendous challenge in running a school with a strong faculty and high-performance students is that even your victories in one area get bad marks from another area. On the one hand, for example, we can see the great pride and joy of some in the rising sports program.

The Affirmative No
October 5, 1977

Gridders, Soccies Crush U. S.

It has been 13 years since any Hawken soccer team has defeated University School. The last victory at the expense of the Preppers was 1964. A member of that team is our present soccer coach, Steve Haas. This 3-2 victory was especially sweet for him.

The football game against University was supposed to be close. At the end of the first half Hawken led 22-0, at the close 28-15. Hawken football is coming of age.

* * *

The same could be said for field hockey. One of the most beloved coaches Hawken ever had is Zoann Dusenbury. In her initial year her team lost to Hathaway Brown 0-10. In 1977 they lost again, but this time 0-1. "This is our best team ever. It's a shame we started our season against our toughest opponent. This is a mature, hard driving squad with tremendous desire." The same could be said of the golf team. The 1977 season climaxed with this team (Todd McCormack, '76; Tom Farkas, '78; Brad Poe, '79; Tom Herdman, '78, and Gary Rusnak, '83) shooting a 676 total and defeating Marion Catholic by thirteen strokes to win the Ohio Class A championship. This marked the first team state championship in Hawken's athletic history.

On the other hand, the winning sports focus disturbed some people.

The Affirmative No
November 9, 1977

Senate Debates Issues

The Senate held this meeting in the presence of the entire Upper School.

Ronald Robinson, Upper School head, asked the Educational Goals Committee to study the purpose of Hawken's athletic program, a subject on which he was receiving many complaints. This committee is trying to determine Hawken's "philosophy of athletics as it relates to the philosophy and goals of the total educational experience of the school." Decision has not been reached.

Several other items of lesser importance were considered.

* * *

The Affirmative No
December 22, 1977

ROBINSON RESIGNS

Ronald Robinson submitted his resignation as head of the Upper School and requested to be permitted to return to full faculty status in the Mathematics Department.

He states as his primary reason for resigning ... "his desire to be deeply involved in the education and activities of our students."

Other reasons: "We human beings are so vulnerable when it comes to needing approval. Deep down one may believe that he has the confidence of those with whom he works, but there remains a finite capacity for the day to day problems, complaints, dilemmas, personality conflicts, hysteria, etc. The defense mechanism is the proverbial thick skin. Unfortunately when the skin becomes too thick it also suffocates passion and caring for the very people for whom one is responsible in the area of morale and well being. When that point is reached it is good neither for the individual nor for the school."

* * *

STUDENT VOICE

The students in the Upper School were given a surprisingly strong voice in school affairs. Douglas Stenberg addressed the student body in December 1977 with great candor about the school finances and the debate about increasing enrollment or holding steady.

To assist him in choosing a successor to Robinson he appointed a committee comprised of three faculty and two students.

Largely because of student voices the instrumental music program was reinstated.

Douglas Stenberg, in addition to holding lunches in his home with all seniors, invited back students who had graduated the previous year to relate how well or poorly Hawken had prepared them for college in various aspects.

Admissions at Hawken had always been a critical activity, constantly fighting problems of balance ever since Jim Hawken based the school on small classes. Small classes boost cost per pupil. Increasing the enrollment dilutes the attention per student. Accepting the children of alumni, faculty, and trustees builds a loyal constituency; on the other hand it may admit some students not equal to the Hawken high pressure education. In other schools such questions would be strictly regarded as the province of management. At Hawken, student voices are invited.

The Hawken Review
December 1977

Accountability, Academic Freedom
And "A Reasoned View"—Compatible?

By T. Douglas Stenberg
Headmaster
(Excerpts)

The major preoccupations of education are in constant flux. The present attractions include the well publicized concerns over basic skills, career education, the continued emergence of egalitarianism and preparatory decision making as palpable forces with which educational administrators must deal—and accountability.

As with all movements today, instant media attention gives them instant importance. The extent to which they remain on the front burner after the passage of time is the ultimate measure of their historical significance.

The Hawken Review
December 1977

Interview With Lincoln Reavis
New President
Board of Trustees

How would you compare the Hawken School you went to with the present school?
I graduated from a one-campus one-

hundred-fifty-boy school which probably didn't have an annual budget much over one hundred thousand dollars. In thirty years, really in the last fifteen, we have added girls, a second campus, a high school, three major new buildings and about two and a half million dollars in overhead. In more important but less visible ways the school has changed surprisingly little. The values have remained pretty much as they were and the quality of education is probably higher.

Higher in what ways?

Hawken has always been blessed with more than its share of great teachers, but we think our present faculty is our best ever.

Additionally, Doug Stenberg has already made a big difference here and will make even more ... He has provided some exciting and welcome leadership.

What are the values that you mentioned?

Respect for the individual. Hawken doesn't have a patent on this, but the school has always made a particular point to search out and develop individual, unique abilities. It's the first objective listed in our new official statement of goals.

What's the financial condition?

Good. No debt. Endowment fund worth about two million. This year we expect to balance the budget for the third year in a row.

* * *

Hawken's rise in the sports world accelerated. In 1978, for example, the spectacular swimming team was off to a fourth undefeated season. Unquestionably good for school morale and public relations and development funding, the school, however, concerned itself with the physical development of those students who were not star athletes, lest they become only spectators in life.

Students were still emphatically involved in policy

via the Upper School Senate when in February 1978 they voted to rank students by numbered class standing. Headmaster Stenberg tabled that legislation, feeling it needed more study. The Senate also voted to discontinue the policy of omitting failing grades from transcripts.

The Affirmative No

* * *

DONATIONS SKYROCKET

"Many people are just now starting to realize that Hawken is an institution worth supporting," stated Morris Everett, Jr., aggressive Director of Development, in connection with this year's spectacular success in the annual giving, thus far $205,000. The proportion of donating alumni has nearly tripled in the last four years, rising from 31 percent to 60 percent. Everett and Stenberg see Hawken as the number one co-educational school in the nation in donations. "Mr. Development" was quick to emphasize that the drive's success was not solely due to his and Stenberg's work, but to the persistent labor of 200 Hawken parents and friends.

* * *

FACULTY TO WRITE STUDENT REPORTS

In a move designed to increase rapport between the school and parents, the Hawken Upper School required teachers to write academic evaluations of all students in their classes.

Many parents missed the written reports they received from Lower School and felt entitled to more than a number grade every six weeks.

The program was not unopposed. Some faculty members disagreed with the usefulness of this paperwork, an estimated total of one hundred thousand words and the potential use of meaningless cliches.

The Affirmative No
February 1, 1979

Holtrey's Crew Loses First

Even after a dual meet loss to power-house Akron-Firestone, the Hawken 1979 swimming team is still the *Plain Dealer's* number one ranked team in the city. This loss which snapped a HAWKEN winning streak of 51 straight dual meets, should be the only loss this year by the powerful tankers.

Faculty Fumes Over
King Day Truancy

Both faculty and students were disappointed in the 96 Hawken students who cut school or left early on the day set to honor Martin Luther King. While many schools closed and made a holiday of it, Hawken celebrated King by holding school and running programs about Dr. King's fight and his work.

These programs were put on by the students. Student Greg Coles, '79, in criticizing the absentees said, "Many think Martin Luther King was a civil rights leader only for black people, but he was for all people."
The assistant head of the Upper School, Bruce Carr, voiced his disgust, "It appears we have some students with a trade school mentality. Their idea of education is one almost exclusively oriented toward the practical ... getting a job or getting into college. Since we weren't holding classes they didn't bother to come."

The Affirmative No
March 14, 1979

Soccer Field Site
Of Aviation Mystery

"Hawken's open field was an inviting view at a critical time. When an engine dies, a pilot looks for an unobstructed landing area," stated flying student Dr. Lester Wyman on the crash landing on the Hawken soccer field Saturday.

The last five minutes of the flight were flown by instructor Randy Peterson. Neither pilot nor student was injured.

Damage to the plane was estimated at sixteen thousand dollars. The engine failed on the plane's return to the Cuyahoga County Airport.

While attempting to land, the two front wheels stuck in the deep snow and the plane flipped over.

Because of the crash the student was not charged for the final five minutes of the flight. Dr. Wyman contended the student should have been charged double for the final five minutes of the flight; "it was a good lesson in emergency landing."

* * *

Obviously the Hawken trustees were involved with the Cleveland community on dozens of boards. It is less well known that the faculty and students also were involved with the city of Cleveland. Douglas Stenberg was keynote speaker in January of 1979 at a Cleveland education symposium: "Proven Educational Services to the City of Cleveland." The chairman of the arts department, George Roby, entered his work in the May Show for ten years. In 1979 he won the one-thousand-dollar first prize in the crafts division.

The director of development, Morris Everett, Jr., was so successful at raising funds for Hawken, he was asked to advise other Cleveland schools and was elected nationwide conference chairman for the

Council for Advancement and Support of Education and also for the National Association of Independent Schools.

* * *

The Affirmative No
November 14, 1979

Chessmen Fourth At Nationals

Facing the best chess teams in the nation our chess team nabbed fourth place in the National High School Chess Tournament in Philadelphia, one half point away from first place.

The team won the Cleveland championship.

* * *

Bequest Boosts
E n d o w m e n t

Development Director Morris Everett reported a major gift to the Endowment Fund of $385,000 from the estate of the late Henry Sheffield. It was Henry Sheffield's money that made possible the first school on Ansel Road in 1915. This latest gift was a credit to Everett's work in regularly contacting Mr. Sheffield, who for the past several years had become displeased with Hawken School, and removed it from his will.

* * *

The Affirmative No
February 13, 1980

STENBERG WRESTLES AND THROWS
FINANCES

The responsibility of balancing the budget, the intake and outgo of $3,300,000, rests on the headmaster. Stenberg has kept the Hawken books in the black since his arrival, the first headmaster in the history of the school to accomplish that. His budget for 1980-81 shows a surplus of $2,401.

* * *

The Affirmative No
June 7, 1980

BULLETINS

—The 86 seniors who just graduated were the largest graduating class to date.

—Charles Marsee, chairman of Science Department since '68 leaves to become headmaster of Andrews School for Girls. How many men have gone out of Hawken to become headmasters?

—Ten year chairman of the History Department, Kenyon "Red " Cramer retires after teaching 34 years.

—University of Michigan drew the largest number of this year's graduates—8. No other college drew more than three. Yale only three. Harvard only one.

22. Operations

The Hawken Review
December 1980

TDS: The Man Behind the Title

It is, as offices go, outsize. Three large tables, each generously spaced from each other. The first is a conference table, the second is a desk, the third is a long slab of wood strung between filing cabinets as one has while in college-stage financial distress.

It is, as offices go, a disaster. Everywhere the eye can rest there is a piece of paper. On each counter top and table, stacks of paper are lined in vertical rows an inch apart. On the floor itself paper is heaped in great piles—under tables, chairs, book shelves.

And it is, amazingly enough, the tidier of the two spaces here. For behind a door is one of life's strangest sights ... a stairwell with paper, paper, paper cascading in slow ooze DOWN some fifteen steps to another door.

The first time visitor stands riveted. What is the meaning of this mess?

The man who calls this paper mill home is according to a headmaster of a competing school, "the best planner and organizer and administrator I know."

He's talking about Douglas Stenberg who says, "Some summer, I'm going to get really caught up."

* * *

The Professional

In five years Douglas Stenberg had made deep tracks. Trustee Lincoln Reavis, as if laying down the last word, said, "What we've got is a real professional headmaster."

Stubbornly courteous, even in sharp one-on-one ideological disagreements, he was unflappable also in the large group hassles. Somewhat aloof, but always listening to opposition, he considered the whole operation his responsibility, including the financial side. "A superb administrator," said Morris Everett, Sr.

Touches of gray now enhanced Stenberg's natural dignity. Some thought he incubated a decision overlong and then drowned it in a swamp of language. But one trustee said, "That's just how he prevents getting stampeded from above or below. You don't ambush Doug into something."

* * *

The Affirmative No
September 3, 1980

STATE OF THE SCHOOL
By Jon Grunzweig ('81)

Following the fifth straight year under a balanced budget, Headmaster T. Douglas Stenberg expects the 1980-81 year to be "a truly unique one."

Several developments have taken place over the summer and long term projects continue on or ahead of schedule.

The Upper School has switched from oil to gas heating. This will save $22,000 a year and pay for itself in two years.

The computer will continue to play a major role. For maximum usage the memory of the Randall mini-computer will be doubled.

The next step toward re-accreditation

will be a 3-day visit to Hawken by a 28 member review team November 16-19.

The campaign to double the endowment was two months into its second stage. In the first phase one hundred people were approached for major gifts in hopes of raising seventy-five percent of the money needed. Part two consisted of three hundred more people and the target—another fifteen percent of the total. The following spring a general campaign was expected to complete the drive.

Stenberg stated that future goals included continued deficit-free operations, increased contact between students and trustees, amendment of the faculty pension plan, and development of master site plans for both campuses.

* * *

The Affirmative No
November 28, 1980

BULLETINS

—Robert Spicer, head football and baseball coach since 1973 and chairman of Physical Education since 1979, leaves to become a stock broker.

During Spicer's seven years his football record is 44-17-2. The 1980 record was 9-1, finishing as the top Class A team in the area. He has been named Independent Coach of the Year four times.

—Morris Everett, Jr., has announced his impending retirement as Development Director after seven years on the job. His resignation will take effect on completion of the endowment fund drive.

—Girls Keep On Winning. Tied for first place in the Private School League and presently holding the second best record among all Hawken teams (10-1) the girls' varsity basketball team far surpassed expectations of students and faculty.

—Debater Sherman 5th In State. Senior Lori Sherman placed 5th in the state among girl extemporaneous speakers and junior Hillary Zellner ranked among the top 16 in the same event in the Ohio High School Speech League state tournament in Youngstown.

* * *

The Hawken Review
May 1981

Dick Davies

Head of the Lower School for 11 years, Dick Davies leaves to become director of the Elizabeth Morrow School, Englewood, New Jersey.

* * *

In a new conservative age, Hawken remained "liberal," continuing to encourage educational experimentation. That experimentation, however, was usually on line with the school's basic philosophy. For example, in one sense Hawken staff considered communication (reading, speaking, writing) as the heart of an education and they treated math as a form of a communication. Witness:

The Hawken Review
May 1980

(Excerpts)

New At The Lower School: Fun for the
Able-Minded
by Linda Gojak, Chairman, Lower School
Mathematics

> "Fantastic!" "Interesting!" "Spectacular!"
> "Creative!" ...

Do you remember describing your elementary math class in such a positive way? These words were used by fourth graders in Connie Palmer's class when they were asked to describe their experiences in the Mathematics Enrichment Center.

The idea for the center was born last year as Lower School math teachers met to discuss ways to meet the math needs of every Hawken student and ways to build a positive attitude toward the subject. The feeling was that the mathematics curriculum was too dependent on a textbook; too often we were fitting the children into the book rather than tailoring the program to the needs of the students.

Another concern was the fact that so many aspects of mathematics could not be found in a basic textbook series. Consensus of opinion was that the solution could easily be found in developing a special place and time where students could have the opportunity to explore and discover many ideas using appealing manipulative materials.

During the summer, games, manipulative materials, and resource books were purchased, constructed, assembled, and categorized. A note book was compiled for all math teachers whose students would be involved in the Math Enrichment Center. The curriculum studied in grades four to six was arranged according to mathematical concepts with available books, materials, activity cards, file folder ideas, and games listed for each concept. Since most of the materials could be used to develop a variety of concepts, a cross reference was included, enabling all math teachers to become familiar with available materials and to use them in their daily math classes. The final task of the summer was to arrange the classroom which would soon be known by the students as the "math lab." All fourth, fifth, and sixth grade students spend at least one forty-minute class a week in the center. Although I plan a lesson for each class, anything can—and usually does—happen. The main emphasis of all work in the center is on doing and thinking, rather than paper and pencil work. The students are always finding new and creative ways of using the materials; smiles and enthusiasm are sure signs of the fun the children are having while they learn. Many ideas and discoveries are taken back to the regular math class the next day for further discussion and extension.

While Connie Palmer's fourth graders are brushing up on facts and estimating, Tom Tenerovich's sixth grade class can be found playing "fraction, decimal, percent concentration," and Signe Forbes' fifth graders might be busy working with fraction bars and cards.

Student interest in mathematics and in the enrichment center is high enough that I have been able to sponsor a sixth grade math club ...

Exit a Brace of Thirty-Two-Year Legends

In a seventy-five-year cast of brilliance, who dares make special notes of the departure of two men?

Certainly not the authors. The alumni, however, did. In dozens of the interviews, alumni revealed salient memories of two contrasting figures ... who were the same in one quality which men wistfully admire and try to emulate.

The quality is a certain bravura ... in one serene, in the other blustering ... a readiness to tell conven-

James A. Hawken; the inscription is to Charles R. Stephens and his wife (1927).

Clockwise (upper left): Wally Wallace; Mr. Wallace; Elmer Sipple; and H. Mortimer Smeed

Fannie Luehrs (upper left); John H. McCarthy (upper right); and the Interurban bus

Carl N. Holmes with Sheldon H. Tolles II, '36 (top photo); and (bottom photo) an unidentified man with Carl N. Holmes and Captain Bill Slocum, the Holmes' Chesapeake Bay Retreiver, inside the Model A Ford station wagon

Clockwise (upper left): Clarke Bruner, '28, and Muriel Bell; Helen Hochstetler and husband Bill; Mac McCarthy; and Winnie McCarthy

Top photo (left to right): John Newell, Char Bolton, Hamilton Eames, and Ed Kast

Bottom photo: looking at plans for the R. Livingston Ireland Building (left to right): Headmaster Ed Kast, Del deWindt, Liv Ireland, and Harry August

(Top photo): Frank "Jack" Dimpsey; (bottom left) Jack Raish; and (bottom right) Lorimer Robey

Charles Poutasse, with students and in action

(Top photo) Leonard Carey; and (bottom photo) Lee Henry (second from left) and friends

(Top photo) Groundbreaking for Phase II renovation (left to right): Tim Bolton, Joan Page, and T. Douglas Stenberg; and (bottom photo) Gretchen Stenberg-Dismukes, '78, Larry Nelson, and Shirley Stenberg (left to right)

(Top photo) Jerry Holtrey; (middle photo) James Bresnicky; and (bottom photo) Ron Hall

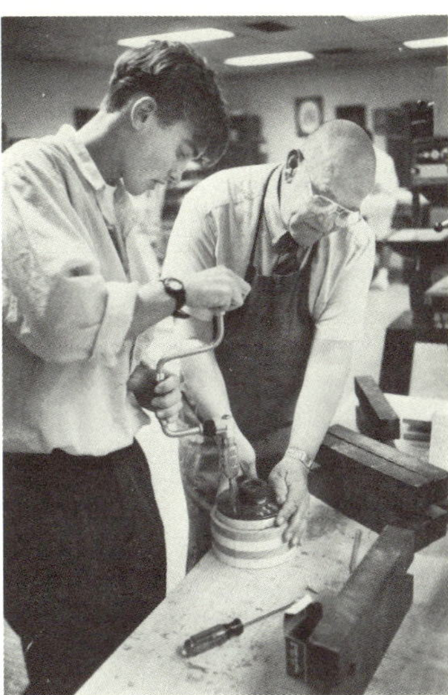

Clockwise (upper left): John Tottenham, Paul Nahra, '81, and Martin Shultz (left to right); Tom Bryan; Larry Nelson; Howard Stirn and Janet Hoerr; and Martha Brown

Clockwise (upper left): Zoann Dusenbury; Keith Warner; Herb Furst; Marjorie Johnson; and Peter Relic

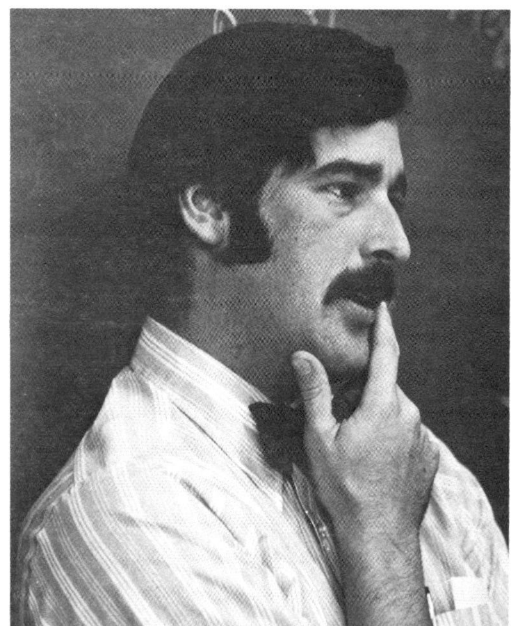

*Clockwise (upper left): Nat Carter; Genevieve Swan;
George Roby; and Frank Brandt*

Clockwise (upper left): Douglas McDonald; David Rosenzweig; Elizabeth C. McCullough and John Sherwin, Jr., '53; and Charles L. Stephens, '46

Clockwise (upper left): Kathleen Carr; Dorothy E. Williams; Mildred R. Smith; Alice A. Zimmerman; and Inez T. Budd

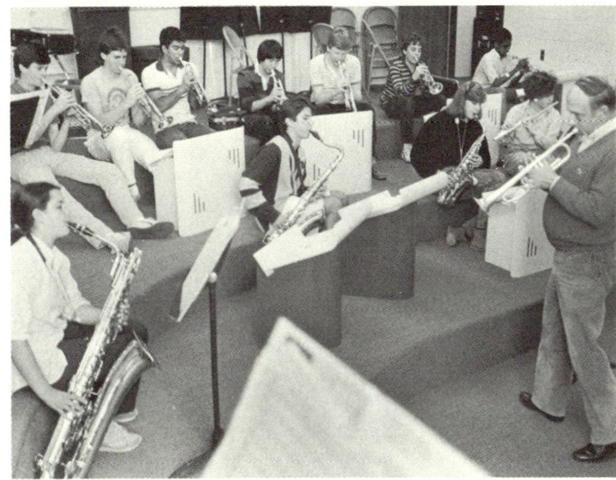

Clockwise (upper left): Sheldon Freedman; Laura R. Zappa; James Snavely; Barbara Dlugosz; and Allen McMickle

Clockwise (upper left): Christopher Fusco, '68; D. Bruce Carr; James Gross; James Whiteman; and Mary S. Eaton

*Clockwise (upper left): Deborah Handy;
Jennifer Mosse; Alan MacCracken; Jacqueline Meyer; and Staci Block*

Clockwise (upper left): Rebecca Jones; Roger Atwell; Patrick Palumbo; Jane Warner-Seik; and Timothy Leslie

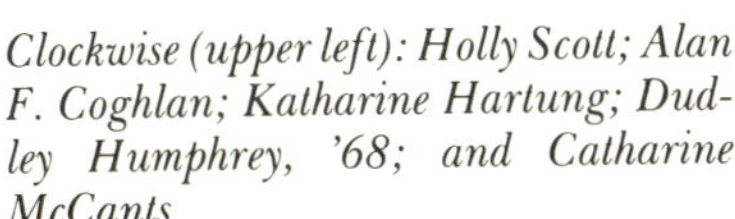

Clockwise (upper left): Holly Scott; Alan F. Coghlan; Katharine Hartung; Dudley Humphrey, '68; and Catharine McCants

Clockwise (upper left): Virginia K. Petrie; Peter Scott; Sally Zarney; Robert J. Kachurek; and Ann I. Dawson

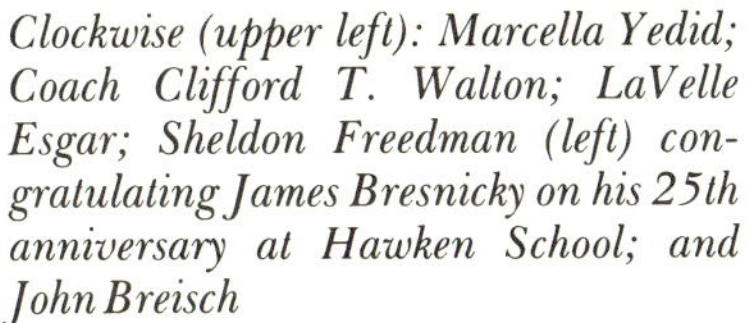

Clockwise (upper left): Marcella Yedid; Coach Clifford T. Walton; LaVelle Esgar; Sheldon Freedman (left) congratulating James Bresnicky on his 25th anniversary at Hawken School; and John Breisch

Clockwise (upper left): Lynn MacArthur; Wendi C. Bomback; Suzanne Kent; Headmaster Stenberg and students; and Meachem Hitchcock, '42 (left), talking with Morris Everett, Sr., '27

tion where to go. Strangely this rebel characteristic in both combined with a remarkable tenderness.

Charlie

The stature is medium and chunky; the face outdoor ruddy. The demeanor—gentle and stubborn. The eyes behind steel-rimmed glasses want to know about you. They are compelling because they are close to the surface and the generous space between eye and brow is vertically corrugated. When he listens to children he is not glancing at his watch. He won't wear one to control his life.

People in general are strangely comfortable in his presence; in two minutes they know who he is.

The exceptions to the comfort are top administrators. Operating in the confined zone among trustees, parents, and faculty, administrators need some flexibility on staff. For them, a teacher who daily lives his principles can be an inconvenience.

Charles Poutasse is Henry Thoreau (and from the same town—Concord, Massachusetts). Like Thoreau he built his own house in the woods, and he loves the woods better than any place but Hawken School. Like Thoreau he built his own code. He left the payroll of the state of Massachusetts in disgust at its politics.

He tries to keep his code from troubling other people. He still wouldn't wear a tie, but to spare his boss, "You can explain about my neck trouble." They said—use a textbook. He still said no. Not defiantly; just quietly. But they were concerned about the outside state evaluator team. "Okay. You could say I use a text if you want because I do know the book well."

Official evaluations are meaningless to him because he is almost daily confronted with extravagant ratings by his alumni. And they are *his*. For example, at a funeral the three Feller brothers came up to him, Steve, '60, Marty, '65, and Bruce, '68. Bruce stuck out his hand, "You're the reason I'm a professor at the University of Chicago."

Charles goes to the funerals, graduations, and weddings of his constituents (*sans* necktie).

And when he travels, which is constantly, he visits

his alumni to see how they're doing. For example he found Randy Taplin is a cabinet maker on a back road in Vermont; Harman McBride, '64, a rancher in Georgia with seven hundred acres of corn, five hundred acres of peanuts, and three hundred head of special cattle; and Paul Vignos, '69, runs an apple orchard in Georgia.

Charles Poutasse, former chairman of the primary school's kindergarten through grade three, follows youngsters all the way to adulthood, and returns to the class reunions. It is important to him to know how they are doing. "The girls from our first coed kindergarten class are now seniors in college."

In the late 1970s the administration planned a reorganization of the Lower School for reasons they considered educationally sound. Charles Poutasse opposed it for reasons he considered educationally sound.

Doug Stenberg believed a better division was kindergarten through grade five, six through eight and nine through twelve. The proposal was controversial. In the ensuing debate, dramatic compromises were offered Poutasse. But his own code left him no slack. He announced his resignation.

"Now the big problem was," Chuck Stephens recalls, "Charlie was beloved." The news spreading through the parents and alumni caused an uproar. "It was really very deeply resented."

"Charles Poutasse Day" was set for December 19, 1980, on the lower campus. Charles was very sick that day, but he didn't want to disappoint people. He had already heard that alumni were assembling from all over the country. So he went to the ceremonies which spread over the day in different buildings. Only Betsy Poutasse knew he was ill.

The crowd overflowed the hall and Poutasse stories exchanged all over the campus. Poutasse went into hiding to lie down between events.

Lincoln Reavis, then vice president of the board, addressed Poutasse from the podium, "For more than three decades you have served Hawken ... as the most caring of teachers."

Water welled in the audience eyes, the same kind "Mr. Poutasse" had brushed off their cheeks thirty years ago. Despite the roster of giant teachers in Hawken's history—from Smeed to Charles R. Stephens—this was the school's most emotional retirement outpouring.

Liv

On Tuesday, April 21, 1981, Hawken lost the old lion.

In the Hawken survival years Liv Ireland must be ranked with Hawken, Bole, Sheffield, and the Boltons for holding the fort. In the deficit years, and those were the only years he experienced as a thirty-two-year trustee, the so-called "anonymous gifts" usually came from Ireland.

Liv Ireland set his own compass from early youth when he decided to drop out of Yale in favor of Navy flying. Natural chutzpah forced leadership on him even then, and he was put in charge of a group of Navy pilots. That leadership role followed him all the way into the coal mining business, managing thirty-three mines in four states, working successfully with the men who followed union giant John L. Lewis. One could say that wasn't leadership, it was great wealth. But the coal business was full of wealthy men, and John L. Lewis was no respecter of individual wealth.

When Ireland delivered a blistering attack on Canada's coal industry pollution, Canada legislated new standards.

And in Ireland's loud leadership of civic organizations, he was dealing with highly statured volunteers who could mutiny any time they disliked Captain Bligh's style. But when he decreed that the last man to arrive for board meetings pay for the drinks, tardiness stopped. When he passed the hat for six figure emergency pledges, the hat filled.

Amid profane management of the coal business and the school, the graying lion wept openly at mine cave-ins. He became the imperious industry whip on mine safety. And at Hawken campuses where he, with Hitchcock, was probably the most active board visitor, he concerned himself with the well-being of the backstage non-professional staff.

As decades rolled down he still led with a menthol cigarette and a martini in hand and an unhallowed phraseology, but the handsome features softened.

Of course, there came the evening when, before a multi-school audience, he cut loose from the podium with a gratuitous evaluation of University School which wilted the podium flowers and chilled the cold war, but . . . "What the hell."

A strong-handed manager of several business and civic boards besides the coal company and Hawken, Liv managed his own exit. In a letter to the school dated February 4, 1981, he explained, "I am in the process of trying to tuck in all the edges in anticipation of an early demise." He inquired about the availability of the Hawken Chapel for a "brief memorial service" and the dining room for "one of Mrs. Helen Hochstetler's goodie spreads and our regular assortment of drinks."

He specified that at this event he wanted sea chanteys played, and later "after the guests have been revived from listening to a eulogy . . . ask Howard Stirn to get silence and make the following toast: 'Please face in whatever direction you imagine Liv has filed his flight plan to get from here to his destination in the hereafter and wish him a rapid flight.' Meeting adjourned. Liv."

At the service, Morris Everett, Sr., told the crowd, among whom were few who could remember first hand, "In the 1930s the school was busted. Liv Ireland carried the school through when it looked like there was no way it could survive."

Of course not many in the audience in 1981 actually remembered the 1930s. They had read about it in their history books. But that's a different thing; it lacks the sting. It required a Liv Ireland to look that Depression monster in the eye and tell it where to go.

Though larger-than-life, Liv was representative of the early trustees. His departure is a good time for a brief look at Hawken trustees in general and in particular the new trustees.

THE TRACK OF A TRUSTEE

Board members tend to be very experienced in other organizations before becoming Hawken trustees, and they tend to be trustees and directors of several other organizations. Hawken has no patent on this of course; but the record of Hawken trustees in that way is striking, even in the newer and younger ones.

Marcia La Riche is representative. When Liv left she joined the board. She was already a trustee on Rainbow Babies and Children's Hospital, a member of that board's chemical dependency task force. She was also a trustee of the Shaker Lakes Regional Nature Center. Previously she had been a foundation associate with the Cleveland Foundation, working primarily in the areas of criminal justice and housing. She was a member of the board of managers of Hough Housing Corporation, and a member of the citizens' advisory committee on community development block grants.

Before coming on the board she was one of the four parents on the CCIS parent study group and she was on the Hawken mothers committee. As she joined the board she was doing graduate work toward a master's degree in applied social science.

This is the kind of background the generations of Hawken trustees generally bring to the job.

23. Introspection

THE ADMIRERS and detractors of Hawken both cite its "liberalism," usually meaning its mechanisms for deliberately giving faculty and students a real voice in school policy.

It is easy to run a hierarchical, authoritarian school. But to run a school with nine hundred possible voters, while holding direction and avoiding chaos, is high art. This is especially true when we realize the high annual turnover in faculty in these latter years. Old hands leave Hawken to head other schools. New teachers, without the Hawken background, come aboard.

INTROSPECTIONS

Some intense self-evaluation took place in February and March of 1984 via independent projects.

COLLEGES' PERCEPTION OF HAWKEN SCHOOL

College Counselor Gary Williams sent a questionnaire to one hundred and twenty-five colleges asking their perceptions of Hawken's academic and social climate. Williams's purpose was to establish a connection between "what Hawken is and what it is perceived to be."

He explained that results indicated a variety of opinions but "common respect for our academic programs."

Some of the more common responses were "quality," "excellent facilities," "academic excellence," "liberal," and "beautiful intimate campus."

Other answers included, "a top prep school," "preppie prep," "less traditional," "laid back learning atmosphere," and "highly personalized."

One admissions officer wrote, "If I lived in the

area it is the first school I would consider for my children."

Some were not so complimentary: "Enthusiastic students feeling their school is superior to others" and "typical private school—fairly good kids."

Colleges responded that the greatest weaknesses at Hawken are "isolation," "homogenous," "sheltered."

Strengths were listed as "strong academic program," "serious student body," "community of faculty and students," "very strong faculty," and "breadth of programs."

The consensus among respondents was that Hawken's academic quality was superior to other schools. One college indicated that Hawken was "superior on a national level." Another responded that "Hawken's best compares to the best in the U.S."

Trustees Review Curriculum

The chairman of the education committee of the board of trustees suggested the committee be brought into the curriculum development loop to assure that Hawken goals translated into courses. This was warily received by faculty.

While this sounds rather routine, it was actually a delicate matter. The board, meaning no interference, was trying to do its overseer job. However, faculty was hypersensitive to the possibility of excessive board interference in curriculum. The air finally cleared, but it becomes an example of two dedicated sets of people not communicating. The board identified deficiencies in Hawken's advanced computer, modern language, psychology, and non-Western history elective offerings.

Stenberg said that the history department may offer electives in Afro-American history or Latin American history next year.

The head of the Upper School, Fred Hoffman, presented a study of school time spent in class.

Hawken's Community Image
Evaluated in Survey

McKinsey and Company was selected to do a study determining whether the perceptions of the community toward the school accurately reflect the image Hawken tries to project. The results, presented to an ad hoc committee of the board, indicated that the community believes Hawken to be a very strong institution. Hawken's academic excellence was shown to be the principal reason parents chose to send their children to Hawken. Other perceived strengths: co-education, diversity, and the accent Hawken places on the individual.

Recommendations from McKinsey indicated that Hawken should not change its purpose but should emphasize academic excellence and should market the benefits of a coed private school.

Later phases of the survey noted unusually good rapport between students and faculty.

The negative comments turned up were: "Academic program too rigorous"; "Hawken changing children's values by making them too materialistic"; "tuition too high."

The study found University School to be Hawken's chief competition for students. And that those parents who favored U. S. did so because it was more conservative, single sex, and more athletics-oriented than Hawken. While they considered U. S. weaker academically, they felt the atmosphere there was more structured. Some felt there is too much opportunity for self-direction at Hawken, the "too liberal" criticism.

Headmaster Stenberg cites evidence that the liberalism is one of the great strengths. "Our alumni, when they go off to college, one to six years out, say to us, 'Don't allow any change at Hawken that would jeopardize self-management of time. We find we're more experienced than other students about managing our free time in college.'"

THE FOUNDER'S CONTINUITY

One powerful testimony is the press of alumni to send their children to Hawken. One dramatic example which can be replicated in many families is the founder's three generations.

Roberta Bole's son, Benjamin Patterson Bole, Jr., known as Pat, was of course in the first class. Pat had four children, three of them sons who went to Hawken: Benjamin Patterson Bole III, known as Ben; Jonathan Bole, and Richard Bole. Ben's four children, Kathleen, Suzanne, Kristin, and Ben Bole IV attended Hawken as did Jonathan's children Jonathan and Abigail. Richard Holden Bole's children Richard, Jr. and Allayne are in Hawken at this writing; his other son, Nicholas Boyleston Bole, is waiting in the wings to enter Hawken primary.

* * *

The Affirmative No
May 2, 1984

Course Offerings Broadened

Every department is adding new courses in response to student demand.

The history department is offering seven new electives.

Two new Spanish electives are added.

In the Math Department, computer instructor Susan Coverdale will teach Advanced Placement Pascal.

Technical director Stegmiller will return to teach a year-long Technical Theater class and Basic Drafting.

The Physical Education Department is offering football officiating.

In the English department, Introduction to Drama replaced Values, a sophomore course. Seniors gained the choice of two drama-related courses, Modern Drama and Plays and Reading. English electives were Oral History as Literature and Nineteenth Century Novel.

The school also introduced a class on bioethics; English teacher Peter Scott made this course enormously popular.

***

The Affirmative No
June 3, 1984

92 Are Graduated

Among the colleges chosen this year by the graduating seniors, Miami University (Ohio) was chosen by the largest number, eight. Harvard only four. Yale—two.

The Affirmative No
September 1984

Lower School Renovated

Phase II of a three-phase development program is nearing completion at Lower School involving the building of Phillips Hall and renovation of Blossom Hall, the South Wing and the West Wing.

Phase II's educational objective was to double the science, music, and art facilities. The new campus configuration would support the Lower School's two division concept of an elementary school and middle school. Kenyon C. Bolton III, '58, was the architect, extending the same physical plant his grandfather had spent so much time building. The chairman of the board was Whitney Evans.

Hawken received a four-hundred-thousand-dollar bequest from the late John Phillips, '25. With this money six new classrooms were built for the fourth and fifth grades.

An all-glass walkway containing student art will be built connecting Phillips Hall to the west wing.

"It is amazing," said Joan B. Page, Lower School

head, "that a major facility has been built in just five months!"

The Hawken Review
May 1985

A Sense Of Wonder
Lower School Science Program

Curiosity is Pervasive ...

... says science teacher Virginia Petrie "and that's partially because of the new Charles Poutasse Science Room which has brought science education in the Primary Building to a new plane. All the paraphernalia is in one central location, an expansion of Charlie Poutasse's 'science cart'. The younger students will see a table of fourth grade science projects and ask, 'Hey, what are the fourth graders doing?' Curiosity is constantly being stimulated at all levels because students are confronted with a variety of science projects all the time."

Too Drunk To Drive?

Students from University School, Laurel, Hathaway Brown and Orange have joined to form *Saferides,* an organization that will provide rides home for people who think they are too drunk to drive themselves home from a party or who do not want to ride with a drunken friend. Rides are free, and the identity of the person picked up is kept in strict confidentiality. Although Hawken is not presently a member of the organization, Saferides president, Jay Novak, said that if a Hawken student called, he or she would not be refused. 831–1566 Friday-Saturday 10 p.m.-2 a.m.

The Affirmative No
June 9, 1985

Stenberg Responds To Letter

Headmaster Stenberg responded to a letter from three juniors questioning the school's non-sectarian policy regarding menus during various religious holidays, decorations around the school at Christmas and music, all of which were Christian in motif.

Dr. Stenberg said, "Hawken must become more sensitive to the needs of all our students who represent the pluralistic community we aspire to be."

Stenberg held a meeting with Suzanne Kent, Charles Stephens, and Marcella Yedid on the subject. The result is a new section of the Hawken handbook mandating ongoing assessment of classroom materials, chapel hymns and prayers, and musical programs and decorative symbols.

In addition, Stenberg proposed to talk with the faculty at the beginning of each school year, bolstering the nonsectarian policy.

The Affirmative No
October 23, 1985

Hail To The Chief:
Gary Williams

College Counselor Gary Williams has been elected president of the National Association of College Admissions Counselors, an organization with over 3200 member high schools and colleges, the pre-eminent organization of college counselors. Williams' election campaign committee was headed by Kevin Sullivan, dean of admissions at John

Carroll University. Williams has been elected to a very prestigious position.

Fall Family Fair Tradition Continues

Mothers' Committee members planned this year's Fair.

Ken Roby's Iron Works, The Hawk's Nest and craft demonstrations filled the booths. Midway games were popular.

A sense of community was strong. Senior Julie Braun expressed it, "Great to see the Upper and Lower Schools together."

There are hundreds of people who comment about Hawken's sense of community, which manifests itself in the active Parents Association and such events as Fall Family Fair, April Hawken Night to Remember, May Antiques Festival, etc. In any event, other local schools have commented often that they observe and admire this. Shirley Stenberg has helped to contribute to that sense of community. She hosts the monthly gatherings of the mothers committee, worked on the annual auction committee (the Hawken Night to Remember) and, though not on staff, she is very much Hawken.

* * *

The Affirmative No
October 30, 1985

Faculty Struts

Faculty held a fashion show satirizing student dressing habits. The lights dimmed and the faculty strutted on stage to flaunt student illegal dress styles.

Latin teacher James Bresnicky wore shorts with boxers hanging out to his knees and math teacher, Kathleen Kuss, wore a very short mini-skirt and a midriff top. The assistant head of the Upper School, Marcella Yedid, wore a tank top and shorts, both too small. There were many other gauche costumes.

The administration felt the show was needed because as school progressed there was noticeable deterioration in student dress habits.

* * *

The Affirmative No
November 20, 1985

Tails Fly

A special meeting of the Hawken Senate on dress codes finally approved the wearing of sandals and shirt tails worn *outside* pants or skirt.

In the heated debate, students pointed out that styles change and Hawken should be with it. Fred Hoffman admitted the students made strong arguments. The "neat and clean" requirement remained in force, but other regulations softened.

* * *

The Affirmative No
January 22, 1986

Facilities Grow

Headmaster Stenberg declared, "It doesn't make sense for a school of Hawken's quality to be so limited in athletic facilities."

The school planned a new Upper School gymnasium to be completed by the end of the decade. Hawken's educational goals include keeping its students physically fit as well as mentally fit.

The new gymnasium would use part of the seven million dollars to be raised in the current campaign for development of the Lower and Upper schools.

The Hawken Review
  Winter 1986

Lerner Visits Russia

"Once we were inside the Moscow airport we immediately felt the pressure of authority," explained English teacher Nancy Lerner, traveling with a group to contact the Jewish "refuseniks." "We were escorted to a small room where we were surrounded by mirrors. A man sat in front of us with our passports and stared at us for 20 minutes."

She explained the intimidating experience: "It would be very dangerous for the Soviets to know our group included two rabbis and a journalist who were billed as teachers. Five members of our group made it through customs. But Rabbi Horowitz was stopped because of American periodicals in his suitcase. The customs officials spent an hour reading every page."

Ultimately the group was able to interview several refuseniks to discover the true situation of these people.

* * *

GOALS RE-EVALUATED

Charles L. Stephens, head of the Middle School, submitted a proposition for that school's renewal, a program to re-evaluate goals and philosophy.

Stephens said, "I am thinking of something very good being developed and polished into something great."

HITCHCOCK DEVELOPS

Meacham Hitchcock was appointed director of the Hawken development office (later associate headmaster for development). Former vice president of the board of trustees, he had resigned from the board to accept this position. Doug Stenberg appointed him because of "his proven organizational skills, superb abilities as a communicator, and his dedication to Hawken and his knowledge of Hawken."

In the period January 1985 to spring 1988 the projected development goal was seven million dollars for physical additions and endowment.

* * *

The Affirmative No
January 8, 1986
> Women Swimmers Capture Third
> State Championship

* * *

> Undefeated Hawks Hoopsters
> Stuff Opponents

* * *

The Affirmative No
June 8, 1986

> Playground
> Construction Completed
> "It's Awesome!"—Larry Richmond

From May 14 to May 19, children and parents and teachers all worked together on the new Lower School playground of fantastic design.

The idea started in 1985 when the mothers committee decided to donate four thousand dollars for new playground facilities. Their committee found out about architect Robert Leathers, who has helped one hundred and eighty communities create dramatic playgrounds made out of heavy timbers with castles, tunnels, mountains, and a veritable amusement park of items for kids to climb, swing on, hide in, and chase around.

Robert Leathers came to the Lower School and talked with the children first. From their dreams he in turn designed a phantasmagoria of interconnected castles, boats, jails, sky walks, climbing apparatus that sprawled across a large area.

This of course outran the four thousand dollars. The Boyer and Gresham families contributed several thousand dollars; the mothers committee came up with a series of fund raising events which produced another five thousand.

This was still not enough for production. Architect Leathers drew up a schedule by which volunteer labor could put the monster together under supervision. Students, parents, and faculty turned out to build the extravaganza with the guidance of some paid professionals.

* * *

The Affirmative No
June 1986

106 Graduate

This year's graduating roster showed an unusual number of graduates heading for state universities, only one to Harvard, two to Yale.

* * *

IKE RETIRES

After twenty-three years Isiah "Ike" Smith retired from the maintenance staff at the Lower School in 1986. He was honored at the Lower School chapel, where he received a tribute from the Lower School faculty. Headmaster Stenberg spoke of Ike's twenty-three years and presented him with a Hawken chair. Ike expects to spend a lot of time fishing and traveling to visit his family.

* * *

The Affirmative No
November 19, 1986

Hawks Reach Play-offs

The Hawken football team captured the Northeast Regional title and extended their winning streak to 24, the longest in Hawken history.

Ireland Hall Re-Dedicated

Ireland Hall was re-dedicated to include the most recent additions. This building honors R. Livingston Ireland, who served for the most terms as president of the Board of Trustees.

The Affirmative No
June 7, 1987

Hawken Adopts Inner-City
School

For the 1987–88 year Hawken will adopt Stephen E. Howe Elementary School, pre-school through kindergarten and 4th-6th grades. Hawken students will help Howe students.

Nadja Deighan, faculty head of the adopt-a-school program, said that by adopting Howe, "we might be able to design a pilot for the entire city. All children deserve hope and opportunity."

ADMINISTRATIVE REORGANIZATION

In the fall of 1989 the ten-year head of the Upper School, Fred Hoffman, was moving up to associate headmaster for administrative services, school-wide. He was beginning his nineteenth year on the faculty. Coincident with that move, Hawken School reorganized its administration functions. The basic change was to make three rather than two fundamental divisions of the school, each with a director—Elementary, Middle, and Upper, giving more autonomy to each.

To free each director for a purely education mission, they were relieved of maintenance concerns, which transferred over to Associate Headmaster Hoffman.

RENOVATION PROGRAM

Planned for 1988-1990 were five important renovations: The Carl Holmes Library to be built in the "brown gymnasium"; the commons room in the existing library; a new gymnasium to the west of Godfrey Pool, and an enlarged dining room. On the Gates Mills campus the plan was to build a comprehensive Upper School sports center in the area of the main parking lot.

The Affirmative No
November 18, 1987

Project CHARLIE Underway

A new program is being introduced to Lower School, called Project CHARLIE. This is an educational approach to drug prevention. Dr. and Mrs. Stenberg will be teachers in one class.

Parents play a large part. The goal is to establish partnership between school and family in the prevention of drug use.

* * *

The Affirmative No
April 27, 1988

Hawken Half Girls?

The Education Committee of the Board of Trustees held a meeting concentrating on the gender issue, reassessing the admissions policy of 40%-60% ratio.

A change in admissions policy would drastically affect the athletic department. Head of Upper School Fred Hoffman said, "If we change to a fifty/fifty ratio, soccer and football will certainly suffer."

Trustee Ted Luntz challenged, "Are boys' teams any more important than girls' teams?"

Committee member Marcia LaRiche added, "There might be other issues that might have as much sway to let athletics go a bit."

No decision resulted. The issue would be pursued.

* * *

The Affirmative No
October 5, 1988

Students Protest Parking Lot

Construction of the new parking lot was to begin this fall: however, protests from students and faculty over destroying 1.7 acres of Hawken woods may delay it.

Another meeting has been initiated by the "Save the Woods" committee of seniors, Megan Sherman, Sean LaRiche and Joe Tait. The committee has banded the large trees with yellow ribbons.

Hawken students grew up with a reverence for woods, partly learned in Lower School in what came to be named Poutasse Woods where teachers taught natural science and conducted bird walks.

Mrs. H

Among the larger statistics of classes taught, books read, points scored, students graduated ... is *meals prepared.*

Helen Hochstetler did not start out at Hawken as dietitian. It is a rather amazing story. Helen was a nurse.

When Hawken was about to launch its kindergarten with twenty-nine boys, Dick Day thought they should have a nurse on premises. Tiny Helen Hochstetler was hired for the job.

During the flu season she lined the boys up every morning to check throats.

She did a good job as nurse, but those who watched her felt she was suited for an even more pertinent job. They asked her if she would be interested in teaching science.

She was delighted, and they added math to her assignment.

"I taught science," she recalled, "with Mrs. Bennett and Zoann Dusenbury. Then Charlie Poutasse and I worked together. Charlie taught science and he taught me a lot of things too. We had a lot of animals that the children cared for. In the spring we would buy four dozen fertile eggs and we had a huge incubator. The eggs had to be turned over every day. My husband built a cage for the ducks. We had baby rabbits, snakes, mice, and gerbils.

"But the greatest time was when it was time for the eggs to hatch."

Helen enjoyed teaching science. But one day she passed Mac McCarthy in the corridor. Winnie McCarthy, dietitian for thirty-five years, had retired. Mac McCarthy was business manager for the school. When Helen passed him in the hall she casually asked, "Find a replacement for Winnie yet?"

"No." Mac kept right on walking, "And I'm tired of looking!"

Suddenly he stopped dead, whirled around and asked, "How about you?"

"Me?"

"Yes. You had dietetics in nursing?"

"Well, yes, but ..."

She did love cooking. She talked it over with her husband, who had reservations about leaving a teaching job for dietitian. But she said, "Bill, I want to try it."

The first year was very trying. "The ladies in the kitchen had worked there for a long time. I wanted to make some changes. No way. They were very set in their ways."

Helen backed off for a year on the changes and downshifted to bring the changes in gradually.

Then it began to become "Helen's Kitchen." She brought the primary children over to the main dining room with the other boys.

Today Helen and her remarkable staff prepare a wide range of cuisine from snacks to elaborate dinners for alumni and board affairs and Family Fair and Christmas events.

She loves to dress up a meal so that it is a fashion show. "I'm a firm believer that you eat with your eyes."

Helen sings the praises of her staff.

WHERE ARE HAWKEN GRADUATES GOING TO COLLEGE?

About ninety-eight percent of Hawken graduates go on to colleges and universities. A four-year analysis ending with class of 1989 (of colleges with above nine Hawken applications) is interesting. (See Appendix XIV.) Notice the results do not weigh heavily toward Ivy League schools.

24. Bench Strength

A school is only as good as its alumni.

Jim Ireland

SUPPORTING the active players on the field ... faculty, staff, and board ... Hawken has great sideline strength.

The small class size had a side effect; the boys, and later the girls, became close friends with classmates, extending close ties years beyond graduation. Malcolm B. (Frat) Vilas, '33, a tireless supporter of Hawken, stayed in regular contact with classmates Peter Hitchcock, Henry Wilhems, Dixon Morgan, Asa Shiverick, Allen House, John Davenport, and Jim Lincoln.

This was not uncommon. Bill Hubbard, '29, belonged to a group known as the Four Horsemen—Joe Eaton, Bob Beatty, Morris Bradley, and Guthrie Bicknell. Most alumni still know their classmates. These small-class friendships could have a bearing on alumni support to the school.

There are a large number of alumni like Clark Bruner, '28, so dedicated that they attend nearly every home event—football, class days, and general ceremonies.

Cal Judson, '31-I, who arrived at the author's interview not very much out of breath from his daily five-mile run, still enjoys the fact that without much practice he always beat Francis Silver, '30, in cross country and he remembers "Benny Schneider got out of sports because he was the smartest kid in the entire world, maybe the universe." Schneider, '31-I, of course, probably was. Anyone seeking a lost Hawken fact is told, "See Ben Schneider. He probably knows."

And he probably does. To this day he can sing the old Hawken fight song.

In various large cities active Hawken groups meet for lunch.

Beyond the sentimental, a practical result is unusually strong alumni financial support. Of course, the strong support did not happen spontaneously. We've seen, previously, certain alumni step up to the podium and set new, higher giving levels. Carl Holmes especially enjoyed alumni contact and constantly exhorted alumni to return to visit the campus.

Even so, strong alumni financial support did not cut in to relieve the struggle during the long Frances Bolton-Liv Ireland era. The consecutive deficit-free years began with Stenberg's headmastership and the establishment of a very active alumni development office.

The functions of the modern Hawken alumni development office today are to organize and coordinate annual giving by alumni, parents, and friends; work with the board's development committee on long-range planning and capital campaigns; arrange for all functions such as homecoming; handle public relations in all media; keep all contribution records; publish the annual report and *The Alumni Review*.

Development works closely, of course, with the alumni association. Many of the heads of that association are names you've met in these pages:

Hawken Alumni Association Presidents

1925	Alvah C. Drake '25
1926	Barnard Prescott '24
1927	Sherman S. Hayden '24
1928-1929	James C. Weir '25
1930	Edgar A. Taylor, Jr. '26
1931	Thomas B. Grandin '25
1932	Henry C. Osborn, Jr. '28
1933	William R. Nash '29
1934-1936	No record
1937	James C. Weir '25
1938	Frederick R. White, Jr. '30
1939	John B. Calfee '31-I

1940	Guthrie Bicknell '30
1941	Frank E. Taplin, Jr. '31-II
1942-1946	No record
1947	Willard W. Brown '32-I
1948	Charles Hickox '31-I
1949	Fayette Brown, Jr. '31-I
1950	Morris Everett '27
1951-1952	Malcolm B. Vilas, Jr. '33
1953	Dixon Morgan '33
1954	Robert Y. White '36
1955	John F. Wilson, Jr. '33
1956	Benjamin H. Taplin '31-I
1957	A. Benedict Schneider '30
1958	Kenyon C. Bolton '30
1959	William B. Chamberlin, Jr. '29
1960	Harry C. Royal, Jr. '31-I
1961	James D. Ireland '32-I
1962	Cyrus S. Eaton, Jr. '34
1962-1964	Meacham Hitchcock '42
1964-1966	John Newell III '40
1966-1967	Stevenson M. Taylor '35
1967-1968	H. William Strong, Jr. '40
1968-1969	Clark E. Bruner '28
1969-1970	Charles O. Newell '41
1970-1972	John Sherwin Jr. '53
1972-1974	Malcolm B. Vilas III '59
1974-1976	Jeffrey M. Biggar '68
1976-1978	Christopher Royan '67
1978-1980	Robert T. Page '49
1980-1982	John B. Calfee, Jr. '60
1982-1984	H. Clark Harvey, Jr. '57
1984-1986	Kenneth Dettelbach '54
1986-1988	Fred Wendel III '67
1988-1990	J. Albert Klauss '66

Many alumni association executives move up the chairs to the Hawken board of trustees. There is no greater board responsibility than financing, on which depends educational goals. Trustee David S. Ingalls, Jr., '49, was a Hawken work horse. But his largest load was probably chairing the board's development committee, charged with raising seven million dollars. By the winter of 1985-86 he reported the drive had reached the $2.7 million mark, and gaining momentum.

HAWKEN FELLOWS

The school very recently further strengthened alumni bonds with a new concept. On a Saturday, September 26, 1987, it created the charter class of Hawken Fellows.

In the arts communication building seventy-five people from all over the country assembled to be honored as Hawken Fellows.

The idea developed in the board of trustees championed by Henry Eaton, under chairman Whitney Evans, '51. The seventy-five men and women thus honored were people who had made giant contributions to Hawken—former board members, former and current life trustees, former mothers committee and fathers representative chairpersons, former headmasters, Head Boys and Charles B. Bolton Award winners, former alumni association presidents and Carl Holmes Alumni Award winners, faculty emeriti, and special friends of the school.

Henry Eaton, co-chairman of the Hawken Fellows committee, with trustee Alton Whitehouse and H. Clark Harvey, Jr., '57, opened the investiture ceremonies explaining that the seventy-five people had given "exceptional contributions, unusual love, devotion, and commitment to Hawken."

It may be useful to future researchers to record here that charter class of Hawken Fellows:

INVESTITURE OF THE CHARTER CLASS OF HAWKEN FELLOWS

Sarah W. Bartlett
Guthrie Bicknell '30
Jeffrey M. Biggar '68
Dudley S. Blossom '56
Nancy A. Bole
Robert J. Brice
Rosemary Brice
Elizabeth Briggs

Harvey Brooks '32
Clark E. Bruner '28
Dorothy O. Bryan
Richard E. Burney '58
John B. Calfee '31
John B. Calfee, Jr. '60
Leonard R. Carey
Roger E. Clapp '35
Ethan H. Cohen '82
Kenneth Dettelbach '54
Zoann L. Dusenbury
Jack K. Easterday
Barbara F. Eaton
Eleanor E. Everett
Morris Everett '27
Leigh L. Fabens
David A. Feingold '83
Constance T. Ford
Michael Friedman
H. Clark Harvey, Jr. '57
Meacham Hitchcock '42
Jo Hoge
Cornelia W. Ireland
James D. Ireland '32
Louise I. G. Ireland
Edward K. Kast
Ross A. Kipka '45
Emilia Korman
Timothy C. LaRiche '59
Robert E. Little '48
Ted M. Luntz
Joseph J. Mahovlic
Lynn R. Mintz
Suzanne M. Murray
Robert T. Page '49
Clara MacKenzie Pelfrey '79
Scott W. Phillips '76
Charles Poutasse
Leann D. Rayburn
Mary E. Reavis
Nancy G. Rome
Adolph B. Schneider, Jr. '30

Elizabeth W. Sedgwick
Ellery Sedgwick, Jr.
John Sherwin, Jr. '53
Asa Shiverick, Jr. '33
Shirley L. Stenberg
Charles L. Stephens '46
Cara S. Stirn
Howard F. Stirn
Herbert W. Strong, Jr. '40
Frederick L. Swetland, Jr. '31
Frederick I. Taft '60
Edgar A. Taylor, Jr. '26
Stevenson M. Taylor '35
Frank Jerome Tone III
Frank S. Treco, Jr.
Malcolm B. Vilas, Jr. '33
Andrew C. Watson '82
Babette M. Weir
David R. Weir
Theodore Wiedemann
Fred R. White '30
Robert Y. White '36
Alton W. Whitehouse, Jr.
James B. Young

Parents

In a sense a mothers committee founded Hawken, Roberta Bole and her friends. And from the beginning mothers were closely involved, assisting school operations and helping the faculty until finally it was spelled with capitals, The Mothers Committee.

Fathers became involved of course, especially through the sports channel. A fathers club developed which organized more formally in 1976 as The Fathers Representatives.

In addition the Class Parents Council developed.

Parent involvement at Hawken, therefore, was intense and very active. Putting order into what could be chaos is the Parents Association which embraces the Mothers Committee, Fathers Representatives, and Class Parents Council.

Beyond this is a very active group of grandparents and friends who are neither alumni nor parents.

All this adds up to a school with remarkable bench strength.

Working Board

Additionally the trustees are a working board. John Sherwin, '53, president in 1990, is on the board of every school he attended and he states, "The Hawken board is a tremendously active board. Two meetings a week for the chairman, because of the committee work, is not unusual." He attended seventy-one meetings in 1989.

Those committees are: (a) the education committee, which meets four times a year. Example of challenges: Gender balance presently sixty/forty boy/girl. Perhaps should be fifty/fifty; (b) the executive committee, which meets twice a year to review performance, salaries; (c) the finance committee, which meets twice a year to oversee budget, tuition, salaries, performance level of scholarship aid, and teacher contracts; (d) the investment committee, which manages the endowment fund; (e) the nominating committee; (f) the personnel committee, which studies employee benefits.

The trustees meet once a month at the Lower School and attempt to hold their meetings to two hours. With trustees serving three-year terms, the average attendance is seventy percent with five members logging one hundred percent. Present at these meetings are representatives of parents groups, faculty, and the alumni association.

* * *

However, amid all the organizational complexity, what makes it all work is an intangible—the loyalty of alumni, typified by the unabashed affection radiating from every sentence of the following written, at the request of the authors, by an alumnus of class of 1931-II and one-time president of the alumni association.

A PERSONAL RECOLLECTION
by Frank E. Taplin, Jr., '31-II

There were five of us in the class—Harvey Brooks, John Cashmen, Jock Collens, John Nash, and I.

Miss Fanny Luehrs was our first-grade teacher. We began an educational adventure that would end, for me at least, with my graduation ten years later from the tenth grade. The elimination of the 11th and 12th grades at the end of the 1930-31 year, owing to the depression, meant the end of the Hawken chapter of our student lives.

After spending our second grade with Mrs. Gillette in temporary quarters on East 96th Street off Euclid Avenue (she introduced us to long division), we moved to the new Lyndhurst campus in the fall of 1923.

Here was paradise—wide open fields, with woods to the south ... and hills nearby for sledding and tobogganing in winter. At the center was the school of elegant proportion.

The Chapel, bathed in light from large windows along one side with its stage at the front and organ loft at the rear, was the moral center of our lives. We started and ended each day with a service in this beautiful place. At the end of the day with "Now the Day Is Over" we would leave the Chapel by a side door, older boys first, and file through the Headmaster's office, each of us shaking hands with Mr. Carney. This personal encounter was one of the forces which tied us into a closely knit community.

Then in fair weather and foul, we walked from the School, along Clubside Drive, to the interurban rail stop on Mayfield Road. There we climbed aboard one of those red ninety-ton electric giants that linked Cleveland with Gates Mills, Chardon, Middlefield and Burton, zipping along their single track line to connect with the Cleveland Electric Railway Company's tracks closer to town. There might be a short pause at Green Road, where an outbound interurban could enter a side track to let an inbound car pass. These were the dying years of the interurbans—such a romantic part of our young lives.

We had a rare group of teachers—Mr. Stephens, Mr. Smeed (Tuffy), Mr. MacMahon (Mr. Mac), and Mr. McCarthy, along with Miss Luehrs and Miss Liebe (who started us on French in the third grade), Mr. Adams (who always said "maysure" and "traysure" for measure and treasure), Mr. Horton (elegant gym teacher), and Mr. Howard ("shiver me timbers!"). And in art, Mr. Motto under whom in the fifth grade we recreated the Parthenon in plasticene green clay.

Each of us had our role—Harvey Brooks was Phidias, the sculptor; I was Ictinus, the architect. And in manual training Elmer Sipple taught us how to work in wood and metal. Some of us still have our pewter plates and copper ashtrays.

These men and women cared about their students and were extraordinarily successful in motivating us to do our best. John McCarthy, for instance, conveyed his love of Latin to some of us (not all) and enriched our lives in a very special way. And so did the others, each in his or her own way. Our English teacher required us to come to class each morning with a paragraph of our own on any subject. Over time this careful scrutiny of our daily work helped us to observe the world around us, clarify our thoughts ... I recall Seward Covert taking us outdoors on a warm spring day to read *The Merchant of Venice*.

I was a Gray; Collens was a Red. Red or Gray, we seemed to feel our identity in this respect had been predestined from birth, and our loyalty to our own side was strong and constant.

If these "high and far off times" seem bathed in a golden glow of reminiscence, I need only recall football practice, where I would be smashed by opposing lineman Bill Osborne, a giant who gave no quarter. And how can I forget that afternoon of baseball, when Cal Judson, our best pitcher, felled me with a bean ball. Then there was the day when I, a third grader, was pinned in a wrestling match by Gilbert (Bud) Humphrey, a mere second grader—a humiliating blow!

On Wednesday mornings we often had a guest speaker. It might be Father Sill from the Kent School; or Joel Hayden, the minister from Fairmount Presbyterian, who stayed on to don a uniform and play baseball with the students; or John Webster, Graham and Bob's father, who regaled us in his proper Scots accent with poems of Bobby Burns.

Music and acting were much encouraged. One fine day Mr. Carney got it into his head that it would be a good thing if the students would put on a production of *Hamlet*. The thought of asking parents to sit through an uncut version of *Hamlet* did not disturb him, nor did he blanch at asking me to play Gertrude, Queen of Denmark, Hamlet's mother. Mr. Carney was a determined fellow; my protests carried no weight. And so, in April 1931, we presented it on the Chapel stage. The Queen's first line is, "Good Hamlet, cast thy nighted colour off." This came out in our dress rehearsal as, "Good Hamlet, cast thy coloured nightie off." There was a certain tension at the per-

The Hawk

Created by artist Emily C. Parkman, mother of Mary R. Parkman, '78; commissioned by William C. McCoy, '38, father of William B. McCoy, '78, and Peter A. McCoy, '84

Carey, Charles A. Poutasse, Herbert F. Furst, Mary S. Eaton, Charles L. Stephens, Suzanne K. Kent, r, Virginia K. Petrie, David A. Coad, Patricia C. Hosmer, Lawrence E. Nelson, Martha Brown, Alan g. Third row: Rena L. Widzer, James C. Whiteman, Ann Ella Rasper, Brian J. Ross, Wendi C. Bom- A. Moser, Robert J. Kachurek, Hugh G. Thompson, Liane N. Beier, Deborah S. Handy. Fourth row: ugosz, Cynthia Guertin, Gregory G. Bobb, Sarah Ann Durn, Ann Mary Bracale, Holly M. Duncan,

Lyndhurst Faculty

Front row (left to right): Constance L. Palmer, Genevieve B. Swan, Elizabeth McCullough, Leonard R
James Lowe. Second row: Jerry I. Holtrey, Douglas L. Smith, LaVelle Pelton Esgar, Lynn M. McArthu
F. Coghlan, Sally M. Zarney, James D. Gross, Anne C. Smith, Robert T. Wiemer, David A. Rosenwie
back, Laura R. Zappa, Susan C. Wilson, Ann I. Dawson, Linda M. Gojak, Marta I. Ferrario, JoAnn
Lynne Raphael, Kathy Crennell Carr, Avis Thrash, Patricia O'Donnell, Inez Venning, Barbara B. D
Sandra L. Kahn, Pamela A. Win, Victoria R. Browne, Mary I. Rule, Christopher L. Fusco.

*. Budd, Dorothy Williams, Dudley Humphrey, Helen Hochstetler, T. Douglas Sten-
orris, Cynthia Kovach, Beatrice Kuhl, Jeri Parks. Back row: Pegi Pyles, Sharleen
Scott, Genevieve Vella, Beatrice Steadman, Clara Pawlikowski, Velma Cunninghan,
illespie, Wayne Zerby, Kurt Rink, Leonard Taylor, Kenneth Weber, Clarence Bon-
enry Ruff, William Doremus.*

Staff – Lyndhurst and Gates Mills

*Front row (left to right): Margaret Widmar, Kathleen Burgess, Mary Podmore, Delores DeNiro, Catherine A. Miller, In...
berg, Alan D. Matta, Mildred L. Smith, Alice A. Zimmerman, Rosetta Pavlik, Donna Nista, Deborah Dykstra, Chery...
Russo, Bette Steimle, Evelyn Paugh, Rose Sciulla, Barbara Perry, Isabell Salvo, Margaret Makarski, Mary Ciraolo, Les...
Priscilla Szabo, Janice Davidian, Frances Rose, Lynore Buck, Donna Drummer, Joyce Brinkerhoff, Kathleen Carr, Jack...
ner, Robert Kolsen, Charles Sekerak, Michael Iorio, Christopher Calo, Anthony Wanner, Frank Bucceri, Joseph Scharfel...*

hat the Bette
and each gen
successor to

Upper School Faculty

H. Hawkes, George A. Roby, James A. Snavely, Alan L. MacCracken, James P. Bresnicky, Frank P.
M. McNamee, T. Douglas Stenberg. Back row: Catherine S. McCants, Fernando Soldevilla, Joaquin
e, Julie M. Handler, Randall R. Dlugosz, Katharine D. Hartung, Marcella M. Yedid, Anne J.
hard Stacy, John G. Breisch, Lawrence M. Seik, Catherine A. Miller, Staci Ann Block, Jacqueline A.

Gates Mills Faculty

*Front row (left to right): Jane E. Warner-Seik, Peter F. Scott, Jesse D. Berenstein, Joan Bresnicky, Rob[ert]
Brandt, Larry H. Banks, Fred Hoffman, David M. McCahon, D. Bruce Carr, Nadja M. Deighan, Sus[an]
Soldevilla, Allen McMickle, Robert C. Wilheim, Robert H. Shurtz, Phillip T. Blood, Timothy C. [...]
Thompson, Clifford T. Walton, Ronald Hall, Merl B. Davis, Patrick J. Palumbo, Roger J. Atwell, W. [...]
Mayer, Mary Ann Gaetano, Eileen M. LaVerde, Sheldon Freedman, Maria Robbins.*

elf shall prevail
ation introduce its
igher plane of life

formance, when Taplin's actor colleagues sweated out his delivery of that line.

Commencement in the Chapel at the end of each school year was a moving occasion. Each class advanced to the pew in front of the one it had occupied for the past year. Prizes were awarded, and the Head Boy was announced, his name to be added to the impressive roster of Head Boys on the varnished wooden plaque on the Chapel wall. Track and field events were held, and I especially remember Char Bolton, our best sprinter, winning the four-hundred-forty yard dash in spectacular style. What a tragedy it was when he was later paralyzed; what a triumph when he went on to lead a fulfilling life in so many ways.

Johnny Ciarlillo: it is all right to call him the janitor, which he was, but he was our pal. His round Italian face was wreathed in a great smile, and the warmth of his bubbling personality never failed.

I treasure my memories of Hawken as a vital and caring place, where friendships flourished in the classroom and on the field; where we were challenged by remarkable teachers to do our best; and where perhaps we partly fulfilled in some small degree Mr. Hawken's famous injunction about each generation. Seventy-five years on is a good point at which to stand back and take a look.

25. Those First Ansel Road Boys?

> That the better self shall prevail and
> each generation introduce its successor
> to a higher plane of life.

AT THE SEVENTY-FIFTH YEAR, the projected influence of that pioneer faculty is visible as is the influence of the pioneer trustees.

What of the pioneering students? With the Hawken education under their hats, what kind of a pace did they set? As a denouement for a small chapter of American education history—what happened to some of those pioneering boys of 1915, 1916, 1917, or what did they make happen?

Benjamin Patterson Bole, Jr., '25, attended Hawken from first through tenth grade.

Pat Bole is an example of Hawken School encouraging a boy's individualism. When the school moved out to Lyndhurst, his teachers let Pat spend some science class time in the woods where he was entranced by its population, especially birds. He brought into class live science material.

While he followed his schoolmates' path, Exeter and Harvard, he then cut an original trail for himself.

Avoiding industry and the tall-money professions, his life was nature.

He took advanced degrees at Western Reserve University, then stayed to become a professor of biology introducing hundreds of young people to the ultimate miracle—life.

He projected that to hundreds more when he instituted a regular series of nature and bird walks, both on his beloved farm and in Gordon Park. He also conducted a famous series of western tours. He ran Three Corner Round, a summer camp for boys in the High Sierras.

Son of the founder, Roberta Bole, Pat became a Hawken patriarch because he had three children and eight grandchildren who attended Hawken.

Pat Bole himself became a trustee. Yet with all of that, he never hesitated to criticize the school when he thought it needed it.

Before and after graduation, the Weir brothers—Jim, David, and William—were and are a powerful presence at Hawken, the fighting Weirs. They went on from Hawken to distinguish themselves in law and medicine and in the armed forces in World War II.

Jim, oldest and toughest, attended Hawken grades three through twelve, went directly into Harvard, then into Harvard Law School. He built a law career at the firm of Bulkley, Hauxhurst, Inglis and Sharp. He headed the alumni association in 1928-29 and again in 1937.

William Weir, Hawken grades one through twelve, went directly into Harvard '31 and then into Harvard Medical School '35. He worked at University Hospitals, specializing in ob/gyn and was a leader in the treatment of infertility.

Today he is still proud of his schoolmates. Drawing on a pipe, he named off Graham Webster, Justin Sholes, Farrand Taplin, Joe Nutt "and a somebody Walsh, I think." He remembers that of his class three went to Harvard, two to Yale, one to Princeton, and one to Williams. Over the years, he met with many Hawken alumni physicians at the Pasteur Club.

David Weir, recipient in 1979 of the Carl N. Holmes Distinguished Alumnus Award, entered Hawken at four-and-a-half. His brother William explains, "He was so little he was just supposed to sit in the back and keep himself occupied and out of trouble. It was soon discovered that he could understand everything very well, so he was included right in." Dave was called Peewee because of his unusually small size, so small that sometimes he would open the lid of his desk, climb in, close the lid, and go to sleep.

Graduating in 1927, David followed his brother to Harvard and Harvard Medical School, interning in Cleveland at University Hospitals. He became a research fellow there and at Western Reserve University. He served in the Fourth General Hospital during World War II, advancing to lieutenant colonel. . After the war he built a distinguished medical career at several Cleveland hospitals and was finally persuaded to become director of medicine at Highland View Hospital from 1953 to 1979. In that time the hospital became world renowned for the care of patients with long and terminal illnesses; even better known around the world than locally.

His professional and civic positions summary requires two single-spaced pages ... titles which "introduce his successors to a higher plane."

David Weir served as Hawken trustee from 1961 to the present, president from 1972 to 1975 during the contentious coeducation decision.

Charles B. Bolton, '27, built a great Hawken record (grades one through ten), then went east to Milton Academy. Beyond a bright mind, he was a superb athlete with a joyous pride in his body and physical action. At a summer camp for underprivileged boys where he was a counselor, he was suddenly paralyzed in a swimming accident.

The laborious and heroic comeback from that accident to enter a life of public service in several fields, especially in dental research, has been chronicled previously here. Known as Char Bolton by most of his friends, he headed the Hawken endowment association, served on the board of trustees, and became its president, relieving Liv Ireland. He opposed and regretted the discontinuance of the Head Boy institution at Hawken. Later, in his honor, the trustees established the Charles Bolton Award for the senior with top commitment to school and community. The first winner was Scott Phillips, '76.

A number of those pioneer students went on to major careers in industry.

Stephens Chamberlin, '25, went on from Hawken to Exeter, Yale, and Harvard Business School. He went to work for Central National Bank in Cleveland and then to the dramatic M. A. Hanna Company. He was killed in World War II.

John Teagle, son of the family who started the school before the school, attended Hawken grades three through nine, graduated from Shaw High and then Cornell. He became an executive in Humble Oil and Manufacturing Company in Texas.

William Palmer (grades four through ten) went to Hotchkiss and Princeton and then to work for Lamson Brothers and Prescott, Biggar and Company in Cleveland.

John Phillips, '25, (grades three through nine) graduated from Roxbury High '27 and Yale '32. He worked for the Werner G. Smith Company in New York after serving as a naval attaché in Korea and Manchuria in forty-degree below zero temperatures.

Norman Ingersoll, '26, (grades two through nine) went to University School and Miami University before entering the advertising business in Philadelphia.

Barnard Prescott, '24, (grades four through eight) went to Taft and Williams and worked for Hord, Curtiss & Company in Cleveland; then became a broker in Florida. He was a pioneering president of the alumni association in 1926.

Sherman Hayden, '24, (grades four through twelve) graduated from Harvard and Harvard Law School and taught at Columbia and at Clark University. He followed Prescott as president of the alumni association and was a Hawken trustee. At this writing, he lives in Massachusetts.

Frederic Allen Whiting, Jr., '24, went on to Deerfield and Harvard and became editor of the combined national journals, *Magazine of Art* and *Creative Arts*. He wrote two novels, many short stories, and articles for the *Washington Post* and the *New York Herald Tribune*.

Thomas Grandin, '25, (grades three through eight) graduated later from Kent School and Yale where he edited the *Yale Daily News*. He worked at the Geneva Research Center in Switzerland where he studied European radio politics. During World War II he broadcast as a CBS radio war correspondent. In 1953 he became a rancher.

OTHER PIONEERS

There were other pioneer students, of course: The first group of girls; the first son of a faculty member; the first ethnic student. Among these pioneering students was Charlie Jordan.

The Hawken Review
May 1989

Portrait of a Pioneer
Charles N. Jordan, Jr., '65
by Suzanne Ringler Jones

Charles N. Jordan was Hawken's first black student. He was somewhat apprehensive about this pioneering, but his father said, "Our family have always been pioneers. I think of our family members who were slaves in Texas, who walked all the way to Ohio, steering their course by dead reckoning, depending only on their inner resources. I think of our family who were freed slaves, who traveled by covered wagon from Lynchburg, Virginia, to Bloomington, Illinois, fifteen years before the Emancipation Proclamation. Can you imagine the terror they must have felt? We have always been pioneers, yes, but the risks we have taken have always been calculated risks."

Charley Jordan remembers, "The pressures at Hawken in terms of making things happen and performing were pretty intense. At the time, Hawken was a school of about two hundred [the Upper School] in which everyone literally knew everything that was going on. It was a bit of a goldfish bowl and I was pretty visible. Also, I sensed that some of the faculty and some of the students were really not ready for this and I think some of their actions indicated their feelings. Subtle things, never a direct statement.

"One funny incident happened when I was playing chess at lunch time. We were choosing pieces and I got my pieces and the person I was playing said, 'Oh, you're black,'—and then embarrassed silence. That sort of thing. But all these things lessened over time."

Young Jordan threw himself body and mind, into life at Hawken. The Phalanx group stimulated his political interests, and he was elected vice president of the Student Council his senior year and captain of the track team. The first fall semester he played halfback on the varsity football team and—it was the first year of the new Upper School's team—scored the first Hawken touchdown. He was the leading scorer during his three years.

Jordan's football prowess is recalled vividly by classmate Kip Horsburgh (later a trustee): "Charley created the turning point for the Hawken football team in a game against Maumee Valley Country Day our junior year. We had just scored a touchdown with seconds to go in the fourth quarter, and the game was tied. Charley was handed the ball for a two-point conversion. He was stopped absolutely cold, but then seemed to reach deep down inside himself for that something extra, something our team needed and hadn't seen before. He ran it through and then was knocked unconscious. After that game, in our senior year, he was a superlative football player, and we as a team became more 'good' then 'mediocre.'"

One might naturally wonder if Jordan felt a pressure to excel beyond the norms, if he felt he must prove his worth, or that he must act according to a different set of rules. "This is very true," he says. "There is a fear of failure; it's a very pronounced thing. I had the perception that had it not worked out for me, this would be the end of the noble experiment, as it were. That is, I think, a fairly significant burden to carry."

The school did not integrate quickly. One black student entered the Upper School during Jordan's junior year, and dropped out, and one other entered his senior year. Life, particularly after-school life, could have been lonely.

Jordan graduated from Hawken the spring of 1965 and entered Tufts University that fall, completed his credit requirements in three years, and spent his fourth year doing independent study and working full-time as an admissions officer.

Jordan's business career was launched back in Cleveland, where he returned in 1971 to take a job with the Cleveland Trust Company as an operations research analyst. During the next few years he moved up quickly in the executive banker's ranks, being made an officer of the bank when he was twenty-four and then joining Bankers Trust Company in New York City in 1974 as an assistant vice president to the strategic planning group, while simultaneously going through the bank's training program for lending officers. He was then recruited by Urban National, a privately owned Boston venture capital fund, where he became vice president. In 1980 Pitney-Bowes, the office equipment manufacturer, hired him as its manager of financial planning and analysis, a position which placed him among the top one hundred executives in a company of twenty-five thousand employees.

* * *

One could credit Jordan only with outstanding personal ambition, and some do. But most know that with that ice breaker record Jordan smashed open paths for his successors up to a high plane.

Thus far approximately four thousand young men and women have experienced the Hawken education. The post graduate records show that although they did well for themselves, most do well for others as well. In the spirit of the Hawken watchword the records show the better selves prevailing as they do the work of hundreds of service organizations dedicated to every human need ... introducing successors to a higher plane.

Authors' Note:

And What of
1588 Ansel?

In the mid-1920s, the house at 1588 was razed and a residential hall for women only, Devon Hall, was built. In the 1940s, Devon Hall changed to Evangeline Hall, a home for underprivileged people.

In 1961 Evangeline Hall became the new home for the Job Corps Center and remained so until Job Corps moved to 107th Street and Carnegie.

Evangeline Hall then became Rockefeller Park Tower, a home for low-income elderly.

Hawken Appendices

Abbey, Robert P. '67
Abbot, Robert A. '44
Abbott, Julian B. '41
Abbott, Kit '88
Abbott, Paul
Abood, Keith T.
Abood, Michele M. '83
Acheson, Malcolm O. '68
Ackerman, Martin R. '56
Acree, Tyshawn '88
Adams, Brian C. '68
Adams, Hazzard '40
Adams, Joseph '84
Adler, Dan '77
Adler, Jacquelyn '89
Adlers, Detlev '66
Affelder, Lewis J. '32-I
Afshrapanah, Andesha
Aikawa, Keiko '87
Aikawa, Taro '89
Akers, Lynn R.
Albee, Alexander A. '74
Albee, Luke S.
Alcott, Franklyn '30
Aldrich, Daniel W. '83
Aldrich, David G. '79
Aldrich, Dean C. '81
Aldrich, Thomas P. III '72
Alemagno, Donna '80
Alemagno, Edmund V. '87
Alemagno, James S. '75
Alemagno, Laura '85
Alemagno, Linda '82
Alemagno, Mario '76
Alemagno, Stephen '79
Alemagno, Thomas '78
Alexander, Edward R., Jr. '34
Alexander, James H. '40
Alexander, Pamela '82
Alexander, William L. '66

Alfred, Bruce '81
Allatt, Peter '95
Allen, DeAnna N.
Allen, Douglas D. '76
Allen, Gilman B., Jr. '53
Allen, Griffin M., Jr.
Allen, Horace Lee '74
Allen, Kenneth L. III '57
Allen, Roderick E. '85
Allen, Walter B. '64
Allen, William S. '42
Alley, Colin K. '87
Allman, David '72
Allman, Donald R. '70
Allyn, Anderson III '88
Almirall, R. Randall '59
Almirall, Robert E. '57
Alpers, Lisa '84
Altoff, Michael R. '58
Altschul, Eric '86
Amarnath, Anand '92
Amarnath, Bindu '90
Ambaw, Getaneh '72
Ambrose, Joseph '84
Amor, Edward '89
Amor, Mary E. '83
Amor, William H., Jr. '58
Amsden, Howard R. '70
Ancker, Eric M. '93
Anderson, A. Chace '71
Anderson, Austin M. '87
Anderson, Charles E. '71
Anderson, Dane O. '66
Anderson, Elliot H. '84
Anderson, Everett, Jr. '71
Anderson, Franz E. '53
Anderson, Herbert R. III '68
Anderson, James B. '40
Anderson, J. Scott '94
Anderson, Jeffrey C.

Anderson, Rolfe '81
Andrews, Horace, Jr. '53
Andrews, Meghan L. '83
Andrews, Oakley '55
Andrews, Robert J. '81
Andrews, Zenas '32-II
Angell, Alan '75
Angell, Darcy Beth '80
Angus, Charles '87
Anikienko, George '73
Anslow, Robert '77
Anthony, Donald '82
Antoine, Albert S. '77
Antoine, Edward S. '79
Antonelli, Jason '95
Aponte, Milton '88
Applebaum, James A. '66
Applebaum, Robert E.
Appling, William '88
Armington, Arthur P. III
Armington, George E., Jr. '48
Armington, George A. '66
Armington, Paul '55
Armington, Peter '72
Armington, Steven E. '69
Armington, Steven G. '74
Armington, William, Jr. '65
Armstrong, Peter '70
Arnoff, Jane '91
Arnoff, Stephen '88
Arnold, Bradford '67
Arnold, Paul, Jr. '45
Arnold, Scott D. '87
Arnold, Stephen '64
Arnold, Wallis D.
Arnos, Guy '73
Arnos, Norman W., Jr. '53
Aronoff, James B. '77
Aronoff, Steven K. '79
Arp, Beth '82
Arrington, Curtis R. '70
Arsham, Michael, L. '72
Arter, Charles K. III '64
Arter, Charles K., Jr. '32-I
Arter, David '77

Arter, Thomas '69
Artz, Megan '89
Artz, Philip '78
Atkinson, Robert A. '78
Atkinson, Timothy W. '76
Atwater, James B. '74
Augustus, Ellsworth '71
Austen, George III '56
Austin, James B. '69
Austin, James W. '68
Austin, Philip '87
Austin, Richard A. '72
Aveni, James '77
Avery, Ann K.
Ayers, David '64
Ayers, Edward B. '65
Ayers, Joseph B. '57
Aziz, Farooq '88
Azzolina, John J. '92

Babcox, Peter C. '52
Babson, Nicholas C. '64
Babson, Stephen H.
Backer, Howard M. '82
Baggott, John G. '86
Bahr, Bruce '50
Bailey, Britt J.
Bailey, Steven J. '67
Bailey, Theodore '75
Baiter, James E. '81
Bakamjian, David '75
Baker, Allan '96
Baker, Allen '68
Baker, Daniel A. '75
Baker, David E. '47
Baker, Douglas C. R. '26
Baker, Kenneth D. '34
Baker, Newton D., Jr. '26
Baker, Reginald '25
Baker, Sherry D.
Baker, Thomas H. '75
Baldwin, Albert '73
Baldwin, Lewis '32-I
Baldwin, William W., Jr. '50
Balester, Mark '84

Ball, Christopher '75
Ball, Flamen, Jr. '29
Ball, Peter C. '66
Ballard, Julie '77
Balog, Aaron '87
Banister, William K. '52
Banks, Brian G. '83
Banks, Deshon '89
Banks, Larissa '86
Bard, Christopher A. '81
Baris, Kenneth '76
Barker, James '80
Barnes, George M., Jr. '43
Barnes, Patterson '47
Barnes, Winthrop '32-I
Barnett, Barbara '89
Barnett, Charles W. '72
Barney, Prescott '72
Barney, William R. III '70
Barney, William R., Jr. '40
Barratt, Henry T. '43
Barrett, Harvey N. III '64
Barrett, Megan '88
Barrett, Todd A. '83
Barris, Anthony '79
Barris, Jonathan '80
Barron, Douglas K. '74
Barron, James J. '69
Barron, Lee W. '72
Barron, William '67
Barrow, Andrew G.
Barrow, Timothy A. '48
Barrows, Andrew K. '85
Barrows, Kristen '89
Barson, Jack '85
Barstow, John '69
Barstow, Todd W. '80
Bartels, David '87
Barthelmess, Thomas J. '83
Bartholomew, Guy E. '45
Bartholomew, James M. '68
Bartlett, Edward T., III '53
Bartlett, Katharine '88
Bass, Howard I. '66
Bass, Jonathan '71

Bass, Stephanie '89
Bassage, David W. '76
Bassett, Arthur '97
Bassell, Larry A. '74
Bassett, Lee II '65
Bassett, Lowell R. '52
Bates, Michael Teague '88
Battle, Gregory '73
Battle, Jeffrey S.
Battles, John W. '39
Bauer, Robin David '77
Bauer, Wendy '82
Bauman, George T. '29
Bauman, Jeffrey P. '58
Bauman, John C. '24
Bauman, William C. '29
Bauschard, Laura A. '89
Baxter, Gordon M.
Baxter, Laura '78
Baxter, Matthew A., Jr. '57
Bayer, William S. II '53
Bazely, Arthur '36
Bazely, John N. '37
Baznik, Daniel '91
Beal, Steven '67
Beard, Jason '90
Bearden, James C. '73
Beatty, David F. '56
Beatty, Robert D. III '68
Beatty, Robert D., Jr. '29
Beatty, Scott M. '77
Beatty, Todd M. '79
Bechkowiak, Michael J. '83
Bechkowiak, Michele '75
Bechkowiak, Russell '73
Bechtel, Richard '71
Beck, Bryan '81
Beck, Scott '74
Becker, Charles, Jr. '75
Becker, Jay W. '81
Becker, Paul H., Jr.. '85
Beckerman, Joseph F.
Beckwith, Hugh '77
Bedol, Brian T.
Bedol, Gregg '74

Black, Robin R. '83
Blackburn, William R.
Blackledge, William K.
Blake, Kenneth '82
Blake, Nancy '77
Blankenship, Jacob '87
Blasko, Manuel G.
Blau, Andrew '86
Blau, Bennett '80
Blau, Julie '89
Blaugrund, Jeffrey '72
Blaushild, Eric L. '64
Blaushild, Steven '67
Bletcher, Thomas E. '55
Blome, George '73
Blome, Randall E.
Blossom, C. Bingham '53
Blossom, Christopher P. '81
Blossom, Dudley S. IV '87
Blossom, Dudley S. III '56
Blossom, Dudley S., Jr. '29
Blossom, Jonathan B. '88
Blossom, Roberts '39
Blossom, Stephen A. '32-I
Blount, Peter N. '60
Blount, Stephen R. '65
Blowe, George S. III
Blum, Adam H. '82
Blum, Anne M. '83
Blum, Jane Fellinger '86
Blum, Kevin R.
Blum, Leslie J. '80
Blum, Peter '81
Bly, Roger '88
Boak, James E. '66
Boardman, Samuel J. M. '99
Boardman, William '27
Boffey, David M.R. '36
Bohme, Arno O., Jr. '46
Boiardi, Mario '66
Boland, Jennifer '89
Boland, Jill Cathleen '86
Bole, Abigail A. '87
Bole, Ben Leslie '76
Bole, Benjamin P. III '50

Bole, Benjamin P., Jr. '25
Bole, David '37
Bole, David C., Jr. '31-II
Bole, Jonathan A., Jr. '85
Bole, Jonathan A. '53
Bole, Kathleen '77
Bole, Kristin A. '81
Bole, Richard H. '60
Bole, Suzanne L. '79
Bolton, Charles B. '27
Bolton, Charles P. '57
Bolton, Hugh R. '60
Bolton, John '67
Bolton, Kenyon C. '30
Bolton, Kenyon C. III '58
Bolton, Oliver P. '32-II
Bolton, Philip P. '60
Bolton, Thomas C. '57
Bolton, William B. '66
Boltuch, Cynthia '86
Bond, Catherine E. '88
Bond, David W.
Bonebrake, Geoffrey T. '58
Bonebrake, Robert A. '49
Boni, M. Allen '66
Bonnie, Sevier III '69
Booze, MacDonald '69
Borden, Karl J. '64
Borges, Norton A., Jr. '47
Borland, Thomas R. '51
Borsellino, Stephanie '92
Bostwick, Robert '74
Botten, Philip E. '67
Boughton, Mark K. '74
Boulware, Leigh '87
Bourne, Frances '84
Bourne, John M. '84
Bouscaren, Pierre '27
Bowen, Scott E. '82
Bowen, Sean A. '78
Bower, Harry F., Jr. '50
Bowerfind, Ellis T. '76
Bowerfind, William '86
Bowerman, Bruce L. '60
Bowler, Franklin '32-II

Bowler, William '71
Boyd, Darrell Thomas '76
Boyd, James M. '43
Boyd, Jonathan '67
Boyer, Chris '84
Boyer, Christopher F. '81
Boyer, Christopher '68
Boyer, Elizabeth '80
Boyer, Jonathan G. '66
Boyer, Markley H. '77
Boyer, Robert J. '68
Boykins, Anthony '69
Boyle, Sascha '89
Bradford, Charles C. III '69
Bradford, Charles C., Jr. '38
Bradford, Preston B. '75
Bradley, Morris A. '29
Bradner, George T., Jr. '59
Brady, Owen A. '39
Bragdon, Allen D. '45
Brainard, Edward C. '47
Braman, Steven '73
Braman, William S. '76
Bramhall, Thomas G. '72
Braming, Scott '89
Bramson, Jonathan '76
Bramson, Michael G. '74
Brand, Gregory '72
Branden, James '81
Branden, Robert '77
Brandt, Aaron '86
Brandt, Amy '82
Brandt, Brady '89
Brandt, D. McGregor, Jr. '68
Brandt, Peter '85
Branham, McElreath W. '72
Braun, Dale R. '85
Braun, Daniel '81
Braun, James L. '89
Braun, John '80
Braun, Julie '86
Braun, Marc '87
Braun, Paul E. '82
Bravo, Mark E. '84
Bravo, Paul M. '85

Brawley, Tony D. '80
Bray, William H.
Bray, Andrew '79
Brayton, John C. '25
Breeding, James H. '65
Breen, Daniel '87
Breeze, Kenneth W. '60
Brendel, Bierce C. '55
Brendel, Frank A.B. '52
Brennan, Terry '88
Brennan, Timothy '85
Breslau, Daniel '79
Breslau, Jonathan '78
Breslau, Joshua A. '83
Bresnicky, Ann '82
Bresnicky, Jack '84
Bresnicky, James '79
Bresnicky, Mary '78
Brettschneider, Lisa A.
Brewer, David N. '45
Brewer, John N. '42
Brewer, Wesley C. '44
Brewin, Bayard '77
Brewin, Michael K. '67
Brewster, Rodman P. '58
Brice, John '80
Brice, Robert A. '78
Bricker, Patrick '82
Bricker, Thomas '78
Bricker, W. Jeffery '76
Brigden, Jeffrey '96
Briggs, John H., Jr. '50
Briggs, Peter S. '71
Brigham, Brian P. '53
Bright, Lee C. '45
Brill, Jeffrey H. '75
Brill, Steven '87
Brinker, John H. III '67
Brinker, Thomas '81
Britschgi, Donald T.
Britt, John E. '66
Brittenum, Lauren '81
Brittenum, Marcus A. '82
Brittenum, Suzanne '79
Brittingham, Thomas E. '38

Brodkey, Daniel '84
Bromberg, David L. '87
Bromberg, Jason A. '84
Brooks, Harvey '32-I
Brooks, James C., Jr. '26
Brooks, Leroy '29
Brooks, Oliver '38
Brooks, Oliver, Jr. '75
Brose, Robert M. '85
Brown, Jacqueline S.
Brown, Alexander C., Jr. '31-I
Brown, Christal '85
Brown, David S. '64
Brown, David '69
Brown, Donald R. '54
Brown, Edward H. '60
Brown, Edward D. '32-II
Brown, Fayette, Jr. '31-I
Brown, G. Gardiner '54
Brown, George K. '71
Brown, Harvey H. '52
Brown, Henry W. III '58
Brown, Laurie '98
Brown, Marcia '82
Brown, Ralph H. '38
Brown, Roger '78
Brown, Ryan J.
Brown, Samuel Robert '88
Brown, Sarah Kane '76
Brown, Steven A. '75
Brown, Theodore S. '38
Brown, Willard '44
Brown, Willard W. '32-I
Brown, Willard W., Jr. '66
Bruch, Amy '86
Bruch, E. Phillip, Jr. '37
Bruch, Edward P., III '67
Bruch, Thomas O. '42
Bruell, Heather '90
Bruere, John M. '73
Brumagin, Edd F. '54
Bruml, Jonathan W.
Bruml, Robert W. '72
Bruner, Clark Evans '28
Bruner, William E., II '67

Bruns, Mark '75
Bryan, Bradric T. '83
Bryan, Tedric '86
Bucci, Philip R. '78
Buchner, David '94
Buckles, Michelle '84
Buhl, Dana '84
Buhl, Kent '79
Bukovnik, Carole '84
Bukovnik, Elizabeth '86
Bukovnik, John A., Jr. '83
Bukovnik, Kathryn '88
Bulkley, Robert '28
Bullen, Anne R. '76
Bunin, Diane '79
Burch, Charles A. '47
Burch, James E. '50
Burch, Robert '71
Burdge, Peter T.
Burdge, Richard '73
Burdge, Scott C.
Burdick, David L. '56
Burgard, Peter T. '65
Burgess, Richard E. '89
Burke, Stevenson '27
Burney, Jon R. '57
Burney, Richard E. '58
Burnham, David C. '75
Burnham, Rufus B. '72
Burns, Allen A. '46
Burns, Howard M. '48
Burnside, Curtiss S.
Burroughs, Timothy '67
Burry, Edward G. '71
Burry, J. K., Jr. '66
Burton, Courtney '30
Burton, John F. '74
Burwell, Richard E. '44
Burwell, Robert W. '37
Busch, Eric '76
Bustamante, Andre '79
Bustamante, Michael '72
Butler, Terrence R. '74
Butler, Timothy W. '74
Buxton, Louis P.

Byrne, James S. '97
Byrne, Rebecca A. '98
Byron, Carl J. III '80
Byron, Matthew '87
Byron, Michael '82
Byron, Stephen '84

Cabot, Christopher '80
Cabot, Kimberly C.
Cadou, Christopher '84
Cadou, Kate Hammond '87
Cagigas, David A. '91
Cagigas, Lisa '87
Cahen, Harley '74
Cahill, Colleen '76
Calabrese, Kristin '92
Calfee, David L. '64
Calfee, John B. '31-I
Calfee, John B., Jr. '60
Calfee, Lee '32-I
Calfee, Mark '72
Calfee, Peter H. '69
Calfee, William L. '32-II
Calhoun, Creed H. II '75
Calhoun, John '36
Calhoun, Stephen '72
Calhoun, Timothy '72
Callahan, Michelle '89
Calo, Christopher '85
Calo, Lynnae '89
Camp, Lawrence H. '69
Camp, Ronald M. '66
Camp, William '58
Campbell, Douglas '50
Campbell, John D., Jr. '60
Campbell, Keith T. '41
Campbell, Margaret '87
Campbell, Tom '79
Campen, Timothy D. '78
Cannon, James M. '69
Canty, James W. '79
Canty, Ronald A. '81
Caputo, James K. '71
Caraboolad, Geoffrey S. '73
Caraboolad, Michael '78

Caraboolad, Richard '72
Carey, Christopher '76
Carey, Paul '78
Carlson, Kimberly '89
Carlton, Bradford R. '88
Carroll, Daniel K. '75
Carroll, Grant T.
Carroll, Mark B.
Carroll, Shawn A.
Carson, Daniel D.
Carter, John H. '45
Carter, Jonathan '51
Carter, Juliet '90
Carter, Leyton E. '38
Carter, Russell J. '83
Caruso, James W. '73
Caruso, Robert T.
Cashin, Christian A. '87
Cashman, John A. '31-II
Cassill, James A. '75
Caston, John '84
Caughey, John L., III '56
Caunter, David H. '43
Cesar, Marcel '80
Chamberlin, John H. '75
Chamberlin, Stephen H. '66
Chamberlin, Stephens '25
Chamberlin, William B. III '59
Chamberlin, William, Jr. '29
Chandler, George N., II '53
Chandler, John R. '49
Chandler, Stephen R. '74
Chandrasekhar, Ashok '81
Chandrasekhar, Jai K. '83
Chandrasekhar, Tamasker '88
Chang, David '74
Chapman, Arnold D. '57
Chapman, David U.
Chapman, J. Kenyon '65
Chapman, Scott B. '58
Charbonneau, Michael P. '71
Charbonneau, Peter U. '69
Charbonneau, Stephen T. '74
Chari, Ravi V. '83
Chari, Sunita '82

Charles, Wilson
Charnas, Stephen Joel '86
Chase, Mark '72
Chattree, Ritu '81
Cheeks, George A. '83
Chen, Curtis '89
Cheeks, Robert R.
Cheney, Thomas '32-II
Cherry, Jessica '83
Chew, David W.
Chiappetta, Stacey '86
Chiappetta, Stephanie '83
Chiffe, Timothy '67
Chirgwin, John M. '64
Chisholm, Alvah II '76
Chisholm, Corning '31-I
Chisholm, Homer David '73
Chisholm, William IV '72
Chism, Scott R. '84
Chopra, Christopher '90
Chrencik, James P. '65
Christian, Jeffrey E. '74
Christie, Daniel C. '83
Christie, John '89
Chu, Isaac '88
Clamp, Charles F. '75
Clamp, Robert W.
Clancy, Raymond H. '68
Clapp, Roger E. '35
Clark, Amy '84
Clark, David S. '31-I
Clark, Edward F., Jr. '42
Clark, Evan '89
Clark, Jeffrey M. '56
Clark, Gerald '36
Clark, John T. '34
Clark, Jonathan E. '57
Clark, Jonathan W., Jr. '69
Clark, Joseph '56
Clark, Junius M. '56
Clark, Raymond S. '53
Clark, Thomas L. '45
Clark, Walter C. '80
Clarke, David G. '71
Clarke, Frederick M. '72

Clarke, Gerald J. '36
Clegg, Lee M. '46
Clegg, Michael A. '53
Clements, Arthur L., Jr. '40
Clements, George T. '82
Clements, Robert M., Jr. '57
Clements, Thomas III '50
Clements, Tyler M. '82
Clements, William W. '41
Cleveland, Robert '26
Clewell, Andre F. '49
Clipsham, Neil '56
Clough, David '72
Clough, Mary B. '85
Clough, William S. '69
Clowes, Alexander W. '64
Clowes, Thomas J. '68
Clowes, Thomas J. '66
Clucker, Warren C. '52
Clyde, Andrew '77
Coakley, Joseph '69
Coakley, Mathew S. '72
Coan, John G. '65
Coaxum, Kofi '96
Coaxum, W. C. '88
Cobb, Ahira, II '40
Coben, Laurel '78
Cochran, Bruce H. '47
Coerdt, Carl D. '69
Coerdt, Henry K. '64
Cogan, J. Kevin '70
Cohen, Adam '80
Cohen, Andrew L. '84
Cohen, Dorit Ann '87
Cohen, Douglas L. '87
Cohen, Douglas '74
Cohen, Ethan '82
Cohen, Flynn M. '89
Cohen, Gwen '95
Cohen, James '72
Cohen, Kacey '98
Cohen, Karla '85
Cohen, Kelly '89
Cohen, Liza F. '83
Cohen, Rick '74

Cohen, Robert A. '76
Cohen, Stephen D. '74
Cohens, Paul D.
Cohn, Donald M. '78
Cohn, Herbert S. '73
Cohn, Kenneth A. '86
Colburn, James M. '48
Coldiron, Michael '85
Cole, Charles E. '26
Cole, David '78
Cole, David '85
Cole, Donald W. '75
Cole, Erik '84
Cole, Harold N., Jr. '33
Cole, Michael Smith '76
Cole, Pamela C. '83
Cole, Stephen W. '65
Cole, Thomas '81
Cole, Victoria '79
Colebrook, Kelly '92
Coleman, Eugene, Jr. '72
Coleman, F. David '69
Coleman, Jason '91
Coleman, Mark E. '67
Coleman, Michael A. '77
Coleman, William '75
Coles, Greg E. '79
Coles, Robert L. III
Colgan, Mark '82
Collacott, Charles M., Jr. '34
Collens, Clarence '28
Collens, Edmund '73
Collens, Granger H. '34
Collens, Jonathan L. '31-II
Collens, Jonathan L., Jr. '68
Collins, John I. '41
Collins, Lester S., Jr. '76
Collins, Mark M. '45
Collins, Rebekah C. '82
Collins, Robert M. '48
Collis, John III '80
Collister, Peter '74
Collura, Thomas F. '69
Colt, Oliver P. '67
Comella, Dominick V. '74

Comstock, Clyde N., Jr. '67
Comtois, Keith '74
Condon, William M., Jr. '70
Coney, Aims C., Jr. '44
Conkey, Albert B. '31-I
Conkey, Guy E. III '49
Conkey, Robert W. '51
Conley, Peter J. '95
Conlin, Marc S. '64
Conner, Thomas '85
Connor, James, W. '65
Connor, Thomas H. '68
Connor, Thomas N. '76
Conomy, Christopher '88
Conomy, John T. '83
Conomy, Lisa '84
Conroy, Aimee P. '83
Consolo, William '77
Conway, Caroline '75
Cook, Dana '91
Cook, Thomas S. '72
Cooley, Richard S. '39
Coolidge, Carlton C. '58
Coolidge, John W. '47
Coolidge, Robert '39
Coolidge, William M. '69
Coon, Steven E. '68
Cooney, Jonathan '74
Coons, Richard F. '41
Cooper, Jonathan '78
Cooper, Thomas C. '50
Cooper, William H. '53
Cope, John R. '49
Copper, Craig M. '47
Corke, Kenyon K. '59
Corl, Michael '90
Corlett, Edward L. '27
Corlett, Thomas '26
Cornelison, John H. '76
Corning, Lawrence H. '72
Corning, Nathan E. '46
Corrado, Mark '72
Corrigan, Wendy J. '87
Cosper, James A. '64
Cosper, John E. '67

Coulton, John W. '30
Coulton, Robert W. '32-II
Courtioi, Marc '88
Cox, Eames '39
Cox, Ronald C.M.R. '42
Coy, Roger T. '70
Crabbe, William D. '40
Crafts, Bryan C. '52
Crafts, David C. '56
Craig, Douglas S. '36
Craig, G. Armour '32-I
Craig, Willis G., Jr. '64
Cramer, Allan M.
Cramer, Kenneth '82
Cramer, Steven '85
Cravens, Kenton '47
Crawford, Christopher M. '58
Crawford, David '35
Crawford, Roland W. '68
Crawford, Willard J. '32-I
Crawford, William W. '75
Crease, Richard '74
Crease, Robert, Jr. '71
Creighton, Katherine '88
Crocheron, Lewis L. '73
Crosby, Jennifer A.
Crossman, Kim R. '68
Crossman, Scott '70
Crowell, Robert H., Jr. '37
Crystal, Brian E. '84
Crystal, Douglas E. '83
Cuddy, Jack '36
Cumming, William N., Jr. '39
Curry, Anthony T.
Curry, Donald '83
Curtis, Benjamin W. '89
Curtiss, Jonathan P. '73
Cusick, Richard '88
Cutler, Anne L.
Cutler, David W.
Cutler, Robert S. '80
Cylar, Lisa A. '87

Da Costa, Charles A., Jr. '46
Daberko, Jeffrey '86

Daigle, David '84
Daigle, James '79
Daily, Allan '93
Daily, Julian '96
Daley, Liza '84
Daley, William A. II '88
Dalton, Calvin B. '37
Dalton, Douglas M. '65
Dandalides, George '76
Dandalides, Steven M. '74
Danforth, Frederick C. '67
Danforth, John P. '31-I
Dangler, Don C. '42
Daniel, Michael E.
Danner, Eric '89
Darling, Bruce L. '70
Darmstadter, Neill '39
Daroff, Robert '81
Daroff, William C. '86
Darr, Omar '89
Darst, Elizabeth '77
Datt, Bonnie '84
Davenport, David N. '72
Davenport, David W. '34
Davenport, John N. '33
David, Pamela '84
Davidson, Charles L. '48
Davidson, William E. '48
Davies, Michael B. '82
Davies, Richard C. '36
Davies, Ross E. '80
Davies, Susan '82
Davis, Benjamin '88
Davis, Byron '88
Davis, Carrie '79
Davis, Christopher Cobb '47
Davis, Daniel '50
Davis, David F. '69
Davis, Frederic L. '34
Davis, Frederick D. '66
Davis, Frederick L. '80
Davis, John D. '50
Davis, Lisa Ann '81
Davis, Rebecca '94
Davis, Robert '79

Davis, Robert '87
Davis, Sarah '90
Davis, Trudi '78
Day, Andrew M. '68
Day, Richard W., Jr. '60
De La Pena, Michael H. '80
Deaner, Robert M.T. '79
Decatur, Sean '86
deConingh, Edward H., Jr. '44
deConingh, Frederick M.
deConingh, Mathew F.
Deighan, Jim '79
Deighan, Lisa '82
Delman, Brent '81
DeLong, Frank N. '56
DeMelto, Paul '91
Demko, Laura '76
Demko, Thomas D. '78
Dempsey, Ernest D. '69
Dempsey, Lawrence '92
Demsey, John D. '74
Denemark, Douglas A., Jr. '68
Denemark, Malcolm A. '71
Denison, Robert F. '47
Dennett, Tyler III '58
Denton, Michael O. '86
Deodhar, Melanie
Deodhar, Neal '80
DeOreo, David '87
Derry, William R., Jr. '60
Dery, Robert B. '58
DesPrez, John D. III '74
Dettelbach, Anne '87
Dettelbach, Carolyn '84
Dettelbach, Eric '86
Dettelbach, Hallie
Dettelbach, Jeffrey '87
Dettelbach, John A. '51
Dettelbach, Kenneth '54
Dettelbach, Kim '84
Dettelbach, Mark '82
Dettelbach, Michael '82
Dettelbach, Steven '84
Deutsch, Andrew H. '84
Deutsch, Mark '81

Deutsch, Paul S. '83
Devere, Rollin R., Jr. '46
Devitt, William E. '36
Dewey, Daniel, Jr. '39
Dewey, Edward A. '46
Dewey, Joseph E. '41
Dewey, Windsor F. '43
deWindt, Dana '66
Dewindt, Edward M., Jr. '79
Dewitt, Clarence A. '37
deWolfe, Peter '71
deWolfe, Robert C. '73
deWolfe, Victor G., Jr. '67
DeWoody, Charles T. '56
Dexter, Richard, Jr. '48
Diallo, Ghainous Idrissa '73
Diamond, Carol '78
Diamond, Cathy '78
Dick, Robert S.
Dickinson, Richard, Jr. '47
Dickman, Elizabeth '79
Diehl, Richard Anthony '86
Diener, Lawrence R. '76
Dilen, David R. '70
Dill, Charles A. '54
Dill, M. Meese, Jr. '52
Dilley, Steven '81
Dimpsey, Don S. '53
Dimpsey, Robert E. '50
Dingle, David R. '70
Dinner, Nicole '86
Discenzo, Kelly '89
Distad, Richard N. '78
Distad, William E. '80
Diwan, Ajay '82
Dixon, George '77
Dixon, Michael '79
Dobbs, Kenneth R. '67
Dodge, David K. '69
Doering, Roger '88
Dolan, Mark '78
Domadia, Sanjay M. '83
Domadia, Sonal '86
Donald, Peter G. '50
Doran, Tom A. '51

Dorer, Frederick E. '48
Dorsky, Steven '76
Dougan, Thomas '55
Dougherty, Ralph E. III '73
Douglas, Richard M. '37
Douglas, Samuel N. '39
Douglass, Malcolm C. '44
Douglass, John P. '68
Doull, Greg '79
Doull, James A. III '78
Doull, James A. Jr. '42
Doustdar, Bobby '86
Dovgan, Jason '89
Dowd, E. Healy '49
Dowd, James '97
Dowd, Katherine '94
Dowie, John R.
Dowling, Amie S. '81
Downey, Kate '78
Downey, Martha '79
Downing, Gwynne '89
Downing, Matthew '88
Dragin, Peter '67
Drake, Alvah C. '25
Drake, Catherine '84
Drake, Elizabeth A. '87
Drake, Robert '84
Drake, Roger W. '51
Drake, Suzanne '80
Drane, W. Harding, Jr. '67
Drechsler, David L. '82
Dreyer, Robert H. Jr. '66
Duber, James '78
Duffy, David '73
Duffy, John '74
Dulaurence, Robert H. '65
Dundon, Brian J. '59
Dundon, Bruce C. '58
Dunning, Bradley '82
Dupuy, Tammy '89
Durn, Sarah A. '83
Durn, Tamara '85
Durn, David R. '82
Dusenbury, Warren C. '71
Dusenbury, Wynne '76

Dutton, Bonny Jane '82
Duvin, Scott A.
Dyer, C. Dickey III '33
Dyer, Marshall '36
Dyer, Marshall, Jr. '65
Dyke, Charles G. '69
Dykema, Kryn K. '70
Dykema, Samuel D.
Dykstra, Sarah '89

Eakin, J. Whitney '88
Ealhan, Anil '89
Earle, Alisha B. '83
Earle, Christopher '82
Easly, Carl E. '78
Easly, James H., Jr. '50
Easterday, Alexander C. '84
Easterday, Dyke '80
Easterday, Jack Jr. '79
Easterday, Tracey '81
Eatman, Janice A. '77
Eaton, Cyrus S. Jr. '34
Eaton, Cyrus S. III '64
Eaton, David '77
Eaton, Dennie '8 2
Eaton, John S. '66
Eaton, Joseph O. Jr. '29
Eaton, MacPherson '41
Eaton, Richard '74
Echols, Robert L. '74
Eckelberry, Tener R. '39
Eckert, David '75
Eckert, Robert A. '79
Eden, Alan L. '65
Edgerton, Robert '80
Edwards, Marcus C. '83
Eells, Samuel III '79
Eells, Samuel, Jr. '50
Eglin, Eric '91
Egeberg, Roger O., Jr. '52
Ehrlich, Jason '95
Ehsani, Farzad '84
Eichenberger, Peter A. '72
Eide, Philip W. '66
Eigendorf, Jorge

Eigner, James R.
Einbund, Karen B. '78
Einhorn, Michael '84
Eisenstat, Aida '79
Eisenstat, David '68
Eisenstat, Debra '81
Eisenstat, Michael '66
Eisenstat, Paul T. '83
Eisner, Elaine '85
Eisner, Jeffrey S.
Eisner, Todd A. '83
Elder, James '78
Elder, John '73
Elder, Rebecca N. '83
Elfvin, Robert R.
Elghanayan, Diana '84
Ellis, Eric T. '82
Ellis, Geoffrey '80
Ellis, John '86
Ellis, Peter '84
Ellis, Robert G. '79
Ellmers, Charles M. '80
Ellmers, David '89
Elmslie, Kenward G. '43
Elrad, Michael '85
Elser, John L. '84
Ely, John M. '36
Emerman, Bradley A. '87
Emerman, Daniel '71
Emerman, James '68
Emerman, John '72
Emert, James O. III '86
Engel, David W. '50
Englander, Julie '89
Englund, Monika '81
Eppes, Carolyn '88
Eppes, Susan
Epstein, Ari '89
Epstein, Dan '77
Epstein, Howard G. '71
Epstein, Jeffrey '75
Epstein, Jonathan '80
Epstein, Steven '66
Ericson, Timothy C. '95
Erin, Brigit '86

Erlechman, David '85
Ernest, Robert T. '58
Erwin, Robert J. '40
Esgar, Ann '78
Esgar, Marla '75
Esselstyn, Caldwell III '86
Esselstyn, Jane H. '83
Esselstyn, Theodore '82
Evans, Andrew W. '59
Evans, David '87
Evans, Dwight A. '71
Evans, James '75
Evans, Michael J. '57
Evans, Peter D. '83
Evans, Scott D. '70
Evans, T. Raymond '50
Evans, Theodore H. '48
Evans, Whitney R. '51
Evans, William, Jr. '75
Evarts, Charles M.
Evarts, Robert A. '82
Everett, Chandler H. '53
Everett, Chandler P.
Everett, Homer '29
Everett, Morris '27
Everett, Morris, III
Everett, Morris, Jr. '56
Everson, John H. '75
Everson, William V. '70

Fabens, Andrew '85
Fabens, Jennie '88
Fader, Cynthia '77
Fader, Deborah '80
Fader, Lora J. '83
Fagan, John '89
Fahey, Darren '89
Fahey, Sean '85
Falkenstein, Robin D. '73
Faller, Kurt '83
Falsgraf, Sherwood N. '51
Faltay, J. Laszlo '86
Fanaroff, Jonathan Mark '87
Farkas, Thomas '78
Farmer, Amy '86

Farmer, David '88
Farrell, David B. '67
Farrell, Michael G. '66
Farrington, Randle '64
Farrington, Robert K. '35
Farrington, Ronald '52
Farris, Joseph J. '83
Favors, John E. '68
Fawcett, James L. '64
Fazio, Carl, Jr. '68
Fazio, Charles M. '60
Fazio, Charles W. '58
Fazio, John, Jr. '70
Fazio, Robert '70
Fechheimer, Mark '88
Feil, Kenneth '85
Feingold, Alisa '86
Feingold, David A. '83
Feldman, Elisabeth Rochelle
    '82
Feldman, Karen '84
Feldman, Stacy '67
Felger, Sara L. '83
Feller, Martin W. '65
Feller, Stephen '60
Feller, Winthrop B. '68
Fennoy, David '70
Fenton, Andrew '80
Fenton, Lewis, Jr. '55
Fenton, Mark '84
Fenton, Todd '90
Fenton, Ward
Ferber, Abby L. '85
Ferchill, Melissa '87
Ferfolia, Mark L. '71
Ferguson, Ray A. III
Fernandez, Felicia '88
Ferris, Richard B. '73
Ferster, David L. '70
Fields, Douglas A. '67
Fields, Richard J. '66
Figgie, Harry E. III '71
Figgie, Mark P. '74
Figgie, Matthew P. '84
Figueroa, Joy M.C. '83

Files, Gregg '72
Files, Marc Alan '65
Finley, John H. '38
Finn, Nicholas B. '87
Finney, Adrienne '81
Finney, Robert W., Jr. '70
Fiordalis, Charles J. '59
Fiordalis, Clifford K. '65
Fiordalis, Gary '71
Fiordalis, Stuart C. '67
Fiordalis, Vincent, II '57
Fiori, Bridget '85
Firman, Royal III '66
Fischer, Lawrence R. '68
Fisco, Dennis '73
Fisco, Ernest '69
Fisher, Christie R. '66
Fisher, Cynthia E. '80
Fisher, Elwood M. '52
Fisher, Robert '81
Fitch, Edward H. Jr. '66
Fitts, Rodney M. '71
Fitts, Ronald W. '66
Fitz-Gerald, Chas. A. III '65
Fitzhugh, William E. '69
Fitzsimmons, Samuel D. '67
Fleek, Henry S. III '37
Fleek, John S. '39
Fleming, Lew III '72
Fleming, Neil S. '70
Fleming, William L. '64
Flesher, Marc '75
Fletcher, Trenton Tipton '85
Flickinger, Erik '89
Floyd, Richard B. '72
Flynn, John R. '47
Fochler, Stephen '85
Fogaras, Zarko P.
Fogg, Daniel T. '69
Folise, Michael '77
Folk, Lawrence '72
Fonda, Albert P. '31-II
Foney, Robert H. '83
Fong, William '86
Fonoroff, Paul '72

Fonoroff, Robert D. '75
Foose, Adrian F., Jr. '31-I
Foote, Charles H. '31-II
Foote, George Ward '31-II
Foote, John D.
Forbes, Dawn '81
Forbes, Shawn T. '84
Forbush, Scott '56
Forchheimer, Martin '77
Ford, Andrew '28
Ford, Charles '77
Ford, Clark '26
Ford, Daniel B. III '86
Ford, Daniel, Jr. '48
Ford, David K. Jr. '73
Ford, Donald '78
Ford, Edward C. '71
Ford, George W., II '44
Ford, James T. '77
Ford, John '75
Ford, Jonathan '31-II
Ford, T. Windsor '30
Ford, Thomas W.
Fore, Darryl '78
Foren, David '89
Formato, Marc '74
Forstner, Gerald '88
Forsythe, Amy '88
Forsythe, William IV '84
Fortthome, Philippe. G. '83
Foskey, Anthony P. '83
Foster, David S. '64
Foster, G. McIntosh '27
Foster, John H., Jr. '74
Fotheringham, Chris A. '83
Foti, Frank '75
Foti, Michael '78
Fotland, David '75
Fox, Rebecca L. '83
Foy, Brian B. '53
Foy, Brian '75
Foy, Richard N. '85
France, Warren '68
Francis, Henry S., Jr. '46
Franck, Sheldon M. '68

Frankel, Jessica S. '87
Frankel, Scott '81
Franklin, Caleb '90
Franklin, Monique L.
Frankmann, Paul '81
Frankmann, Thomas '89
Franz, James N., Jr. '40
Frayne, Tara '84
Frayne, Thomas '82
Frederick, Alan S. '71
Freedman, David B. '75
Freedman, Jonathan '89
Freedman, Randall G. '87
Freeman, Todd L.
Freer, Mark G. '76
Frees, Lewis D. '75
Freimark, Adam '95
Freimark, Joel '98
French, Edward S. '27
Frey, Gregory N. '64
Friedell, Richard A. '60
Friedland, Jessica '89
Friedland, Jonathan '86
Friedlander, John A.C.
Friedlander, Matthew L. '73
Friedman, Ben W. '83
Friedman, Dennis G. '65
Friedman, Gerald '79
Friedman, Joel D. '67
Friedman, Jonathan R. '72
Friedman, Josh M.
Friedman, Matthew S. '86
Friedman, Roger '84
Friedman, Samuel '95
Friedman, Wendy '87
Frisse, Joseph Jon '58
Frisse, Samuel J. '70
Fritz, Edward R. '68
Frolking, Peter H. '52
Fromson, Alan S. '79
Fromson, Lisa '83
Frye, Philip '31-I
Fryer, Jane E. '87
Fuelling, Bruce C. '68
Fuller, Duncan R. '74

Fuller, Kenneth '50
Fuller, Lawrence
Fulton, Robert L. '82
Furrer, Ernest '35
Fusco, Christopher '68
Fusco, Timothy '70

Gaag, Ehren '86
Gaag, Jennifer L. '83
Gaddis, Robert J. '79
Gaetano, John C. '88
Gale, Benjamin '53
Gale, Frederick K. '68
Gale, Robert I. III '59
Gale, Robert I., Jr. '32-II
Gale, Thomas '58
Gallin, Paul '71
Galvin, Thomas E. '58
Gambetti, Francesca '90
Gamundi, Renaldo '65
Garcia, Manuel B. '67
Gard, Andrew '93
Gardner, Anne '92
Gardner, James R. '38
Garfield, Daniel B.
Garfield, Edward W., Jr. '45
Garner, Monique Y. '85
Garnett, William B. '55
Garrett, William C. '36
Garson, Jennifer '82
Garson, Michael J. '60
Gary, Andrew R. '83
Gary, Douglas E. '85
Gascoigne, Patricia '84
Gascoigne, Virginia '81
Gates, Jeffrey C. '76
Gates, Robert McNair '57
Gates, William N. III '45
Gatewood, Joi '89
Gaudio, Anthony Jr. '67
Gaynor, Lisa '82
Geer, James H., Jr. '67
Geier, Timothy G. '65
Geller, Daniel '81
Geller, David '81

Geller, Robin '77
Gellman, Jeffrey '84
George, Edwin B. II '75
George, Karen '79
George, Michele '85
George, Philip, Jr. '68
George, Thomas '80
George, Timothy M. '70
Gerard, Bryan S. '92
Gerboc, Philip M. '79
Gerbracht, John C.
Gerhauser, Frederick F. '45
Gettig, Hugh R. '83
Ghose, Lynken '79
Ghose, Saelen '81
Gibans, Amy '78
Gibans, Elizabeth '80
Gibans, Jonathan '76
Gibson, Daniel '98
Gibson, Frank S., Jr. '45
Gibson, H. W. Birkett '68
Giegerich, Gary D. '81
Giegerich, Paul T. '77
Giegerich, Steven S. '83
Gilbert, Brian '86
Gilbert, Charles W., Jr. '80
Gilbert, Derrick '70
Gilbert, Haley '89
Gilbert, Norman '80
Gilchrist, Robert G. '37
Gill, Kathleen '79
Gill, Liam L. '69
Gillam, James K. '76
Gillespie, David A., Jr. '89
Gillett, Kenneth '50
Gilliam, David C.
Gilliam, John D., Jr. '76
Gillies, Donald B., Jr. '35
Gillinov, Marc '80
Gillinov, Melissa A. '95
Gillinov, Michael D. '83
Gillis, Roderick '38
Gillison, Elizabeth A. '80
Gilman, Scott '79
Ginis, Brian K. '82

Girty, Glenn '81
Giunta, Philip J. '58
Glass, Mark Alan '76
Glass, Matthew '77
Glassman, Virginia M. '76
Glavac, Douglas E. '75
Glazer, Greg S.
Glazer, Robert '77
Gleason, David F. '64
Glenn, Jody E. '88
Glenn, Jonathan '86
Glenn, Peter V. '72
Glick, Thomas F. '53
Glover, William '86
Godfrey, Edward B., Jr. '39
Godfrey, Robert D., Jr. '38
Goff, Channing T. '35
Goff, Frederick H. '41
Gold, Laura Ann '86
Gold, Roger '84
Gold, Steven '73
Goldberg, Daniel '79
Goldberg, Lindsey '87
Goldsmith, Jessica '92
Goldner, Bruce A. '75
Goldner, Laura '84
Goldsword, William E. '58
Goldthwait, David '74
Goldthwait, Loren '70
Goler, Michael '70
Goler, Robert '74
Goodfellow, Timothy S. '73
Goodfriend, Harry A. '71
Gooding, David B. '86
Goodlow, Robert '71
Goodman, Bruce '78
Goodman, Christina B.
Goodman, Gary '80
Goodman, Greer E. '83
Goodman, Jennifer '80
Goodman, Stephen '77
Goodrich, Thomas R., Jr. '51
Goodwillie, Andrew K.
Goodwillie, John P.
Goodwin, Cheryl '77

Gordon, David '38
Gordon, Huntly '39
Gorick, Adam E.
Gorman, Jeremy W. '72
Gorovitz, Erik K. '84
Goslee, George, Jr. '89
Goslee, Kimberly L. '87
Goss, Richard, Jr. '74
Goss, Thomas E. '38
Gottlieb, Adam D. '82
Gottlieb, Samuel D. '82
Goulden, Neil '78
Goulder, Robert III '47
Graber, Gretchen L. '01
Graber, Melinda '98
Graf, Michael C. '70
Graham, Eugene C. '83
Gramentine, James G. '79
Grandin, George B.
Grandin, Robert '28
Grandin, Thomas B. '25
Grandin, Thomas B., Jr. '56
Grano, Robert H., Jr. '76
Grant, Benton '28
Grant, Christopher L. '68
Grant, William R. '65
Grasselli, Harry '26
Gratry, Oliver C. '92
Gray, Christopher A. '67
Gray, Delbert '84
Gray, James G.
Gray, Matthew '80
Gray, Maurice '86
Gray, Meldrum III '67
Green, Gregory L. '83
Green, Richard J. '83
Greenberg, Glenn H. '64
Greenberg, Michael '81
Greenberg, Steven '66
Greenburg, Melinda '78
Greene, Anne M. '93
Greene, Brian T. '95
Greene, Darryl M. '67
Greene, James L. '38
Greene, James N. '91

Greenlee, Megan '82
Greenspan, Aaron J. '01
Greenwald, Lewis J.
Greicius, Michael '87
Greiner, Joseph C. III '64
Gresham, Dan '87
Gresinger, Thomas H. '48
Gressel, Jonathan '71
Gressel, Keith '48
Gressle, Alan K. '45
Gries, Donald S. '80
Gries, Robert D. '44
Gries, Robert D., Jr. '76
Gries, Thomas H. '50
Grinnell, Richard L. '69
Groenstein, Lisa '89
Grohol, Jennifer L. '83
Grohol, Robert '82
Gross, Paul N. '64
Gross, Robert I.
Grosser, Aaron W.
Grosser, Jeremy D.
Grossman, Charles L. '87
Grossman, Joe '89
Grossman, Matthew '89
Groth, Charlotte '89
Groth, Katherine '86
Grove, Troy G. '85
Groves, David K. '83
Groves, Matthew R.
Groves, Philip G. '87
Groves, Robert H.
Grubb, Sheldon G. '31-II
Grullemans, Winslow C. '70
Grunden, Brent '87
Grunzweig, Jeremy '89
Grunzweig, Jonathan '81
Grunzweig, Julie '89
Grzep, Christopher V. '89
Guba, Joseph P. '76
Guggenheim, Jonathan '80
Gullia, Andrea '83
Gunde, Edward J. '74
Gunning, David '85
Gunning, Paul '88

Gunton, Gary E. '65
Gunton, Jeffrey R. '68
Guren, Jon D. '69
Gutterman, Scott L. '79
Guyer, David G. '40

Haas, Bernard F.
Haas, Blair K. '72
Haas, Douglas E. '69
Haas, Greg '75
Habiby, Reema L. '83
Hable, Timothy F. '73
Hackenberg, J. Scott '86
Hackenberg, Susan L. '83
Hadden, Alexander H. '39
Hadden, David A. '73
Hadden, John
Hadden, John A., Jr. '37
Hadow, Michael C. '47
Haffey, Brendan M.
Hairston, Maria '77
Hale, Timothy R. '74
Halisak, Kathleen '95
Hall, Amy '88
Hall, Charles C. '72
Hall, Thomas Allen '72
Hallaran, Michael T. '65
Hallaran, Peter '33
Hallaran, Timothy R. '86
Hallaran, William G. '52
Hallaran, William P. '83
Halle, Chisholm '47
Halle, Chisholm, Jr. '75
Halle, Howard '70
Halle, Samuel H. '79
Hallowell, John W., Jr. '51
Hallstein, Harold III '68
Hallstein, Robert '72
Halpern, Cory '77
Halpern, Jeremy D. '83
Halpern, Keith '74
Halpern, Kriss '79
Halsted, Henry M. III '40
Hamblin, James B. II '76
Hamilton, Brent '68

Hamilton, Eric '82
Hamilton, G. Richard, Jr. '66
Hamilton, Scott '84
Hamilton, William
Hamlett, Lavita '91
Hammond, Peter '89
Handel, Douglas A.
Handel, Stephen E. '58
Handlon, Anthony '81
Hanger, Clay '50
Hanna, Daniel R. III '37
Hanna, Howard '26
Hanna, John R. '38
Hanna, John '87
Hanna, Mark D. '80
Hanna, Timothy C. '52
Hannan, John, Jr. '59
Hannon, Michael N.
Hansen, Grover C. '37
Hanson, Adam '84
Hanson, Amy '88
Hanson, Jennifer '85
Hanson, Matthew '89
Harasaki, Yasuaki '87
Hardacre, Jon '85
Hardesty, Jack '68
Hardy, Jennifer '89
Hare, James '74
Hare, Ted D.M. '70
Harik, Nahla '87
Harkins, Derrick '76
Harlen, Sandra '82
Harnett, David '69
Harris, Charles A. '71
Harris, Francis '31-I
Harris, Frederick S. '76
Harris, Gregory '88
Harris, James A. '29
Harris, John R. '72
Harris, Matthew '69
Harris, Russell '75
Harris, Terry D. '73
Harris, Todd S. '72
Harrison, Darryl E. II '99
Harshaw, John '32-I

Hart, George E. '44
Hart, John N., Jr. '71
Hart, John, Jr. '40
Hartel, Edward J. '69
Harter, Richard L. '51
Hartford, Brian P.
Harthun, Jill M. '85
Harthun, Matthew '81
Harthun, Nancy L. '83
Harvey, H. Clark, Jr. '57
Harvey, Henry C. '32-I
Harvey, Michael '94
Harvey, Perry A. '59
Harvey, Perry A., Jr. '83
Harvey, Sarah '95
Haseltine, Scott D. '70
Hassouna, Mohamed A. '65
Hastings, Nancy '82
Hatch, Lawrence H. '77
Hatch, Thomas C. '79
Hatchadorian, Michael '98
Hatfield, Kendra S. '83
Hatfield, Kevin '85
Hauserman, Lance R.
Hauserman, Larry '75
Hawke, David A. '68
Hawkey, David R. '67
Hawkey, Thomas C. '73
Hawkey, Tim S. '48
Hawkins, John W. '69
Hawkins, Robert L. III '65
Hawley, David W. '50
Hawley, Dudley A. III '79
Hawley, Dudley A., Jr. '41
Hawley, E. Washburn '45
Hayden, Sherman S. '24
Hayes, Arthur B., Jr. '72
Hayes, James '73
Hayes, Michael S. '79
Hayes, Scott '71
Hayes, Timothy '76
Haynes, Arthur '86
Hays, Alden '39
Hays, Carrie '76
Hayward, Geoffrey H. '69

Hayward, Philip C. '68
Hazlett, George H. '47
Hazlewood, Jackson, Jr. '56
Heald, David M. '69
Heald, Seth G. '71
Healy, Douglas T. '83
Healy, Jeffrey A. '81
Healy, Scott '78
Healy, Thomas E. '49
Heath, Adam M. '99
Heath, B. Isaac '96
Hecht, Shawn '91
Hecker, John, Jr. '78
Heffern, Richard '80
Heffernan, John A.
Heilman, James B. '84
Hein, Dale '68
Hellegers, Wesley M.
Hellerstein, Daniel K. '75
Hellerstein, David '71
Hellerstein, Elizabeth '81
Hellerstein, Jonathan '73
Hellerstein, Susan '77
Hellman John A. '72
Hellman, Peter S. '67
Hellmuth, Ted '69
Hendershot, Harold J. III '84
Hendershot, Kirsten P. '86
Henderson, Warren S. '43
Henighan, Cota D. '82
Henighan, Ronnie '76
Henkel, Ben '85
Henkel, David '88
Henkel, Peter '82
Henninge, Robert '85
Henninge, Wendy Marie '86
Henriques, Horace F. '44
Henry, Benjamin J. '72
Henry, David L. '69
Henry, Frank C. '69
Henry, John L. '66
Henry, William '58
Herbruck, Christopher '88
Herbruck, Robert '87
Herbruck, Thomas B. '87

Herdman, Thomas '78
Herlands, Lee '73
Herlands, Scott A. '72
Herman, Benjamin '76
Herman, Gregory Scott '79
Herman, James L. '70
Herman, Kathryn M. '94
Hermann, Robert E., Jr. '72
Herndon, Charles L. '64
Herndon, David N. '67
Herpel, Karen '89
Herrick, Craig W. '83
Herrick, Henry '30
Herrick, Kristen '85
Herrick, Myron '26
Herrick, Parmely '28
Herron, Edward B. '51
Hershelman, Douglas B. '85
Herzig, Brian '74
Hexter, Andrew D. '88
Hexter, James R. '84
Hexter, Jeffry '88
Hexter, John B. '60
Hexter, Michael L. '57
Hexter, Sarah '01
Heyman, Brian L. '82
Heyman, Mark '85
Heyman, Todd '88
Hickok, Michael '86
Hickox, Charles '31-I
Hickox, Charles, Jr. '66
Hickox, Fayette B. '69
Hickox, Patrick C. '67
Hildebrandt, Nancyann '86
Hildt, Daniel '69
Hildt, David T. '64
Hill, Bruce, Jr. '77
Hill, Frank R. '54
Hill, Jerome IV '52
Hill, Samuel R. II '65
Hill, Tim John R. '57
Hillenmeyer, Edward F.
Hillenmeyer, Henry R. '83
Hills, David '72
Hills, Frederick '36

Hills, Geoffrey '69
Hills, James C. '69
Hitchcock, Andrew M. '75
Hitchcock, Christopher '70
Hitchcock, Daniel A. '65
Hitchcock, Douglas '72
Hitchcock, Eleanor '79
Hitchcock, Eric A. '70
Hitchcock, Lawrence, Jr. '42
Hitchcock, Meacham '42
Hitchcock, Morley '34
Hitchcock, P. S., Jr. '65
Hitchcock, Peter S. '34
Hitchcock, Reuben, Jr. '36
Hnatko, Harry '74
Hnatko, Michael '75
Hoadley, Jeffrey '80
Hoadley, Todd '82
Hoagland, Laura L. '81
Hoagland, Richard S. '83
Hobson, Stephan '54
Hochstetler, Charles '75
Hodges, Richard '68
Hodnett, Eric E. '84
Hoerr, Charles M. '65
Hoerr, Mark '72
Hoerr, Stanley O., Jr. '56
Hoffman, Alan B. '64
Hoffman, Howard T. III '67
Hoffman, Jeffery '82
Hoffman, John H. '69
Hoffman, Junius '70
Hoffman, Mark '81
Hoffman, Michael W. '72
Hoffman, Nicole '88
Hoffman, Peter '69
Hoge, Robert '79
Hoge, Thomas '78
Hoge, Wendy '75
Holden, Frank M. '55
Holden, John D. '53
Holden, Stephen '71
Holdrege, Elizabeth A. '87
Hollister, Clay '65
Hollister, John B. III

Hollister, Martin S. '64
Hollister, Michael E. '67
Holmes, Carl N. II '72
Holmes, George H., Jr. '59
Holmes, Pamela T. '83
Holmes, Peter C. '41
Holtrey, Deborah '81
Holtrey, Kimberly A. '83
Holtrey, Sheryl '89
Hontas, Byron '78
Hontas, Mark '82
Hooker, Richard, Jr. '29
Horn, Todd '73
Hornbeck, Donald W., Jr. '47
Horner, Douglas '78
Horner, James A., Jr. '75
Horner, James '47
Horner, John M.
Horrigan, Brian '87
Horsburgh, Chas. R., Jr. '64
Horsburgh, Chris W. '67
Horsburgh, James '88
Horsburgh, Kenneth P., Jr.
  '65
Horsburgh, Sarah '87
Horth, Thomas O. '75
Horth, Timothy W.
Horton, Justin '93
Horvat, Diana '80
Horvat, George '87
Horvat, Zoran '82
Horvitz, James H. '76
Horvitz, John '80
Horvitz, Peter A. '72
Horvitz, Thomas '74
Horwitz, Jonathan '73
Hosford, Peter M. '68
Hosmer, Elizabeth '84
Hotchkiss, Charles '31-II
Houck, John C.
Houck, Lewis D., Jr. '47
Houghton, Alanson B. III '83
Houghton, Alexander S. '74
House, Allan C., Jr. '33
House, Frank E. III '36

House, Tim '39
Houser, Glenn D. '80
Houser, Keith '85
Houston, Stephanie Jo '85
Howard, Daniel M. '69
Howard, Edward D. '64
Howard, Elizabeth '76
Howard, John G. '65
Howard, John T. '28
Howard, John T., Jr. '57
Howard, Matthew J. '79
Howard, Nathaniel R. III '74
Howard, Nicole '89
Howell, Harry W. '40
Howell, Neil '80
Hoyt, Elton III '36
Hoyt, James '32-II
Hoyt, James H. '67
Hoyt, James W. III
Hoyt, Peter H. '69
Hruby, Charles H. '39
Hruby, Ferdinand '34
Hruby, Thomas '76
Hruska, James '89
Hsieh, May Chuen '86
Hsu, Griffith '86
Hsu, Jeffrey T. '78
Hsu, Timothy '88
Hubbard, Sterling W. III '67
Hubbard, Sterling W. Jr. '29
Hudgin, Richard H. '64
Hudspeth, Lonnie J. '76
Huff, Carlos '80
Huff, Thomas R.
Hughes, James A. '66
Hughes, Thomas S. '65
Hukill, Emory G., Jr. '32-I
Hulbert, Richard S. III '82
Hull, Jonathan '71
Humel, James B.
Humphrey, Calvin '78
Humphrey, David C. '66
Humphrey, Dudley, Jr. '68
Humphrey, George M. II '57
Humphrey, Gilbert W., Jr. '59

Humphrey, Gilbert '32-II
Humphrey, Kimberly '80
Humphries, A. MacArthur '71
Hunt, Nicholas B. '58
Hunter, Ashley P.
Hunter, Benedict '50
Hunter, Christopher '89
Hunter, Dale Pistilli '82
Hunter, James A. '73
Hunter, Mary Jane '79
Hurd, Peter '67
Hurd, Timothy I. '70
Hurlock, James B. '48
Hurwitz, Eric '93
Hurwitz, Hallie '88
Husband, Sandra M. '77
Husk, Benjamin W. '54
Huston, Christopher '86
Hutchin, Richard A. '64
Hutchinson, Chrissy '84
Hutchinson, Ethan '81
Hutchinson, Matthew '88
Hyams, Robert N.
Hyatt, Daniel '69
Hyde, Brinton L.
Hyde, Elizabeth '79
Hyde, Magreger G.
Hyde, Nate '80
Hyde, Pamela '81
Hyde, Paul L. '47

Illingworth, Walter '68
Ingalls, Albert S. III '45
Ingalls, Bruce '73
Ingalls, David S., Jr. '49
Ingersoll, Norman '26
Inglis, Richard, Jr. '29
Ingraham, Robert N. '49
Ingram, Eric '87
Inkley, Dale '41
Inkley, Scott R. '36
Inkley, Scott R., Jr. '70
Ireland, Frederick D. '68
Ireland, George R. '74
Ireland, James D. '32-I

Jones, Timothy H. '75
Jones, William C.
Jordan, Alf '55
Jordan, Charles N., Jr. '65
Jordan, Erik C.
Jordan, John E. '68
Jorgensen, David H. '89
Jorgensen, Simon N.
Joseph, David '91
Joseph, William R., Jr. '87
Joslyn, Mark R. '79
Judson, Calvin, Jr. '31-I
Judson, Franklyn S. '31-II
Junod, Henri Pell, Jr. '59

Kadish, Matthew F. '80
Kafka, John '70
Kafka, Thomas '70
Kahane, Stephen N. '75
Kahn, Robert '79
Kalberer, Christa '85
Kalberer, Gwenn '75
Kalberer, Lisa '88
Kalberer, Lori '77
Kalina, Mark '80
Kane, David '88
Kane, Michael S. '86
Kanter, Jeffrey M. '73
Kantz, Dale '88
Kaplan, Douglas '80
Kaplan, James F.
Kaplan, Lee '86
Kaplan, Peter S. '86
Kaplan, Richard H., Jr. '78
Kaplan, Roberta '84
Kaplan, Ronald D. '83
Karch, Geoffrey A.
Karch, George F. III '83
Kates, Dale '81
Kato, Mosami '68
Katovsky, Jon '77
Katz, Brett Elizabeth '86
Katz, David '85
Katz, Deborah '80
Katz, Douglas A. '88

Katz, Peter '86
Kauffman, Lizbeth '78
Kaufman, Deborah '75
Kaufman, John S. '45
Kaufman, Richard S. '45
Kaufman, Stephen '77
Kavuru, Mani
Kay, David '59
Kay, Thomas B. '73
Kazmer, Andrew J., Jr. '83
Kazmer, David '86
Keenan, Sean '92
Keeny, Steve '88
Keeney, Michael C. '71
Keeney, Stephen B. '66
Keller, Michael L. '76
Keller, Winchell '34
Kelley, Alfred K., Jr. '42
Kellogg, John W. '93
Kellogg, Justin
Kelly, Armin '69
Kelly, David S.
Kelly, George D.
Kelly, Stephen E. '75
Kelly, Tara K. '86
Kelly, William B. '69
Kelsey, Henry B. '53
Kendall, Richard R.
Kendrick, Bruce '42
Kendrick, Peter '75
Kennedy, Alexander W. '67
Kennedy, Claire E. '99
Kennedy, John '69
Kennedy, Mark '72
Kennedy, Mark '70
Kennedy, Sarah L. '79
Kent, Anne '88
Kent, Jennifer Metz '86
Kerek, John '89
Kerester, Scott '75
Kern, Lorri '86
Kerr, John S. '34
Kersey, Hal C. '45
Kersey, James M. '58
Kest, Richard L.

Khol, Mark S. '76
Kickel, Graig '89
Kilbane, Katherine '79
Kilroy, Edward A. III '70
Kim, Patricia '89
Kim, Robert J. '87
Kim, Sharon '89
Kinchen, Morris A. '67
Kinder, Gordon D. '66
Kinder, John C.
King, Alan B. '79
King, Cecilia '76
King, Christopher '83
King, David S. '64
King, Dennis D. '58
King, Douglas '75
King, John M.R.
King, Preston P.
King, Ralph T., Jr. '74
King, Richard C.
King, Rollin W. '46
King, W. Griffin III '70
King, W. Griffin, Jr. '40
King, Woods III '75
Kinney, Charles E., Jr. '51
Kinney, George R. '58
Kinney, Sam E. '53
Kinsey, Lance G. '71
Kipka, Robert E. '48
Kipka, Ross A. '45
Kirby, John '88
Kirkham, Edward P. '84
Kirkham, George D. '48
Kirkham, Gib '81
Kirkham, Hall II '83
Kirkham, Peter W. '84
Kirkham, Samantha '89
Kirkham, W. Gates '87
Kirkham, Walter R. '49
Kirkpatrick, Amonica '84
Kirkpatrick, James B. '69
Kish, Karen '76
Kitchel, William L. III
Kittredge, Donald '67
Kittredge, Douglas E. '73

Kjellgren, Bengt H. '46
Klaus, Alisa '75
Klaus, David '70
Klauss, J. Albert '66
Klein, Deborah '77
Klein, Elizabeth '77
Klein, Jonathan '76
Klein, Krista '88
Klein, Michael '73
Klein, Paul '77
Klein, Stephen T. '66
Klein, Susan '80
Kline, Jeffery T. '69
Kling, J. Bradley '52
Klunder, Douglas B. '78
Kneale, Todd '81
Kneen, Brewster B. '48
Kneen, Jamie F. '56
Knerly, Stephen J., Jr. '68
Knight, Charles D. '64
Knight, Christopher '58
Knight, Jonathan L. '60
Knight, Peter T. '55
Knight, Samuel B., Jr. '59
Knowles, Harold '60
Knuth, Richard G. '89
Knuth, Todd R. '86
Knutson, David E. '75
Knutson, Jon W. '77
Ko, Kathleen Lim '76
Koblenz, Brian '79
Koch, Carl W. II '67
Kocur, Kevin '76
Koehler, James '66
Koehler, John A. II '65
Koeller, Katie '91
Koenig, Kari '87
Kogan, Craig '88
Kogan, Dana '86
Kogan, Mindi '84
Kohn, Adam P. '82
Kohn, Jonathan '80
Kohn, Norman V. '68
Konigsberg, Charles '76
Koontz, Wesley '95

Koplow, Bret '77
Korecki, E.J.
Korecki, William S.
Koreness, Gregory '84
Korman, Amy B. '80
Korman, David '84
Korman, Laura '82
Kovel, Lee '69
Kozman, James S. '67
Krall, Roy '81
Kramer, Mark '74
Krasner, James D.
Kratovil, Jason '96
Kraus, Grace '76
Kraus, Robert '75
Krause, James R. '64
Kravitz, Eric T. '85
Kreger, C. Stoddard '38
Krejci, Richard S. '74
Kreps, John E. '25
Krotinger, Jonathan '72
Kroto, George F.
Krug, William '88
Krulak, Robert L. '84
Krulak, Roger '82
Krupkin, R. Scott '75
Kuechle, Peter '89
Kukafka, Arielle Long '81
Kumin, Jeremy R. '82
Kuntz, Robert J., Jr. '78
Kushleika, Karen R.
Kuss, Edward M. '64
Kuth, Melinda '84
Kuzma, Robert '84
Kykena, Raymond '71
Kyman, David C. '83

LaBarre, Polly '88
Lacey, Richard S. '57
Ladds, Herbert P., Jr. '48
Lader, David '82
Lader, Deborah '79
Lader, Ellen '86
Laffer, Arthur B. '55
Lake, Heather '87

Lamb, Philip H. '67
Lamb, Todd '76
Lamon, Robert '85
LaMond, John W. '36
Landers, Aimee B. '89
Landers, Rodger D. '85
Landsman, Brian '75
Landsman, Jonathan '79
Landsman, Lisa '77
Landy, Kevin P. '72
Landy, Philip '66
Landy, Robert '66
Lanese, John G. '48
Lang, John A. '57
Langholt, Jonathan '70
Lanphear, Jeffery B. '69
Lantz, Robert '77
Lantz, William G. III '68
LaPine, Jamie '87
Lardas, John '89
Large, Henry '28
Large, James '79
LaRiccia, Frank J. III '88
LaRiche, Jeffery T. '65
LaRiche, Sean '89
LaRiche, Timothy C. '59
LaRiche, William, Jr. '57
Larkins, A. Richard, Jr. '58
Laronge, Craig J. '66
Lasky, Eric '79
Lasky, Neil '81
Lasky, Pamela '78
Latina, Robert '94
Lauer, Alisha '93
Laughlin, Douglas '76
Laughlin, Thomas '60
Laven, Michele '78
Lavin, Gordon K. '68
Lavrich, Philip L. '77
Lavrich, Richard J. '75
Lawrence, Dana '94
Lawrence, Elssy '97
Lawrence, Johnathan M.
Lawrence, Michael '84
Lawrence, Wayne '84

Lawson, Eugene A., Jr. '50
Layson, Conrad '80
Lazo, Peter '76
Le Fevre, Robert E. '55
Leathers, John '72
Leavitt, Alysia J. '87
Leavitt, Richard I. '67
Lebit, Leslie '89
Lederman, Michael '90
Lebit, Lynn '86
Lee, Anthony J.
Lee, Christopher P.
Lee, Grant '86
Lee, James A.
Lee, Jeffrey A.
Lee, John '86
Lee, Jonathan S. '85
Lee, Michelle '88
Lee, Richard '89
Lee, Thomas J. '70
Lee, Thomas W. '74
Lee, Warren W. '40
Leeds, George H. '46
Lees, James '55
Lees, Thomas M., Jr. '50
LeFevre, Robert '55
LeFevre, David Eaton '59
Lehrich, Marc D. '78
Leigh, Armistead M. '68
Leighton, Kenneth '70
Lcizman, Amy B. '83
Leizman, Daniel J. '80
Leizman, Debra Sue '78
Lemmon, Jane Macdonald '76
Lemmon, Martin E.
Lemmon, Pax W. '71
Lenihan, Edward F., Jr. '32-II
Lenihan, Ernest W. '26
Lennon, James P.
Leon, Hayden '85
Lerner, Barron '78
Lester, Leslie R.
Lester, Lisa R.
Lesy, Michael '60
Levi, Jonathan A. '73

Levin, Margot '81
Levin, Stephanie L. '83
Levin, Stephen '79
Levins, James '31-II
Levy, Charles E. '73
Levy, Donald '66
Levy, Sharon '85
Lewis, Ben M. '82
Lewis, Halle G. '80
Lewis, Ian A. '83
Lewis, Kenneth '88
Lewis, Matthew '68
Lewis, Peter C. '49
Lewis, William '86
Lewis, William '83
Libbey, Charlotte '01
Lichtig, Caroline '79
Lichtig, Howard A. '75
Lieber, Andrew W. '52
Lightbody, John C. '64
Lightbody, Richard '65
Lightbody, William '68
Lillie, Walter '27
Lincoln, G. Russell '64
Lincoln, James B. '38
Lincoln, James D. '91
Lincoln, James F., Jr. '33
Lincoln, Kirke P., Jr. '26
Lindan, Nicholas O. '71
Lindblad, Robert W. '73
Lindblade, Carl '57
Linden, Richard '72
Linderme, Edwin G., Jr. '50
Lindgren, John H. '71
Lindsay, Mark E. '81
Lindsay, Scott R.
Lingl, Angie '78
Linsay, Ernest C. '56
Lintern, Richard '67
Lipscomb, M. Keith '92
Lis, James '87
Lis, John J. '83
Liston, Tracey '79
Little, Dwight H. '74
Little, Hubbard '32-II

Little, James J. '74
Little, John C. '48
Little, Mark '71
Little, Mary L.
Little, Raymond E. '78
Little, Revere '59
Little, Robert E. '48
Little, Sam R. '57
Livingstone, Raymond S., Jr. '50
Loehr, Carrie A. '95
Loehr, Cynthia M. '89
Loftiss, Jeffrey W. '79
Logan, Jimmy '79
Logan, Junius '77
Logan, Keith '81
Logan, Nelson A. '39
Loizos, Chrysanthe '89
Long, David '79
Long, Ilana M. '83
Long, Jonathan '90
Long, Samuel D. '83
Long, Tammy '87
Longstreth, Frank H., Jr. '68
Loomis, Muffy '77
Loop, Alison '81
Loop, Fred '85
Loop, Kendall '86
Lord, Robert W. '83
Lorenz, George '65
Lorenzo, Sofia L. '83
Lovelace, Ernest '77
Lovelace, Joyce L. '83
Lovell, David J. '82
Lovell, Douglas C. '78
Loveman, Alex J.
Loveman, Brian '78
Loveman, Courtney '88
Loveman, Kristy '82
Loveman, Shari '79
Lowe, Evan '85
Lowe, Kerie '80
Lowe, Marcia M. '85
Lowell, Irwin '31-II
Lowell, Jeffrey F. '60

Lowell, Jon M. '58
Lowitt, Joel B.
Lowry, Mark '70
Lowry, Robert K. '44
Lubman, Alex '67
Lucas, John T. '49
Lucas, Peter B. '72
Lucas, Robert R., Jr. '70
Luce, David '95
Luce, James '92
Lucier, Kathryn '85
Ludwick, David D. III '82
Ludwig, Kathleen '87
Luke, Alexander M. '50
Luke, James L. '47
Lundgren, Helena
Luntz, Brian '79
Luntz, Jill '89
Lustig, Michael '85
Lutherer, Lorenz O. '51
Lutton, John M., Jr. '53
Lutton, Michael L. '57
Lux, Edward Michael '76
Lux, Michael '78
Lux, William K. '41
Lyles, Beverly '81
Lyles, Charlise '77
Lynch, Patrick '85
Lyngard, Matthew W. '89
Lyons, Sherri D. '83
Lytle, David '88
Lytle, John '85

Ma, Michael '84
MacArthur, Steve '68
MacAyeal, Douglas '72
MacCracken, Alan, Jr. '54
MacKay, Michael P. '70
MacKenzie, Gordon A. '65
Mackenzie, Clara '79
MacKenzie, John E. '71
MacKenzie, Malcolm W. '75
Macko, Joseph J., Jr. '51
MacNab, Thomas E. '73
Macomber, Lowell Peter '48

McBride, Malcolm Jr. '32-II
McBride, Richard '36
McBride, Richard F. '67
McCabe, Edwin P. '56
McCahey, Mary Lorraine '83
McCahey, William '82
McCarthy, John P. '39
McCaskey, James J.
McChesney, Samuel P. III
McClimon, Jon J. '64
McCloud, Julia '85
McConnell, David H. '77
McConnell, Frederic S. III '73
McConnell, Michael '85
McCormack, Scott B. '76
McCormack, Todd H. '78
McCoy, Bruce P.
McCoy, Peter A. '84
McCoy, William B. '78
McCoy, William C., Jr. '38
McCreary, Lewis S. '66
McCreary, Peter '71
McCreery, David '81
McCreery, James '98
McCreery, R. Douglas '70
McCrory, Michael '81
McCullam, Jessie D. '87
McCullam, Rebecca '86
McCullough, Kevin P. '58
McDaniel, Abner '74
McDaniel, James E.
McDevitt, Frank J., Jr. '55
McDougal, Molly K.
McDowell, Bridge
McDowell, Spicer
McDuffie, Otis J. '88
McElliott, Erwin '33
McElrath, Christopher '89
McElroy, Alan '78
McGarry, Jeffery '82
McGaw, Wilbert H., Jr. '43
McGean, Charles '28
McGinness, Margot '87
McGowan, Thomas C. '41
McGuire, Frederick T. III '59

McGuire, James F., Jr.
McIntosh, Gregory '53
McIntosh, Henry P. IV '51
McIntosh, Leonard H. '55
McIntosh, Price M. '58
McIntosh, Scott '77
McKay, Hugh '74
McKay, Jacqueline '84
McKay, Stuart '36
McKay, William '71
McKearney, Miles C., Jr. '64
McKenzie, Bryder A.
McKenzie, Pierre J.
McKinney, Dennis W.
McKinney, Price '28
McKinney, Rigan '26
McKinney, William Jr. '73
McKinsey, Stewart R.
McKitterick, Thomas S.
McKitterick, William G. II '64
McLaughlin, John T.
McLeod, Julie A. '85
McMillan, James E. '87
McMillan, S. Sterling IV '88
McMillin, Scott '89
McNabb, James '25
McNaughton, Dale K.
McNeill, Brett A. '85
McNulty, Peter D. '85
McWilliams, John P., Jr. '55
McWilliams, Thomas '75
McWilliams, W. J. Barlow '44
McWilliams, Walter J. Jr.
Mecaskey, Douglas '80
Mecklenburg, Emily '99
Meeks, Thomas O.
Meigs, Jennifer '84
Meisel, Michael '72
Meisel, Peter '77
Meisel, Robert S. '80
Meisel, Scott I. '67
Meket, Terry A. '56
Melcher, Daniel H. '64
Mellen, Louis III '75
Mellinger, Benton D. '31-II

Melton, Brady A. '84
Menefee, John J. '83
Menefee, Terrell '87
Merkatz, Kenneth A. '80
Merkel, Benjamin '73
Merkel, Henry H. '74
Merkel, Nicholas B. '65
Merkel, Thomas M.
Merkel, William E., Jr. '65
Merrill, Barrant V. '45
Merritt, Andrew L. '73
Merritt, Elizabeth '77
Merritt, William F. '45
Merryweather, George E. '30
Merryweather, George '68
Merryweather, Hubert '34
Merszei-Clark, Justin '90
Merszei-Clark, Trevor '91
Merts, George K. '58
Mesch, Robin '77
Messerman, Karen '78
Messerman, Lawrence '76
Metzger, Anthony E. '89
Metzger, Christopher '56
Metzger, George R., Jr. '53
Metzger, Gregory W. '83
Metzger, Kris '81
Meyer, Henry L. II '41
Meyer, Matthias '64
Meyfarth, George H. '58
Meyfarth, Philip F. '48
Michels, Stephan '91
Middleton, Brock '91
Middleton, Christopher C. '85
Mierke, Sara '84
Mihalik, Egon '34
Milbourn, Jane E. '87
Milbourn, Michael J. '91
Milde, Gordon T. '55
Milde, W. Lyall '48
Miles, Robert J. '85
Milewski, Paul D. '66
Milholland, James
Milholland, Peter B.
Millan, William H., Jr. '65

Millar, Alan B.
Millard, Maxwell D., Jr. '59
Miller, Ann '86
Miller, Cary
Miller, Charles H. '55
Miller, Christopher J.
Miller, Christopher '89
Miller, Clifford '72
Miller, Clinton B. '68
Miller, James C. III '74
Miller, Jeff '71
Miller, Jeffrey S. '74
Miller, Kenneth A.
Miller, Laura '77
Miller, Loren C. '68
Miller, Lynn H. '58
Miller, Nicholas '88
Miller, Philip N. '55
Miller, Randall '70
Miller, Richard T. '41
Miller, Roy J.
Miller, Scott Alan '74
Miller, Steven E. '67
Miller, Timothy W. '76
Miller, Tyler '71
Miller, William C., Jr. '76
Mills, David O., Jr.
Milovanovic, Michael '86
Miltz, William J. '66
Minchin, Nicholas H. '71
Minnick, Don C. '79
Minotti, Michael L. '74
Mintz, Daniel C. '83
Mintz, Scott A.
Mintz, Steven '81
Mitchell, Heather '76
Mitrovich, Laura K. '83
Mobasseri, Sara '86
Mock, David G. '40
Moffet, Kenneth W. '77
Mohler, William C. '42
Molnar, James '72
Moltz, Douglas '72
Moody, Robert W. '66
Moon, Robert B. '46

Moonan, Daniel W. '82
Moonan, William S. '58
Moore, Derek S. '74
Moore, Dan T. III '55
Moore, David B. '73
Moore, Gary
Moore, Halley '89
Moore, Heather B. '87
Moore, Nelson B., Jr. '66
Moore, Robert H. III '81
Moore, Wendy Lewis '85
Morehead, John '91
Morgan, Christopher '98
Morgan, Dixon '33
Morgan, Dixon, Jr. '64
Morgan, Junius '56
Morgan, Michael '68
Morgenstern, Donald '75
Morgenstern, Joel
Moritz, John A. '45
Morley, Dan G. '70
Morman, Todd '88
Morrill, Ferdinand G. '28
Morris, Charles '88
Morris, Daniel M. '60
Morris, Marian '80
Morris, Patrick '77
Morris, Peter J. '79
Morris, Stephen C. '42
Morris, Warren '75
Morrison, John '72
Morse, Arthur S. D. '37
Morse, Dean '35
Morse, Donald R. '73
Morse, James '71
Morse, Leslie '76
Morse, Philip W. '32-II
Morse, Reid '76
Morse, Robert H. '33
Morse, Thomas T. '47
Morton, Herbert L., Jr. '70
Morton, John E. '70
Morton, Robert '89
Morton, Wendy S. '86
Moss, Bruce M. '71

Moss, Jeffrey '75
Motch, Elton F., Jr. '56
Motta, Antonino '73
Motta, Joseph Louis '76
Motta, Paolo '82
Moyar, David '86
Moyar, Mark '89
Mueller, Felice '78
Mueller, Frederick '71
Mueller, John M. '73
Mueller, Omar '81
Muhlhauser, John '29
Munger, Jeffrey H. '77
Munger, Myron W. '73
Munger, Robert L. III '72
Murch, Boynton '35
Murch, Rachel '92
Murck, Christian C.
Murck, Edward V.
Murfey, James J. '65
Murfey, Latham W. III '67
Murfey, William H. '70
Murley, Charles E. '50
Murphy, Gregory R. '80
Murphy, Thomas '89
Murray, Dean '77
Murray, Gregory B. '83
Murray, Jenny '80
Murray, LaTonia '82
Murray, Lawrence N. '74
Musselman, Peter R. '42
Myers, H.A. '74
Myers, Malcolm R. '49

Nahra, Carol '85
Nahra, Diane '85
Nahra, Joseph '87
Nahra, Kirk J. '80
Nahra, Paul '81
Naiden, Jason E. '89
Najarian, Ara J. '78
Najarian, Armen '81
Najarian, Rafi G. '83
Nakamoto, Donna '81
Narten, Andrew B. '89

Olds, Marshall C. '67
Oliva, George III '72
Oliva, Leigh '81
Oliva, Mark '77
Oliva, Todd '83
Olmsted, Christopher C. '66
Olson, Stuart B. '68
Omerza, Raymond J. '78
Oppmann, Harvey G. '64
Oppmann, Justin '93
Orr, Kevin '75
Orr, Parker, Jr. '71
Orrick, Stuart S., Jr.
Osborn, Edmund P. '60
Osborn, Henry C., Jr. '28
Osborn, Henry C. III '57
Osborn, Tracy '32-I
Osborne, David A. II '43
Osborne, David H., Jr. '58
Osborne, James M., Jr. '40
Osborne, William '32-I
Osborne, William III '72
Osborne, William IV '79
Osburn, David H., Jr. '58
Ostendorf, Edgar L., Jr. '49
Ostergard, Derek '70
Ostheimer, Alfred J. IV '46
Otis, William E., Jr. '40
Otto, Shawn '86
Ouhlahan, Richard '60
Overbaugh, Richard C. '74
Oversmith, Jason '92
Oversmith, Kristin '89
Oviatt, David '85
Owens, James R. '40
Owens, Lloyd H. '78

Pacini, Lauren R. '59
Pacini, Lauren '85
Padolik, Peter A.
Paepke, C. Owen '72
Page, Dudley H. '44
Page, Kristin '81
Page, Robert T. '49
Page, Robert T., Jr. '83

Painter, Kenyon
Pak, Daniel '83
Pakis, Courtney '99
Pakrashi, Neil '89
Palevsky, Keith '81
Palevsky, Penny L. '84
Pallat, John E. '78
Palmer, John '77
Palmer, Joseph F. '80
Palmer, Thomas '87
Palmer, William P. '24
Palmer, William P. III '47
Paltza, Gordon C. '70
Pamula, Kara '86
Pamula, Sarah '88
Panosian, Daniel D. '87
Park, Kimberly R. '89
Parker, Horace D.
Parker, John MacRea, Jr. '38
Parker, Leonard J. '83
Parker, Patrick S. Jr.
Parker, Susan '78
Parkhurst, Walter
Parkman, Mary '78
Parks, Barbara '79
Parks, Ronald B. '54
Parks, Tom '77
Parran, Michael '82
Parran, Theodore V., Jr. '74
Partington, Rex C. III '75
Pasalis, Dean '89
Pasalis, Dina '88
Passalacqua, Edele '79
Passov, Joseph '80
Patchan, David '86
Patchin, Darian M. '83
Patchin, Dorian M. '83
Paterson, Thomas '70
Patterson, Dudley W. '72
Pavlich, Craig '96
Pavlovic, Kelly Herron '84
Payne, Angela '88
Pearl, Lisa S. '79
Pearl, Stephen '77
Pease, James V. '54

Pease, Thomas F. '57
Peay, Elizabeth '82
Peay, Gordon Andrew '88
Peay, Nicholas '48
Peay, Nicholas, Jr. '84
Peck, Claude J. '32-II
Peck, Edward I. '32-II
Peck, Herman B. '32-I
Peck, Peter S. '59
Peck, Theodore T. '36
Peck, William A. '37
Pekay, Lars A. '82
Pelton, Robert S. '33
Pelton, William '31-I
Peltz, Elana R. '79
Pender, Katie M. '87
Pender, Mark M. '82
Penland, Edward '71
Peppercorn, Susan B. '83
Perkins, Charles B. '24
Perkins, David D. '75
Perkins, Jacob '32-I
Perkins, John '32-I
Perkins, Leigh H., Jr. '71
Perkins, Leigh H., Sr. '43
Perkins, Maurice '30
Perkins, Ralph '31-II
Perkins, Ralph II '69
Perkins, Roger '28
Perkins, Scott '92
Perla, Bernard '80
Perlick, James '75
Perrin, David T. '69
Perris, David '69
Perrotti, Leonard '73
Perry, A. Wade '55
Perry, Clayton '47
Perry, Edward Lee '65
Perry, George W. '42
Perry, John S. '72
Perry, Michael C.
Perry, Paul-Hilbert W.
Perry, Ray P. '36
Peskin, Lawrence F. '71
Peskin, Robert '86

Pesuit, Edward W.
Pesuit, Roger G. '67
Peters, Deborah '87
Peters, Scott '85
Peterson, Jerome '89
Petrenchik, Jeffery '71
Petrovic, Steven '82
Pevaroff, Lisa, A.
Pfaff, Susan '76
Phan, An Tri '88
Phelps, Alexander G. '84
Phelps, Christopher W. '84
Phillips, Benjamin '89
Phillips, Daniel M. '48
Phillips, Grant '73
Phillips, James L. '75
Phillips, John J. '71
Phillips, John '25
Phillips, Marc '85
Phillips, Scott W. '76
Phillips, Steven '82
Phillips, Stuart '80
Phypers, William T. '43
Pickering, Anthony F. '77
Pickering, Jason W. '84
Pickering, John M. '74
Piczer, Michael '88
Pien, Richard '75
Pierce, Edwin H. '35
Pierce, Raymond '76
Pierson, David S. '65
Pierson, Don Carlos Jr. '78
Pignolet, Nancy '80
Pike, Christopher J. '83
Pike, Laura E. '86
Pilloff, Steven '85
Pinkett, Jeffrey '84
Pinkham, Steven H. '71
Pischel, Robert '87
Pittman, Thomas
Platt, Stoddard D. '49
Player, Jennifer M.
Pleska, Kenneth W. '72
Podrygula, Stephan '69
Podway, Karen H. '83

Poe, Bradley C. '79
Poe, R. Jeffrey '75
Polansky, Greer '88
Pollack, Cathy '88
Pollack, Elizabeth A. '86
Pollock, Daniel P. '67
Polt, William A. '51
Pomar, David '84
Pomeroy, Cleve H., Jr. '44
Poore, Charles M.B. '70
Pope, Helen Osborn '85
Port, Eric W. '71
Porter, Alexander '84
Porter, Chris '89
Porter, Edwin R. '74
Porter, Frederic S. '51
Porter, Heather '77
Porter, Lindsay B. '87
Porter, Michael E. '79
Porter, Robert S. '86
Porter, Scott D.
Porter, Steven '77
Portman, Albert F. III '58
Posch, James J. '79
Posch, Thomas '84
Posner, David '82
Posner, Laura '84
Post, Anthony B.
Poutasse, Andy Charles '73
Poutasse, Douglas '74
Powar, Sherri '81
Powell, Brook H.
Powell, Cedric M. '80
Powell, Charles Q. '99
Powell, George L. '52
Powell, Jolyon B.
Powell, Thomas A. '68
Power, Robert W. '65
Power, William R., Jr. '59
Prescott, Barnard '24
Prescott, Edward P., Jr. '44
Prescott, Orville '24
Prescott, Thomas M. '67
Presley, William '84
Preston, Frederick M. '52

Preston, Henry N. '59
Preston, James F. III '54
Price, John L. III '66
Price, John L., Jr. '36
Price, Robert D. '36
Price, Robert M. '74
Price, Scott '92
Price, Sean '94
Prior, Daniel C. '41
Prior, Emery Carr, Jr. '52
Prior, Peter C. '45
Prior, William C. '46
Proctor, John D. '67
Prufer, Keith M.
Prugh, Clayton '72
Pryor, Carl A. '69
Ptacek, David '70
Ptacek, Paul B.
Purdy, Melissa '84
Purdy, Samantha '88
Putman, John E. Jr. '36
Putnam, Peter '42

Quarles, Pamela '83
Quartullo, Rebecca '84
Quigley, Thomas J. Jr. '79
Quimby, Conrad L. '40
Quimby, William C. '43
Quintrell, Ella Stecher '76

Raach, Frederick E.
Raaf, Sabrina '89
Rabinovich, Kevin '93
Radke, Larissa D. '85
Raffel, Cynthia '82
Raffel, Deborah '79
Ragone, Christine '81
Ragone, Peter V. '83
Rahim, Ayad '80
Raible, John M. '44
Raish, David L. '65
Rajapakse, Vinodh '89
Rakita, Robert '75
Ralston, Sarah '86
Ramsey, James M. '58

Ramsey, John M. '42
Rander, Christopher A. '83
Randorf, William S. '83
Rankin, Abbie '87
Rankin, Alfred M., Jr. '56
Rankin, Bruce T. '74
Rankin, Claiborne R. '68
Rankin, Henry R. III '54
Rankin, Roger '70
Rankin, Thomas T. '65
Ratner, Kevin '85
Ratner, Rachel '88
Ray, Charles A. '68
Rayburn, Andrew K. '73
Rayburn, James D. '66
Rea, John '27
Ready, Robert C. '77
Real, Ralph A. '45
Reavis, David L. '83
Reavis, James O. '81
Reavis, John W., Jr. '43
Reavis, Lincoln '48
Rebel, Larry '71
Reed, John M. '65
Reed, John '75
Reed, Malcomb W., Jr. '47
Reed, Norman J.
Reed, Steven '81
Reeves, Clifford A., Jr. '55
Rehm, Marc '72
Reich, Kristian '90
Reich, Stephanie '87
Reichenbach, Alexander P. '86
Reichenbach, Glen '85
Reichert, David M. '53
Reichert, James '46
Reichert, John F. IV '50
Reichle, Harrald H. '82
Reid, John H., Jr. '47
Reid, Michael '78
Reid, William '73
Reik, Terri '88
Reinartz, John P., Jr. '75
Reinberg, Bonnie '77
Reinschreiber, Jonathan P. '69

Reinschreiber, M. R., Jr. '71
Reiss, Geoffery S. '79
Reitman, Alayne L. '82
Reitman, Scott '78
Rekate, Jason W. '89
Relyea, John '84
Renner, Reed R.
Resnick, Stuart '91
Resseger, John R. '68
Resseger, William E. '64
Reuse, Charles '86
Reuter, James '67
Rezaee, Rod '88
Rezaee, Roya '86
Rhinelander, Eric '71
Rhodes, Kristen '87
Rhodes, Michelle '81
Rice, Amy '90
Rich, Lauren '77
Richards, Jonathan '73
Richardson, Claudia '82
Richey, S. Hunter, II
Richman, Elisa '88
Richman, Eric B. '85
Rickard, Jonathan S.
Rickards, Charles H.P. '73
Riddle, Jeffrey '71
Riemenschneider, Thomas A. '51
Rigg, Jonathan '54
Rigg, Peter W. '59
Rim, Alexander '88
Rim, Sharon K. '87
Rinaldi, Eric '85
Rinaldi, Heather '88
Ring, M. Tamarin '79
Rippner, Betsy Jo '79
Riser, John Robert '72
Riser, Ted, A. '75
Ristau, Kevin '88
Ritter, John A. '57
Rizor, Joel H. '75
Rizor, Randy F., M.D. '70
Rizor, Russell '73
Roalsen, David H.

Roalsen, Merritt '76
Robbins, Bradley '84
Robbins, Brooke A. '66
Robbins, F. O. III '59
Robbins, Peter M. '60
Robbins, Prescott A. '69
Robbins, Sonya '89
Robbins, Tyler '67
Roberts, Dawn Marie '84
Roberts, Ellen '76
Roberts, Gregory '89
Roberts, J. Timmons '79
Roberts, James O.
Roberts, Jonathan '76
Roberts, Stephen J. '73
Roberts, Steven H. '77
Roberts, Thomas C. '73
Robertson, Scott '86
Robey, Bryant '55
Robey, Christopher '56
Robey, Daniel '59
Robey, Richard K. '64
Robins, Lawrence H. '75
Robins, Steven '80
Robinson, Alexander C. IV '41
Robinson, Alvin '73
Robinson, Calvin B. '67
Robinson, Daryl L. '83
Robinson, James M. '81
Robinson, John '78
Robinson, Kenneth '77
Robinson, Laura L. '80
Robinson, Peter D. '46
Robinson, Ted '29
Robinson, Thomas S.
Roblin, Christopher '79
Robrock, Richard B. II '56
Roby, David L. '42
Roby, Kenneth '81
Roby, Leslie Ann '86
Rodgers, David N.. '44
Rodriguez-Antunez, Juan '81
Rodriguez, Iris '90
Roger, Randall K. '78
Rogers, Edward S. III '42

Rogers, Edward S. IV '71
Rogers, Herbert S. '30
Rogers, M. Bradley '46
Rogers, Randolph '47
Rogers, William M. III '77
Roginsky, Marc A.
Rogus, William Tyler '88
Roland, Gregory '81
Roland, James '73
Roller, Kenneth A. '69
Roller, Lyndsey '96
Roller, Morgan '99
Rollins, Richard M. '72
Rome, Peter Alan '77
Romp, Richard '73
Rorick, Mark B. '72
Rose, Jennifer D. '84
Rose, Jonathan C. '56
Rose, Marshall '67
Rose, Mary B. '85
Rose, Nelson Henry '60
Rosen, Jodi K. '78
Rosen, Lisa J. '77
Rosen, Stacy Lynn '87
Rosen, Steven '88
Rosenberg, Garth '75
Rosenberg, Todd O. '79
Rosenfeld, Laura '84
Rosenfield, Jonah '89
Rosenfield, Marla '85
Rosenthal, Diane '78
Rosenthal, James '80
Rosenthal, Lynn '81
Rosenthal, Terri S. '78
Rosewater, Robert D. '53
Rositano, Donald F. Jr.
Rosner, Mark H. '75
Ross, David B. '76
Ross, David '82
Ross, George S., Jr. '49
Ross, Heather '79
Ross, Robert L. '81
Ross, Steven '84
Rossabi, Anthony R. '89
Rossi, Christopher D. '83

Rossman, Reid D.
Rostmeyer, Richard C. Jr. '80
Rotatori, Margaret '89
Roth, Allen S. '75
Roth, Grant '85
Roth, Julie '88
Rothman, Holly '95
Roudebush, Kristin '81
Roulston, Scott '75
Roulston, Thomas H., III '77
Rowden, Mills
Royal, Harry C. '53
Royal, Harry C., Jr. '31-I
Royal, Prentice B. '56
Royan, Christopher '67
Royan, David M. '70
Royer, Thomas R. '66
Rozhin, Maria A. '80
Rubin, Bradley '01
Rubin, Jared '98
Rubin, Paul '84
Rubin, Steven '72
Rubinstein, Charles '84
Ruch, Michael '77
Ruckel, Collin '84
Ruckel, Noal '88
Ruckman, Nicole '88
Ruckman, Samantha '85
Rule, Adrian O. IV '73
Runyon, Walter '28
Ruple, F. William III '65
Ruple, Thomas '75
Rusch, Douglas '88
Rusch, William '89
Rusnak, Gary M. '81
Rusnak, Greg A. '83
Russell, Tracey '88
Russick, James C. '69
Rzepka, Lisa '82

Saarel, Douglas A. '80
Saarel, Edwin E. '82
Sachs, Charles '67
Sachs, Peter '75
Sacks, Patricia '77

Sadowski, Stephen S. '60
Saefkow, Thomas '75
Saegh, Sheila '89
Safford, Platt R. '68
Safford, Thomas '72
Safier, Kerry D. '68
Safran, Mindy '77
Saha, Robin K.
Sahley, A. Douglas '66
Sahley, Richard M. '71
Saint-Amour, Craig E. '71
Saint-Amour, John R. '73
Saks, Daniel Holtzman '58
Saks, R. Steven '71
Salamone, Paul '73
Salanga, Edward '92
Salanga, Matthew '94
Sambrook, John E.
Sammon, Dan '86
Sammon, Leslie '84
Sammon, Samuel B.
Sampath, Sheila '86
Sampson, William J. III '45
Sancetta, Scott R. '76
Sanders, Eric '00
Sanderson, David '31-II
Sands, Linda J.
Sands, Mark F. '72
Sangdahl, Robert Forbes '86
Sankey, Richard B. '55
Sankey, Roger C. '60
Sargeaunt, Mark E. '68
Sargent, David C. '56
Sargent, John A. III '80
Sargent, John A., Jr. '53
Sarlson, Katherine '82
Sarlson, Mark '79
Saron, Terry Lance '66
Sarstedt, Gordon A., Jr. '41
Sato, Sam E. '68
Sato, Steven Douglas '67
Saunders, Elizabeth C. '78
Saunders, James D. '84
Saunders, Peter '75
Saunders, Scott J.

Sawyer, Charles B. '51
Sawyer, Charles B. '72
Sawyer, John '36
Sawyer, Samuel P. '49
Sayre, Harold '75
Schaefer, Albert T., Jr. '67
Schaefer, Kristen '91
Schaffer, Jonathan L. '75
Scharf, David '81
Scharf, Gary '76
Scharf, Laura '78
Schauffer, Frederick S. '32-II
Schauweker, Robert E. '43
Scheele, John '69
Scheele, Paul '70
Scheele, William G. '66
Scheid, Cornelius G., Jr. '66
Scheid, Peter W. '67
Schell, Christine D. '91
Schenk, Christopher '71
Schenk, Richard B. '67
Scher, Katherine E.
Schick, Brian S. '79
Schick, Jeffrey '77
Schiller, Jennifer '87
Schilling, Lewis R., Jr. '64
Schirm, Jay C. '71
Schlang, Bradley '85
Schlang, Leigh C. '83
Schlendorf, John W., Jr.
Schlesinger, Michael D. '64
Schloss, Morley '56
Schloss, R. Christopher '69
Schloss, Thomas M.
Schmalzer, Victor '74
Schmelzer, Cary '85
Schmemann, William E. '58
Schmidt, Christopher '86
Schmidt, Edwin J. Jr. '79
Schmidt, Greg '84
Schmidt, Heidi '76
Schmidt, Keith '87
Schmidt, Robert J., Jr. '86
Schmidt, Stacy '89
Schmitt, Andrew E. '48

Schnackel, Jay F. '55
Schneider, A. Benedict '30
Schneider, Mark '66
Schneider, Philip M. '68
Schnittger, Robert E. '33
Schoenbart, Tamra M. '87
Scholley, James F. '55
Schoonover, John '78
Schramm, David M. '67
Schreiber, Cathy L.
Schreiber, Robert A.
Schreibman, David C.
Schreibman, Eric '89
Schreibman, Michael J. '81
Schroeder, James O. '68
Schulman, Charles K. '74
Schulz, Insa '85
Schulz, Martin '82
Schumacher, Donna '75
Schupp, Karin '83
Schurger, Jon C. '50
Schuster, Richard '80
Schutter, David '89
Schwartz, Anne '80
Schwartz, Dale '79
Schwartz, Jeffrey '81
Schwartz, Leslie R. '83
Schwartz, Lori Reisman '80
Schwartz, Todd '79
Schweickert, John M. '81
Schweikert, James M. '84
Scofield, William '30
Scott, John T., Jr. '39
Scott, Malcolm F. '34
Scragg, George H., Jr. '49
Scullion, Howard
Seay, Stephanie '92
Sedgwick, Theodore '66
Sedgwick, Walter C. '64
Seely, Worcester W. '38
Segerson, James '87
Seidemann, Teri Lynn '85
Seidman, Jeffrey '88
Seidman, Kenneth N. '80
Seidman, Peggy '77

Seidman, Peter '79
Seith, Marjorie R. '86
Seith, Nancy '79
Selden, Daniel '72
Selden, Kenneth '75
Selis, Jane '81
Selis, Leslie '85
Selis, Mary '79
Selis, Susan '82
Selker, Gregory L.
Selman, Kelly '91
Semple, William J., Jr. '52
Semrad, Kurt '94
Semrad, Roderick Q. III '88
Semrad, Susan '89
Senkfor, Steven H. '77
Senor, Stephanie D. '89
Seymour, Geoffrey '53
Seymour, Richard S. '57
Shaffner, Winifred '86
Shafron, Howard A. '85
Shahabi, Albert
Shallenberger, Walter J. '55
Shane, Robert A. '56
Shannon, Edward G. '67
Shannon, Molly H. '83
Shapiro, Clifford J. '74
Shapiro, Mark E. '79
Shapiro, Richard O. '69
Sharlet, Michael J. '87
Sharp, Charles W.
Sharpe, Lee N. '55
Sharpley, DeShawn '86
Shaw, John T.
Shaw, Peter T.
Shaw, Thad '75
Shaw, William G. '54
Sheffield, Duncan
Shelby, Amelia '87
Shelden, Clark L. '73
Shelley, Charles L. '74
Shensa, Robert '85
Shepard, David A.
Shepard, Jack '34
Shepard, Paul C. '43

Shepard, Robert L. '41
Shepherd, Peter '45
Shepherd, Richard '28
Sherman, Charles E. '72
Sherman, John '27
Sherman, Lori '84
Sherman, Megan '89
Sherman, Scott A. '76
Sherman, William R. '86
Sherwin, Dennis
Sherwin, Francis '88
Sherwin, John, Jr. '53
Sherwin, John III '83
Sherwin, Pamela '86
Sherwin, Peter '46
Sherwin, Tyler '89
Shiff, Natalie A. Lowe '83
Shimskey, Donna Sue '81
Shipley, Craig E. '82
Shively, David '69
Shively, Thomas A. '72
Shiverick, Asa III '69
Shiverick, Asa, Jr. '33
Shiverick, Charles '40
Shiverick, David '71
Shiverick, Paul Coombe '71
Shiverick, Reginald C. '74
Shoals, Malcolm E. '88
Sholes, Everett '32-I
Sholes, Justin G., Jr. '27
Shorr, Scott H. '74
Shubert, John M. '74
Shuler, Kenneth A. '68
Shury, Donald P. II '83
Siegel, Barbara '77
Siegel, Laura M. '80
Siegel, Laurence '71
Siegel, Phillip A. '87
Sill, Shari '78
Silver, Ernest '35
Silver, Francis F. '30
Silver, Jonathan M. '75
Silver, M. Theodore '64
Silver, Michael '77
Silver, Richard Blau '64

Silver, Sarah '79
Silver, Theodore '32-II
Silver, Timothy '67
Simeon, James W.
Simeone, Timothy A. '69
Simmons, David O. '82
Simon, Howard A.
Simone, Michael J. '79
Sims, George R. '33
Sims, Harry D., Jr. '34
Sims, John '36
Singer, W. Enrest '70
Singerman, Seth '95
Sipple, Peter W. '54
Skeggs, David C. '74
Skelley, George J. Jr. '70
Skidmore, Daniel R. '58
Skidmore, Joel '66
Skidmore, John A. '67
Skylar, Dean M. '71
Slater, Emily '89
Slater, Mark T. '86
Slavin, Roger S.
Slesh, Dereck '84
Slesh, Kevin '86
Sloan, Peter G. '69
Sloane, Nathaniel '71
Slodov, Leonard '82
Slomak, Erica '99
Small, Caroline '88
Small, Charles '69
Small, William R.
Smeed, James Hawken '43
Smellow, Edwin M.
Smiley, Ghainous W. III '73
Smith, Anthony '87
Smith, Antonia '87
Smith, Bradley '76
Smith, Bruce '70
Smith, Carl '74
Smith, Christopher B. '81
Smith, Clark
Smith, Colin E. '52
Smith, David A. '58
Smith, Dennis '84

Smith, Drew '88
Smith, Dwight '27
Smith, Ethel '82
Smith, Jamil '93
Smith, Jeffrey '77
Smith, Joel '88
Smith, Kimberly N. '86
Smith, Kyle A.
Smith, Leonard B.
Smith, Marcie '78
Smith, Margaret '80
Smith, Meredith W. '85
Smith, Neal '81
Smith, Peter C. '55
Smith, Richardson B. '54
Smith, Russell Y. '53
Smith, Scott '78
Smith, Standish H. '46
Smith, Susan '78
Smoots, Bryan T. '82
Smoots, David '81
Smyser, Andrew '91
Snavely, Jeff '79
Snavely, Molly '78
Snavely, Scott '82
Snavely, Timothy G. '73
Snyder, James H. '49
Snyder, John F. III '69
Snyder, Julie '80
Snyder, Noel K. '80
Snyder, Robert J., Jr. '45
Sobol, Elizabeth '84
Sobol, Steven '81
Sodja, Cheryl L. '83
Sogg, Daniel R. '83
Sogg, Elise '79
Sogg, Stephanie
Sokolski, Anatoli '85
Soles, Jeffrey S. '57
Sones, Frank M. III '66
Soule, Anne '80
Soule, Robert '78
Southgate, Martha E. '78
Southworth, Gregory '79
Southworth, Jeffrey L.

Spacek, Laura '87
Spacek, Lisa A. '86
Spaeth, Douglas '79
Spaeth, Franklin '77
Spangler, Todd K. '84
Spears, Sara McConnell '87
Spellman, Michael W.
Spencer, Christopher '45
Spencer, Michael J. '49
Spiegle, Scott '89
Spiri, Anthony M. '73
Spitz, Lawrence '64
Spivack, John '51
Spock, John '59
Spotz, John D.
Sprey, Malcolm '80
Sprey, Pieter A. '83
Spring, Herbert A., Jr. '36
Springer, Jeffrey J. '65
Springer, Mark L. '66
Springer, Matthew '92
Stack, Andrew '82
Stack, Charles, Jr. '72
Stahl, Arden '49
Stakich, Brian '75
Stakich, Gregory L. '69
Standeven, Warren E. '46
Stanger, Cynthia '80
Stanley, George A., Jr. '29
Stanley, Maureen '86
Stanley, Thomas J. '82
Stanley-Brown, Edward G. '38
Stanzel, Klaus A. '73
Stark, Bradley '73
Stark, Brian D. '67
Stark, Robert '69
Starr, Jonathan E.
Startzman, James '73
Stay, Everitt P. '81
Stay, Finley S. '45
Steadman, Charles T. '65
Stearns, Daniel C. '68
Stearns, James P. '46
Steck, Julie Sharon '86
Steck, Peter C. '57

Steck, William L. '52
Stecker, Mitchell '84
Steckler, Richard L. '70
Steele, Jane E.
Steele, Walter, Jr. '80
Steffee, David W. '88
Steffey, James '85
Stein, Benson M. '73
Stein, Grant T. '74
Stein, Richard '69
Steinbreeder, Harry, Jr. '45
Steinen, Frederick A. '75
Steinen, Philip A. '73
Stenberg, Gretchen S. '78
Stenberg, Sara, O. '79
Stephens, C. David '78
Stephens, Charles L. '46
Stephens, Susan '78
Stephens, Wayne L. '75
Sterling, Benjamin '89
Sterling, Robert L., Jr. '48
Stevens, David F. '69
Stevens, Peter W. '75
Stevenson, Bruce G. '74
Stevenson, David H. '76
Stevenson, John F.
Stevenson, Thomas B. '60
Stewart, Andrew '90
Stewart, Floyd M. '50
Stewart, James B. '55
Stewart, Jeffrey '76
Stewart, John P. '55
Stewart, William P. '54
Stickle, Ralph, Jr. '34
Stief, George H. '58
Stienon, Christopher L.
Stirn, Bradley A. '68
Stirn, Ellen '76
Stirn, Kelvin H. '73
Stites, John C., Jr. '64
Stitt, Douglas F. '69
Stockstill, Raymond III '70
Stoddard, Brooke C. '65
Stoddart, Benjamin '89
Stoddart, Richard '81

Stoker, David H. '54
Stokes, Dana '72
Stoltz, Sheldon D. '70
Stone, Brian '89
Stone, Marc '72
Stone, Michael C. '70
Stone, Sidney J., Jr. '44
Stone, Sidney III '72
Stone, Stanley III '68
Stone, Steven '79
Story, Jennifer L. '81
Stouffer, Christopher F. '66
Stoughton, Roland B. '72
Stowell, Jeremy A. '55
Straffon, Andrew '84
Streeter, Jonathan '86
Streeter, Matthew J. '83
String, Jansen '70
String, Kevin '74
Stroempl, Peter J. '70
Strong, David W. '66
Strong, H. William III '69
Strong, H. William, Jr. '40
Struja, George '76
Studsgaard, Peter K. '70
Stuelpe, Casey '93
Stumpf, Jed '75
Stumpf, Jeffrey R. '74
Stumpf, Jennifer '77
Stumpf, Jeremy R. '81
Stumpf, Joshua R. '79
Stvan, Carol '82
Subel, Jack '84
Stvan, E. Reed '75
Suber, Everett E.
Suckau, Igor N.
Suess, Jessica H.
Sugiuchi, Mark '82
Sukenik, Mark '84
Sulentich, Scott M.
Sullivan, David '81
Sullivan, Ellen '88
Summers, Kurt C. '70
Sundman, Bruce C. '73
Supplee, Theodore L. '45

Surso, James D. '75
Suzuki, Mayo '82
Svete, Jacqueline '82
Swain, Roger '67
Swann, Tiffany '85
Swanner, David A. '82
Swanson, Carl H.
Sweet, John M. '56
Sweet, Richard A. '55
Swetland, David S. '66
Swetland, David W. '32-II
Swetland, F. L., Jr. '31-I
Swetland, Paul H. '36
Swetland, Polly '79
Swick, Alan '81
Swick, Karen A. '83
Syme, John '84
Szabo, Joseph J. III '78

Taber, Thomas C., Jr. '58
Taddeo, Gina '89
Taddeo, Ronald M. '87
Taft, Frederick I. '60
Taft, S. Tucker '70
Taft, Thomas P. '66
Tait, Joseph '89
Takaoka, Butch '85
Takaoka, Charlie '89
Talbot, Jennifer '89
Talley, Kenneth '78
Talley, William, Jr. '76
Tank, Graeme A. '83
Tank, Trevor '85
Tanner, Harvey '35
Taplin, B.H., Jr. '66
Taplin, Benjamin H. '31-I
Taplin, C. Farrand, Jr. '27
Taplin, Charles F. '56
Taplin, Courtenay O. '67
Taplin, David F. '67
Taplin, Frank E., Jr. '31-II
Taplin, Jonathan T. '65
Taplin, Robert '69
Taplin, Thomas E. '35
Tarrant, Bruce A. '80

Tatalick, Laurie M. '83
Taylor, Anthony M. '57
Taylor, Britt '85
Taylor, Camilla B. '89
Taylor, Charles R. '68
Taylor, Donald B. '87
Taylor, Edgar A., Jr. '26
Taylor, George L. '74
Taylor, John C. '41
Taylor, Kristie '89
Taylor, Linda '78
Taylor, Mark '66
Taylor, Myron J. '74
Taylor, Priscilla '89
Taylor, Sarah B.
Taylor, Stevenson M. '35
Taylor, Tobin E. '70
Teagle, Frank H., Jr. '32-I
Teagle, John '25
Teague, Marcus '88
Teitelbaum, Daniel '75
Tennen, Robert S. '71
Tepper, Bennett J. '79
Terkel, Marc A. '73
Terry, Todd B. '92
Testman, Robert J.
Testman, Tamara M. '79
Tewksbury, Michael K., Jr. '66
Tewksbury, Peter A. '59
Thailing, Bruce A. '82
Thal, Mindi '79
Thaler, Jon F.
Thayer, Roger W. '58
Thibodeaux, Page W. '74
Thoburn, Jon S. '86
Thomas, George F. III '66
Thomas, John C. '68
Thomas, Keith '78
Thomas, Markiest '89
Thomas, Scott '89
Thome, Gerald '89
Thompson, George G. '58
Thompson, Jennie '86
Thompson, John '70
Thompson, John '71

Thompson, Maxwell T. '87
Thompson, Michael C. '77
Thompson, W. Hayden '42
Thompson, William '72
Thomson, Alexander '88
Thomson, Bruce M. '70
Thomson, Douglas K. '60
Thomson, Hanna '92
Thornton, John M., III '88
Thorp, John '72
Thorpe, John M. '75
Thynne, Alexis '89
Times, Melissa '88
Titgemeier, Carl J. '81
Todd, James W. '56
Toguchi, Joseph S.
Tolles, King, Jr. '37
Tolles, Morley '39
Tolles, Sheldon H. II '36
Tomaino, Christopher '79
Tomaino, Gregory '80
Tomb, Donald F. '65
Tomlinson, Maurice III '52
Tone, F. Jerome IV '73
Tone, Wolfe '84
Tong, Henry '84
Tong, Michael '86
Toomey, John '78
Toomey, Mary Rita '79
Torch, Christopher '70
Torch, Leland F.
Towell, Garrett Winsor '52
Towell, Timothy L. '50
Towl, Peter '39
Tracy, David F. '60
Tracy, John
Tracy, John '66
Trattner, Marsha '81
Trattner, Robert B. '85
Traub, Ronald M. '69
Trautman, Jonathan K.
Trautman, Michael S. '72
Travis, Camille '85
Travis, Ingrid '87
Traxler, Martino

Treco, Frank III '72
Treco, Gordon '77
Treco, James D. '73
Tremain, H. Alan '51
Treuhaft, Jeff '87
Treuhaft, Jennifer '94
Trigg, David M. '72
Trigg, Eric B. '70
Troccolo, Grace '90
Troyan, Douglas '74
Trumbo, James W. '75
Tschetter, Philip G. '88
Tubman, Charles S., Jr. '69
Tucker, Christopher W. '73
Tucker, Dan S. '45
Tucker, David E.
Tucker, Paul L.
Tucker, Peter C. '83
Tucker, Robert '93
Tucker, Seth '80
Tuckerman, John L. '43
Tuckerman, Robert W. '48
Tufts, Jonathan V. '70
Tupta, Robert R. Jr.
Tupta, Robert '77
Tupta, Rosemary R.
Turi, Jeffrey '81
Turner, Gregory C. '68
Turner, Jack '34
Turner, Robert '36
Turner, Sherrie '85
Turocy, Gregory '82
Tuteur, John, Jr. '56
Tuttle, Howard M., Jr. '67
Tuttle, William O. '73
Tyler, Bartlett, Jr. '43
Tyner, Christopher E. '87
Tyner, Laurel '89
Tyner, Sarah '84
Tyus, Ivan '87
Udelson, Thomas '69
Uebele, Curtis D. '86
Uebele, Jennifer A. '83
Uebele, Victor '87
Uible, David '57

Uible, Frank R., Jr. '50
Ullman, Harlan '81
Umans, Stephen '66
Unger, Alison L. '81
Unger, James '85
Upson, David R., Jr. '75
Urban, George J. '24
Urban, Keith A.
Uytterlinde, Michael '64

Vail, Lawrence J.W.
Vail, Thomas V.H., Jr. '73
Valerio, Melanie '87
Van, Thavy '91
Van Antwerp, John M. '82
Van Dijk, Gerard P. '82
Van Dijk, Leo '80
Van Dijk, Raymond
Van Duzer, Ashley Mac '66
Van Erp, Peter '73
Van Horn, Donald R., Jr. '59
Van Horn, Thomas H. '64
Van Landeghem, John '79
Van Nest, Thomas L. '65
Van Ordstrand, John S. '66
Van Osdol, Peter '74
Van Sicklen, Charles '32-II
Varanese, Anne '87
Varanese, Kathleen '84
Varonoff, John O. '64
Vasil, Jennifer '97
Vasil, Stacy '95
Vasil, Stephen '92
Vasilopoulos, Pelops '45
Vazquez, Heidie '89
Veale, Tinkham, III '65
Velick, Jeffrey '84
Venable, John E., Jr. '47
Verga, John L. '68
Vermillion, Randall L. '74
Vernon, Traci '84
Vese, Rodney '71
Vignos, Paul J., III '69
Vilas, Malcolm B. IV '88
Vilas, Malcolm B. III '59

Vilas, Malcolm B., Jr. '33
Vilas, Towar N. '65
Vincent, Elvin B.
Viny, Joseph '80
Visconsi, Anthoni II '71
Visconsi, Charles '89
Visconsi, Dominic, Jr. '77
Visconsi, Elliott '90
Visdos, Edward J. '81
Vitale, Richard
Vitale, Theodore H., Jr.
Vogel, Andrew D. '86
Vogel, Perry K. '59
Volk, John A. '70
Volk, Larry '80
Volk, Michael '79
Von Faulkenhausen, K. '84
von Koschembahr, Daniel '70
Von Weise, Bradford '81
Von Weise, Charles W. '82
Votaw, John F.
Wachs, Jay Daniel '86
Wade, Jeptha H. III '39
Wagenlander, James F. '66
Wagenlander, Robert L. '65
Wagenlander, William '56
Waggoner, David Edward '87
Waggoner, Gregory '89
Wagley, Ernest N., Jr. '57
Wagley, John R. '46
Wagner, Michael '81
Walborn, Warren '81
Walentschak, Erich M. '89
Walker, David S.
Walker, Willard F., Jr. '36
Wallace, Hume '33
Wallace, Mark S. '74
Wallace, Robert '36
Wallace, William '39
Wallach, David L. '55
Wallen, Drew R. '65
Wallich, David M. '74
Walsh, Philip K. '45
Walters, Jeffrey '84
Wang, Douglas '74

Wang, Richard
Ward, Daniel '75
Ward, James Gary '76
Ward, Jeffrey '78
Wareing, William A. '36
Wargo, Edward H. III '69
Warner, Andrew '54
Warner, David E. '42
Warner, Diane E. '78
Warner, Greg '75
Warner, Hoyt D. '53
Warner, Jeffrey '77
Warner, Karen J. '83
Warner, Steven '81
Warnke, Daniel C. '50
Warren, Daniel '74
Warren, Edward L. '79
Warren, James A. '83
Warren, Mark J. '71
Warren, Martha '75
Warren, Thomas '84
Warshawsky, Jon M. '85
Warshawsky, Beth '88
Warshawsky, Kittie '85
Warshawsky, Steven '87
Washington, Christopher '89
Washington, Michael '70
Wasserstrom, David '85
Wasserstrom, Kay '78
Watkins, George H., Jr. '70
Watson, Andrew '84
Watson, David '81
Watson, Gregory C. '67
Watson, Jay '78
Watson, Susan '88
Watson, William L.
Watt, Alan '94
Waxman, Gregg E. '88
Waxman, Todd '84
Weathers, Donna R. '78
Webb, David '78
Webb, Douglas '72
Webb, George T., Jr. '35
Weber, Julie '80
Weber, Kathryn '82

Weber, Walter T. '50
Weber, Wayne A.
Weber, William M. '54
Webster, David G. '65
Webster, Graham T. '27
Webster, Graham '72
Webster, Harvey '69
Webster, John F.
Webster, John T. '66
Webster, Judd '45
Webster, Paul '68
Webster, Ralph B., Jr. '67
Webster, Robert C. '32-II
Webster, Robert C., Jr. '59
Wechsler, Steven A. '69
Wedren, Andrea D.
Wedren, Craig B. '87
Weidenkopf, David W. '42
Weidenthal, David '80
Weidlein, John F. '51
Weil, Alice Elizabeth '86
Weil, Matthew J. '89
Weil, Michael '85
Weil, Robert H. '84
Weinberg, Richard '70
Weingold, Beth '78
Weinstein, David A. '69
Weinstein, James, N. '67
Weinstein, Martin B. '65
Weir, David R. '27
Weir, David R., Jr. '56
Weir, Gordon C. '55
Weir, James C. '25
Weir, James R. '57
Weir, William C. '27
Weir, William E. '54
Weisberg, Vickie '77
Weisblat, Heidi Jo '85
Weisblat, Jodi '86
Weisblat, Joel '82
Weiskopf, Bernard B. '71
Weisman, Mark A. '74
Weisman, Mitchell '76
Weiss, Andrea '82
Weiss, Anne '92

Weiss, Christian A. III '83
Weiss, Ellen '79
Weiss, Jill '88
Weiss, Jonathan D. '79
Weiss, Leah '89
Weiss, Loren '81
Weiss, Michael '75
Weit, L. Ramsay '65
Weitz, Donald A. '46
Weizman, David '76
Weizman, Robert '80
Welch, Charles A. '74
Welch, Peter T. '68
Weld, David A. '76
Wellman, Daniel T. '30
Wellman, Daniel T. '56
Wendel, Fred III '67
Wengerd, Scott '88
Werme, Eric J. '68
Wert, James W. '99
Wertz, Orrin B., Jr. '43
West, Deborah B. '88
West, Frederic W. '68
West, Howard L. '86
West, Nycole '98
Westbrook, Charles '81
Westbrook, Leslie '85
Westbrook, William L. '83
Whelan, Kerry '79
Whelan, Michael '82
Whisler, Sandra '79
Whisnant, Isaac
White, Barney C. '72
White, Bradford '76
White, C.J. '94
White, Charles B. '40
White, Charles L. '68
White, Christopher G. '75
White, Clifford '78
White, Daniel '82
White, David '65
White, David '73
White, David '85
White, Erick D. '83
White, Frank F., Jr. '71

Winston, Martin B. '65
Winterhalter, Kelly L. '00
Winterhalter, Kristen '97
Wirt, Robert E. Jr. '83
Wischmeyer, Henry G., Jr. '36
Wise, David '72
Wixom, Andrew H. '82
Wolf, Josh '91
Wolf, Peter H.
Wolpaw, Dierdre J. '88
Wolpaw, Erik F. '85
Wolstein, Scott '70
Wood, A.Wilson '35
Wood, Alexander T., Jr. '46
Wood, Charles A., Jr.
Wood, David B. III '83
Wood, Gretchen '88
Wood, Kathryn '91
Wood, Lindsay W. '55
Wood, Robert A., III
Wood, William '75
Wood, William '84
Woodburn, David '89
Woodridge, Harold '77
Woodward, Robert B. '36
Wormly, Carl M. '87
Worsoe, Niels '70
Worthington, Edward E. '35
Worthington, Edward E. '67
Worthington, John '34
Worthington, Randall W.
Wright, Edward M. '71
Wright, Emily E. '87
Wright, Evan A. '83
Wright, Herbert T. '51
Wright, John D., Jr. '50
Wright, John H. '50
Wright, Katherine '82
Wright, Michael '79
Wright, Norton W. '50
Wright, Tom '51
Wyatt, Elizabeth '89
Wykoff, Peter C. '48
Wykoff, Thomas W. '48
Wynne, Craig '74

Wynne, Thomas '69
Wyse, Robert B. '73
Wyse, Scott B. '85

Xavier, Patrick G. '81

Yang, Allison '02
Yang, Jonathan '98
Yankovic, Gerald '69
Yankovic, Mark J. '70
Yankovic, Robert A.
Yarus, Jeffrey M. '69
Yarus, Susan '78
Yen, David '76
Yen, Dominic '75
Yocom, Nathan T. '70
Yoon, Edward '87
Yoon, Frederick '86
York, Frederick W.
York, Robert H. '43
Young, David '69
Young, Jordon '96
Young, Matthew C. '83
Young, Stephen '78
Yulish, Daniel J. '83
Yulish, David M. '77
Yulish, Jonathan '80

Zabell, Jeremy '91
Zabell, Kurtis '87
Zaller, John '88
Zeefe, Justin '95
Zeit, John '70
Zeit, Paul '69
Zellinger, David W. '82
Zellinger, Deborah '87
Zellner, Hillary '85
Zellner, Naomi Beth '86
Zelman, Henry L. '72
Zevin, Robert B. '52
Zigman, Frank J.
Zimmerman, Henry A. III '74
Zimmerman, Warren '72
Zimring, Matthew '84
Zingale, Laura '86

James A. Hawken	1915-1924
John J. Carney*	1924-1925
James A. Hawken	1925-1926
John J. Carney	1926-1931
Charles R. Stephens**	1931-1932
Carl N. Holmes	1932-1955
Charles R. Stephens**	1955-1956
Richard W. Day	1956-1964
Edward R. Kast	1964-1970
James B. Young	1970-1975
Ralph T. King**	1975
Edward M. Read**	1975-1976
T. Douglas Stenberg	1976-

*James A. Hawken was on sabbatical during the 1924-1925 school year.
**Interim Headmaster

	Term
Raymond Q. Armington	1963-68
Sandra H. Austin	1988-Present
Everett M. Baker	1944-47
Edward T. Bartlett*	1951-70
Jeffrey M. Biggar	1982-Present
James C. Boland	1985-Present
B. Patterson Bole, Jr.*	1936-70
Roberta A. Bole	1929-31
Charles B. Bolton***	1947-76
Charles P. Bolton	1976-Present
Frances P. Bolton	1929-31
Willis B. Boyer	1963-70
Chester K. Brooks	1932-38
Harvey H. Brown, Jr.	1944-51
Willard W. Brown	1965-67
Alvin T. Burch	1942-45
Howard F. Burns*	1941-67
Robert M. Calfee	1931-38
Stephens Chamberlin	1937-45
John R. Chandler	1939-51
Richard S. Cole	1971-82
E. Mandell deWindt	1967-72
Henry F. Evans	1951-58
Whitney Evans**	1980-87
Morris Everett**	1951-83
Leigh Fabens	1982-Present
Daniel B. Ford*	1941-71
Robert I. Gale, Jr.	1967-71
Myriam Gresham	1986-Present
Sally P. Gries	1983-Present
Ray J. Groves	1977-86
John A. Hadden	1937-42
James A. Hawken	1929-30
Joel B. Hayden	1929-31
Sherman S. Hayden	1931-36
Horace F. Henriques	1932-38
Meacham Hitchcock	1963-86
Kenneth P. Horsburgh	1989-Present
David S. Ingalls, Jr.	1969-Present

*Former life trustee
**Current life trustee
***Chairman of the board of trustees

	Term
James D. Ireland**	1962-75
R. Livingston Ireland, Jr.	1931-81
Ronald J. James	1989-Present
Ralph T. King**	1970-77
George D. Kirkham	1978-88
Hall Kirkham	1952-66
Harold F. Kneen	1947-52
Marcia LaRiche	1982-Present
John F. Lewis	1977-89
Ellen Long	1976-82
Ted M. Luntz	1978-88
William P. Madar	1989-Present
Joseph J. Mahovlic	1986-Present
William C. McCoy, Jr.**	1969-86
John P. McWilliams	1937-38
Dixon Morgan*	1955-75
Robert W. Morse	1967-71
Suzanne M. Murray	1973-80
Joseph R. Nutt, Jr.	1939-52
George Oliva, Jr.	1970-79
William J. O'Neill, Jr.	1984-Present
Harvey G. Oppmann	1983-Present
Nicholas Peay	1988-Present
David V. Ragone	1981-85
Alfred M. Rankin**	1958-83
Charles A. Ratner	1986-Present
Lincoln Reavis	1974-Present
Nancy G. Rome	1975-84
John T. Scott	1937-62
Ellery Sedgwick, Jr.**	1958-73
Henry E. Sheffield	1929-31
John Sherwin, Jr.	1972-Present
Asa Shiverick	1931-32
Howard F. Stirn	1971-Present
C. Farrand Taplin, Jr.	1943-67
Andrea Taylor	1979-88
Frank S. Treco, Jr.	1967-77
Robert E. Vinson	1929-31
Willard F. Walker	1937-38
John T. Webster	1931-46
David R. Weir**	1960-82
Thomas H. White	1931-51
Alton W. Whitehouse, Jr.	1970-79
Lawrence J. Wilker	1987-Present

*Former life trustee
**Current life trustee

320

Appendix V: Carl N. Holmes Award Recipients

Harvey Brooks '32-I	1963-1964
Charles B. Bolton '27	1965-1966
David R. Weir '27	1979-1980
Morris Everett '27	1981-1982
Meacham Hitchcock '42	1983-1984
Scott R. Inkley '36	1985-1986
Frank E. Taplin, Jr. '31-II	1986-1987
James D. Ireland '32	1987-1988
Willard W. Brown '32	1988-1989
Lincoln Reavis '48	1989-1990

Scott W. Phillips	1976
Kathleen R. Bole	1977
Mary Bresnicky	1978
Clara Mackenzie	1979
Elizabeth Gibans	1980
Kenneth Roby	1981
Ethan H. Cohen	1982
David A. Feingold	1983
Andrew C. Watson	1984
Robert Henninge	1985
Griffith Hsu	1986
Jessica S. Frankel	1987
John Zaller	1988
Jennifer Talbot	1989

Appendix VII: Hawken Alumni Association Presidents

Alvah C. Drake	1925
Barnard Prescott	1926
Sherman S. Hayden	1927
James C. Weir	1928-1929
Edgar A. Taylor, Jr.	1930
Thomas B. Grandin	1931
Henry C. Osborn, Jr.	1932
William R. Nash	1933
No record	1934-1936
James C. Weir	1937
Frederick R. White, Jr.	1938
John B. Calfee	1939
Guthrie Bicknell	1940
Frank E. Taplin, Jr.	1941
No record	1942-1946
Willard W. Brown	1947
Charles Hickox	1948
Fayette Brown, Jr.	1949
Morris Everett	1950
Malcolm B. Vilas, Jr.	1951-1952
Dixon Morgan	1953
Robert Y. White	1954
John F. Wilson, Jr.	1955
Benjamin H. Taplin	1956
A. Benedict Schneider	1957
Kenyon C. Bolton	1958
William B. Chamberlin, Jr.	1959
Harry C. Royal, Jr.	1960
James D. Ireland	1961
Cyrus S. Eaton, Jr.	1962
Meacham Hitchcock	1962-1964
John Newell III	1964-1966
Stevenson M. Taylor	1966-1967
H. William Strong, Jr.	1967-1968
Clark E. Bruner	1968-1969
Charles O. Newell	1969-1970
John Sherwin Jr.	1970-1972
Malcolm B. Vilas III	1972-1974
Jeffrey M. Biggar	1974-1976

Christopher Royan	1976-1978
Robert T. Page	1978-1980
John B. Calfee, Jr.	1980-1982
H. Clark Harvey, Jr.	1982-1984
Kenneth Dettelbach	1984-1986
Fred Wendel III	1986-1988
J. Albert Klauss	1988-1990

James C. Weir	1923
Sherman S. Hayden	1924
Charles B. Bolton	1925
Edgar A. Taylor, Jr.	1926
David R. Weir	1927
Henry C. Osborn, Jr.	1928
Richard Inglis, Jr.	1929
A. Benedict Schneider	1930
Frederick L. Swetland, Jr.	1931
G. Armour Craig	1932
Robert H. Morse	1933
Peter S. Hitchcock	1934
Roger E. Clapp	1935
Douglas S. Craig	1936
John A. Newman	1937
Richard M. Douglas	1938
Leyton E. Carter, Jr.	1939
Samuel N. Douglas	1940
David G. Mock	1941
William S. Allen	1942
William C. Mohler	1943
Sidney J. Stone, Jr.	1944
Ross A. Kipka	1945
William C. Prior	1946
William P. Offenbacher	1947
John C. Little	1948
Walter R. Kirkham	1949
John F. Reichert IV	1950
Joseph R. Nutt III	1951
Robert B. Zevin	1952
Brian B. Foy	1953
Frank R. Hill	1954
Kim D. Mann	1955
Dudley S. Blossom III	1956
William S. Manuel III	1957
Richard E. Burney, Jr.	1958
Timothy C. LaRiche	1959
Nelson H. Rose	1960
David L. Calfee	1961

Adams, Mary T.	1926-1934
Adams, Robert S.	1925-1934
Ahrendt, Agnes	1922-1923
Akers, Robert H.	1937-1939
Aldred, Richard	1961-1963
Aldrich, Wells E.	1922-1923
Allman, Helen	1965-1980
Anderson, George A.	1961-1965
Anderson, Katherine (Friedell)	1968-1975
Armbruster, Cynthia (Reid)	1967-1974
Armington, David E.	1949-1964
August, Harry W.	1968-1970
Aylard, Horace R.	1923-1942
Baker, Howard P.	1964-1969
Baker, William T.S.	1924-1933
Baldwin, David J.	1964-1965
Bassage, Winfield J.	1965-1968
Beatty, Edward F., Jr.	1952-1953
Beck, Carl T.	1971-1975
Beecher, Eugene L.	1959-1961
Bell, Muriel S.	1942-1968
Bennett, Ruth R.	1935-1967
Benning, Hazelle	1935-1964
Bentley, Bradford M.	1939-1940
Berchek, Susan	1982-1984
Berry, Jane G.	1971-1972
Bickford, [Miss]	1917-1919
Bidlack, Nancy	1981-1982
Bird, Jackson	1941-1947
Blau, Zeda W.	1964-1975
Blount, Viola M.	1958-1963
Bluhm, Leonard D.	1952-1954
Boethelt, Martha L.	1952-1953
Bogart, Cornelia	1963-1969
Bogatay, Ruth B.	1953-1972
Boles, Laurence H., Jr.	1964-1965
Bolton, Douglas W.	1922-1927
Bonhomme, Georges	1966-1967
Bonhomme, Renee	1966-1967

Boyle, Louise S.	1965-1971
Bradley, Rosie	1978-1988
Bragdon, Clifford R.	1928-1938
Bramble, Guy A.	1972-1975
Breisch, Mary A. (Wolfe)	1979-1986
Brewer, John N.	1950-1953
Brewer, Richard	1969-1970
Brewer, Robert B.	1926-1936
Brewer, [Mrs. Robert]	1926-1932
Bridgeman, James	1952-1953
Britton, Lynda R.	1961-1962
Brooks, Elias	1966-1972
Brown, Calvin	1975-1977
Brown, Jeffrey L.	1974-1978
Brown, Martha K.	1969-1989
Brown, Stanley C.	1971-1973
Brugnoletti, Claire	1974-1979
Buchanon, Penelope (Draper)	1958-1974
Budd, Inez	1968-1986
Buehl, Lydia S.	1952-1960
Burditt, Eleanor C.	1937-1942
Burger, June M.	1951-1952
Burgin, Charlotte	1978-1979
Butcher, Joanne	1973-1975
Buynak, Angeline	1965-1984
Campbell, Jeffrey	1970-1971
Canfield, Barbara H.	1965-1966
Caprez, Marian (Koenig)	1978-1979
Carey, Leonard R.	1956-1987
Carney, John J.	1917-1930
Carr, Charles M.	1966-1967, 1984-1985
Carr, Jan N.	1968-1977
Carter, Nathaniel	1970-1981
Carter, Warren T.	1928-1930
Cassill, Jean K.	1964-1965
Cerutti, Paul J.	1980-1981
Cervenka, Mary	1971-1978
Charbonneau, Manon P.	1959-1966
Chordas, Mary Ann	1979-1980
Christian, Guy N.	1925-1931
Christopher, Mike	1963-1977
Ciarlillo, John	0000-0000
Clawson, Emeline	1964-1981

Clements, Robert M.	1965-1966
Cleminshaw, Russell H.	1961-1962
Clowes, Margaret	1959-1961
Coffey, Douglas 1962-1967	
Coffin, Mark T.	1974-1977
Cohen, Margot	1970-1972
Coles, Alice	1969-1974
Conkey, Albert B., Jr.	1936-1939
Connelly, Edward M.	1951-1953
Corke, Kenyon	1965-1970
Coulton, Stewart D.	1961-1969
Coverdale, Susan C.	1981-1987
Covert, Seward	1927-1929
Cox, Waymon	1966-1977
Cramer, Kenyon C.	1969-1980
Crawford, Elizabeth S.	1946-1959
Crink, Jeanette M.	1951-1953
Critchlow, Florence	1966-1977
Crosby, Jean A.	1958-1959
Cumming, William N.	1971-1975
Cutler, Margaret	1976-1979
D'Amato, Kaye	1980-1985
D'Amico, Maria	1978-1982
Danforth, [Mr.]	1943-1945
Daniels, Mildred H.	1948-1958
Davies, Richard A.	1963-1981, 1988-1989
Davis, Sally M.	1963-1964
Day, Katherine M.	1958-1964
Day, Richard W.	1956-1964
Deluca, Sarah	1963-1983
Depalma, Anthony	1962-1971
Deter, Deneise C.	1979-1982
Dexter, Richard	1923-1927
Dial, Richard B.	1944-1945
Dickenson, Richard H.	1942-1947
Dietrich, George R.	1963-1964
Dimpsey, Frank J.	1944-1963
Dirks, John W.	1973-1974
Dodd, Kathy	1977-1979
Dowling, Glenn A.	1921-1922
Drabek, James	1980-1982
Droese, Nora	1943-1945

Dunlop, Katherine M.	1961-1975
Durfee, Rodman H.	1951-1952
Dusenbury, Zoann L.	1961-1987
Eames, Hamilton	1937-1947,
	1954-1967
Eells, Elizabeth M.	1959-1962
Egeberg, Roger O.	1933-1942
Eivers, Lois	1956-1957
Esselstyn, Erik C.	1963-1964
Evans, Helen	1944-1946
Everett, Cynthia T.	1962-1964
Everett, Morris, Jr.	1974-1981
Ewers, Lois G.	1956-1957
Fairfield, Mary C.	1974-1980
Farwell, James E.	1964-1970
Fatica, Domenic A.	1968-1972
Ferris, Gerald L.	1962-1964
Fields, Louise M.	1957-1969
Filkins, Nadia	1982-1986
Fiordalis, C. Keith	1969-1970
Fiordalis, Stuart C.	1970-1972
Fiordalis, Vincent II	1964-1970
Fioritto, Pauline M.	1959-1971
Fleming, Nehemiah	1980-1987
Foley, Pamela S.	1980-1981
Forbes, Signe W.	1979-1981
Fouts, Zoe L.	1929-1932
Fraley, [Mr.]	1918-1922
Franklin, Roger C.	1947-1948
Freudenberg, [Mr.]	1916-1917
Friedell, Katherine	1968-1971
Friedlander, Barbara R.	1969-1971
Frye, William D.	1974-1976
Furrer, Arnold F.	1928-1930
Furst, Herbert F.	1945-1984
Fusco, Henry	1967-1969
Galemmo, Eleanor	1978-1982
Gallagher, Kathryn M.	1968-1977
Gandee, Charles	1962-1964
Garfield, Edward W., Jr.	1953-1957
Gerson, Frederick	1959-1963
Giles, Robert H.	1964-1965

Hildebrande, Arthur	1986-1987
Hines, Frank B., Jr.	1937-1960
Hinman, R. Bruce	1924-1925
Hoerr, Janet U.	1961-1981
Hoerr, Stanley O., Jr.	1961-1964
Holden, Cora	1917-1921
Holden, Herman L.	1971-1973
Holmes, Carl N.	1932-1955
Hopkins, Margaret A.	1981-1982
Horn, Todd	1977-1979
Horton, Thayer	1923-1944
Horvat, Eugene	1976-1978
Hough, Graydon M.	1937-1939
Howard, Edna A.	1917-1926
Howard, Maurice C.	1923-1928
Hruby, Joseph, Jr.	1980-1984
Huffman, Eugene	1984-1986
Hunter, Chandu H.	1979-1984
Ibsch, Raymond	1966-1968
Inglis, Anne E.	1958-1960
Inglis, Richard, Jr.	1934-1937, 1958
Ingwersen, Sheila (Murphy)	1974-1977
Inzano, Anna	1956-1969
Iorio, Louise	1960-1981
Ismail, Yuksel M.	1962-1966
Itschner, Daniel D.	1959-1960
Jackson, Samuel B.C.	1960-1970
Jackson, Sarah	1970-1982
Jeffery, Jay M.	1969-1985
Johnson, Arnold B.	1953-1954
Johnson, Marjorie H.	1970-1988
Johnston, Sarah	1978-1981
Joiner, Inez S.	1964-1966
Jones, Joyce A.	1974-1976
Jones, Lucretia B.	1922-1929
Jones, Malcolm K.	1947-1951
Jones, Robert J.	1967-1968
Jones, Suzanne	1979-1984
Jopling, Anita	1926-1928
Jordan, Glenn C.	1945-1947
Joslyn, Robert I.	1965-1969

Judson, William V.	1938-1941
Junod, Henri P.	1966-1967
Jusseaume, Richard	1974-1979
Kark, Stephen J.	1968-1971
Kast, Edward R.	1964-1970
Kaye, Michael	1961-1966
Kelly, Elizabeth F.	1958-1960
Kenepp, Paul L.	1964-1965
Kennerdell, Martha (Barker)	1947-1952
Kimmel, Judith	1972-1978
Kinel, Jon P.	1973-1984
King, Ralph T.	1975
Kingdon, [Mr.]	1917-1918
Kirchhoff, Berta	1982-1986
Kittredge, Eileen	1968-1972
Klein, Stephen	1974-1977
Kleve, Tim	1980-1988
Knutson, Elton H.	1961-1970
Kovel, Terry	1960-1971
Kuss, Kathleen	1979-1987
Lako, Carol	1976-1978
Law, S. Peter	1949-1951
Lazarus, Mary Kay	1965-1966
Leece, Dorothy L.	1925-1926
Leishman, A. Irwin	1924-1925
Lerner, Nancy	1982-1989
Lewis, John R.	1962-1967
Lewis, Ward	1925-1926
Liebe, Edel T.	1923-1927
Lightbody, Patricia C.	1958-1967
Lightbody, Thomas	1963-1964
Lindblad, Barbara S.	1960-1963
Lindblade, Eric N.	1951-1956
Lipscomb, Jeanne	1987-1989
Long, Jane	1954-1955
Loud, Robert L.	1961-1964
Lovell, James G.	1969-1978
Lowe, K. Elmo	1922-1923
Luehrs, Fannie M.	1917-1946
Lusk, Patricia	1981-1988
MacDonald, Douglas	1954-1989
MacIntyre, Maureen	1980-1985

MacMahon, A. Ross	1917-1951
MacMaster, Joseph	1971-1975
MacMaster, Ruth W.	1961-1976
McArthur, Lucille M.	1964-1974
McCabe, Jeanette	1934-1938,
	1949-1959
McCarthy, Francis E.	1933-1970
McCarthy, John H.	1924-1940
McCarthy, Winifred E.	1933-1968
McCloud, Ludella	1967-1978
McCormac, Virginia	1970-1973
McCormack, Valerie (Fawcett)	1980-1984
McCullough, Elizabeth	1962-1989
McCully, Gail	1981-1989
McElroy, Michael I.	1970-1973
McGraw, Frank	1970-1978
McInvaille, William	1984-1986
McMahan, Betteanne	1981-1985
McNealy, Lincoln	1962-1964
Makepeace, Gabriella	1968-1971
Malburg, Raymond L.	1962-1968
Mamere, Herbert L.	1950-1968
Mann, Dianne G.	1967-1968
Mann, John	1967-1968
Mann, Philip	1973-1977
Mann, Robert	1978-1979
Manning, Christine	1981-1982
Manuel, Richard	1958-1959
Marcus, Herbert L.	1951-1952
Marks, A. Louise	1971-1978
Marrapodi, Frank	1952-1955
Marsee, Charles	1968-1980
Marsh, Richard L.	1970-1972
Martin, Alice B.	1977-1980
Martin, Donald H., II	1969-1974
Martin, Phyllis	1972-1974
Mastroine, Mario J.	1972-1973
Mattingly, D. Kevin	1980-1984
Mekota, Mark	1980-1986
Mekota, Michael	1978-1982
Melcher, Daniel	1978-1979
Melzer, Barbara O.	1972-1974
Mercer, Russell B.	1921-1923
Meyer, John B.	1967-1968
Meyer, Niklaus E.	1967-1968

Miller, Frances E.	1946-1947
Miller, Sally A.	1985-1986
Miltz, William J.	1981-1986
Mineo, Ann	1952-1953
Mlakar, Betsy B.	1977-1978
Mohlo, Anthony	1959-1960
Moody, Barbara C.	1962-1964
Moore, Charles K.	1951-1952
Moore, Patricia H.	1959-1964
Morlock, Geraldine	1942-1950
Morrison, Stephen A.	1970-1974
Motika, Peter T.	1986-1987
Motto, Joseph C.	1915-1928
Moviel, Dorcas	1968-1983
Mulroy, John R.	1964-1969
Murray, Suzanne M.	1981-1989
Nagle, Ashely P.	1916-1917
Nemeth, Charles D.	1970-1980
Newcomb, [Mr.]	1920-1921
Nezovich, Ann N.	1971-1979
Nold, Marcella	1973-1979
Nordstrom, Joan T.	1963-1969
Nulsen, Gabriella (Makepeace)	1968-1971
O'Flaherty, Sharon	1977-1979
O'Rourke, Janet S.	1966-1972
O'Rourke, Thomas C.	1967-1969
Ozier, Artie	1964-1976
Page, Joan B.	1981-1988
Palansky, Charles	1972-1977
Parent, Carolyn B.	1967-1971
Parker, Harlan	1963-1964
Patch, Ralph	1927-1931
Paull, Carol	1970-1971
Payne, Gerald	1988-1989
Peck, Hermon	1938-1939
Peckler, Barbara V.	1972-1974
Perry, [Mr.]	1921-1922
Petersen, Curtis E.	1962-1971
Petronzio, Mary	1972-1987
Phelan, William F.	1915-1924
Pickering, John K.	1961-1973
Pierce, Daniel	1984-1987

Pierson, William H., Jr.	1936-1938
Pierson, Agnes	1922-1923
Pietsch, Ewald C.	1924-1925
Pope, Patricia (Crane)	1958-1961
Porrata, Mary Ann (Isles)	1981-1989
Porter, Nancy	1965-1966
Poutasse, Charles A.	1948-1980
Pryor, Judy	1974-1979
Putnam, D. Neil	1976-1979
Raish, John E.	1939-1962
Read, Edward M.	1975-1976
Redmond, Barbara T.	1966-1969
Relic, Peter T.	1959-1969
Rich, George E., Jr.	1971-1972
Richardson, ?	1944-1945
Rickard, Rodger S.	1958-1968
Rico, Francis M.	1981-1984
Riser, George J.	1970-1975
Robert, [Mr.]	1918-1919
Roberts, David C.	1961-1970
Robey, Lorimer	1941-1969
Robinson, Ronald D.	1968-1984
Rosen, Jerome P.	1962-1963
Rosewater, Gail A.	1969-1971
Ross, Jeanne A.	1971-1985
Rossman, Edward	1962-1964
Roundy, Paul C.	1929-1932
Roush, Linda F.	1971-1973
Rowan, F. Jack	1968-1970
Rowlands, [Miss]	1918-1921
Ruff, Henry	1977-1989
Russell, David W.	1928-1934
Russell, Gerald	1978-1985
Rycik, Mary	1980-1983
Sabroff, Melissa	1984-1985
Safford, Margery	1966-1979
Saha, Prosanta K.	1957-1962
Sanders, Ollie	1982-1984
Sanford, [Mr.]	1917-1918
Sawyer, George G.	1916-1917
Schilling, Susan	1878-1980
Schlesinger, Michael	1968-1972
Schmidt, Andrew	1958-1959

Schwartz, David L.	1970-1971
Schwartz, Martha W.	1959-1970
Seidel, Mary Lee R.	1966-1968
Servis, Mark E.	1979-1980
Sheffield, [Mr.]	1921-1922
Shelar, James W.	1967-1968
Sherwin, Brian	1961-1970
Short, Ambrose	1959-1960
Simpson, J. Fletcher	1970-1972
Sipple, Elmer P.	1925-1959
Slavin, Robert A.	1924-1925
Sloane, Marcia (Elbrand)	1977-1979
Small, Ellena C.	1968-1972
Small, Robert J.	1968-1972
Smeed, H. Mortimer	1916-1960
Smith, Geraldine F.	1944-1948
Smith, Gilbert M.	1929-1936
Smith, H. Alan	1970-1971
Smith, Isiah	1964-1986
Smith, Mildred L.	1968-1986
Smith, Paul J.	1984-1987
Sokol, Gene	1967-1968
Somerville, Jeanie F.	1922-1933
Somerville, [Mrs. D.]	1922-1933
Spahn, Elizabeth D.	1969-1972
Spicer, Robert	1975-1981
Sprague, Bruce	1978-1980
Stanard, Keith	1984-1988
Starr, Naomi	1960-1962
Steadman, Beatrice	1970-1978
Steadman, Charles, Jr.	1975-1977
Stegmiller, Robert F.	1984-1985
Steinen, Ramon F.	1960-1964
Stephens, Charles R.	1916-1959
Stephens, Charles L.	1960-1987
Stoudnor, Jan	1982-1988
Stoughton, Gwen	1960-1962
Strauss, Jill L.	1972-1973
Strong, Claudia (Fulton)	1978-1981
Strong, David W.	1971-1972
Stuyvesant, Mary Ann	1962-1966
Swain, John D.	1977-1986
Taylor, Paul	1970-1978
Thauer, Nancy (McHenry)	1950-1952

Thomson, Chilton	1962-1969
Timoteo, Robert J.	1965-1974
Titus, Carol F. (Arnold)	1963-1966
Tomaino, Annette T.	1968-1970
Tomaino, Bruno J.	1968-1970
Towell, Timothy	1958-1961
Trautman, Frank S.	1962-1971
Travis, Fern (Gordon)	1928-1936
Tricky, [Mr.]	1918-1919
Tucker, Barbara H.	1967-1973
Tupta, Robert R.	1970-1978
Tweedy, [Mr.]	1919-1920
Valentine, [Mrs. Harry]	1925-1926
Vogel, Emma K.	1952-1970
Vogel, Roberta (Liston)	1959-1960
Wallace, Robin S.	1918-1921, **1928-1934**,
Walton, Constance	1984-1986
Warner, Keith L.	1966-1979
Watkins, Elizabeth	1964-1980
Webb, Martha	1978-1981
Webster, Robert S., Jr.	1968-1970
Webster, Susan S.	1987-1989
Wendel, Joyce	1985-1986
Weske, Katherine	1962-1982
West, Leroy	1963-1973
West, Polly (Ayers)	1969-1971
Weston, Simon H.	1962-1965
Wheeler, Jan K.	1984-1985
Wheeler, Robert B.	1962-1977
White, Earl	1974-1977
White, George A.	1941-1952
White, George R.	1953-1958
Whittaker, Howard	1958-1966
Whittier, Whittmore	1958-1959
Wible, John R., Jr.	1962-1965
Wichart, Eugene	1959-1972
Wiedemann, Nancy	1980-1981
Williams, Byron P.	1943-1961
Williams, Dorman L.	1965-1966
Williams, Dorothy	1961-1988
Williams, Gary L.	1978-1988
Wilson, Gerald D.	1960-1962

Winzer, Helene M.	1959-1968
Wise, Roanne	1967-1968
Wonnacott, Lee	1973-1980
Wood, Virgil F.	1962-1963
Woodlee, Minnie	1978-1988
Woodruff, Cora	1979-1980
Wysocky, Stanley	1979-1986
Yanock, Richard	1967-1968
York, Susan J.	1961-1967
Young, C.W.	1952-1954
Young, James B.	1961-1975
Young, Lillian	1951-1962
Zavitz, Peter	1987-1989
Zerby, Wayne	1980-1985
Zieske, Donald	1960-1970
Zimmerman, Alice A.	1959-1987
Zucker, Richard A.	1972-1973

Appendix X: The Hawken Administration and Faculty

ADMINISTRATION

T. Douglas Stenberg
Headmaster
A.B., Bowdoin College; Ed. M., Boston
University; Ph.D., University of Minnesota

D. Bruce Carr
Director of the Upper School
B.A., Miami University; M.A., Ph.D., Case
Western Reserve University

Suzanne Kent
Director of the Lower School
B.A., Ohio State University

James C. Whiteman
Director of the Middle School
B.S., Bowling Green State University;
M.Ed., Kent State University

Roger J. Atwell
Director of the Arts Communication Building
B.A., M.A., University of Missouri-Kansas City

Lucinda Baker
Director of Publications and Public Information
B.S., Ohio State University

Frank P. Brandt
Assistant Headmaster for Admissions and Special Programs
B.S., Duquesne University
M.S., Oregon State University

Thomas B. Bryan
Director of Hawken Camps
B.A., Baldwin-Wallace College;
M.A., Kent State University

Meacham Hitchcock '42
Associate Headmaster for Development
B.A., Yale University
M.B.A., Harvard University

Helen Hochstetler
Dietitian

Fred L. Hoffman
Associate Headmaster for Administrative Services
B.S., Purdue University;
M.Ed., Kent State University

Dudley S. Humphrey, Jr. '68
Associate Director of Development
B.A., Hamilton College

Rebecca Jones
Dean of Students
B.A. Mary Washington College
M.Ed. University of Virginia

Alan D. Matta
Assistant Headmaster for
Financial and Support
Services
B.S., University of Pittsburgh
M.B.A., Kent State University

Holly B. Scott
Assistant to the Headmaster
B.S., Williams College
M.Ed., John Carroll
University

Jane D. Wiemer
Director of the Afternoon
Care Program
B.S., Edinboro State College;
M.F.A., Kent State University

Marcella Molho Yedid
Director of Educational
Planning
B.S., Indiana University
M.A., Brown University

HAWKEN FACULTY
1989-90

Lower and Middle Schools

Ann Mary Bracale, 1989
B.S.Ed., Ohio State University
M.Ed., John Carroll
University
Kindergarten Teaching
Fellow

Liane N. Beier, 1980
A.B., Vassar College
M.S., Wheelock College
First Grade

Gregory G. Bobb, 1984
B.A., Ohio Northern
University
M.Ed., Xavier University
Instrumental Music

Wendi C. Bomback, 1984
B.S., University of Maine at
Orono
Head Kindergarten Teacher

Victoria R. Browne, 1987
B.A., Norbert College
M.A.T., University of Chicago
Mathematics 7, 8

Kathy Crennell Carr, 1989
B.S., Miami University
Associate Director of
Admissions, Middle School

David A. Coad, 1972
B.A., Baldwin-Wallace College
M.Ed., Cleveland State
University
Physical Education K-8

Alan F. Coghlan, 1970
B.S., Ohio State University
Science 5, Mathematics 6

Lynne Raphael, 1989
Teaching Diploma, Froebel
Institute
University of London,
England
Head Kindergarten Teacher

Ann I. Dawson, 1979
B.S., M.L.S., Kent State
University
Librarian

Barbara B. Dlugosz, 1985
B.E.D., University of Toledo
Second Grade

Holly M. Duncan, 1989
B.S., Georgia Southern
College
M.Ed., Georgia State
University
Kindergarten Teacher

Sarah Ann Durn '83, 1988
B.A., Northwestern University
M.Ed., John Carroll
University
English 7, 8

Mary S. Eaton, 1960-67, 1972
B.A., Case Western Reserve
University
Reading and Study Skills 5-8
Language Arts 7-8
Chairman, Reading and Study
Skills Department

LaVelle Pelton Esgar, 1973
A.B., Flora Stone Mather
College of
Western Reserve University
M.A.T., John Carroll
University
Reading and Study Skills K-4
Calendar Coordinator

Marta I. Ferrario, 1979
B.A., El Salvador University
Spanish 7, 8

Christopher L. Fusco '68, 1987
B.A., Rollins College
M.Ed., Kent State University
History 7

Linda M. Gojak, 1978
B.S., Miami University
M.Ed., Kent State University
Mathematics 5, 6,
Chairman, Mathematics
Department

James D. Gross, 1973
B.S.Ed., Bowling Green
University
English 4, History 4
Associate Director of
Admissions, Lower School

Cynthia Guertin, 1988
B.F.A., Tufts University
M.A., New York University
Diploma, School of the
Boston Museum of Fine Arts
Art 3, 5, 7

Deborah S. Handy, 1982
A.B., Connecticut College
English 8, Writing 6
Chairman, English
Department

Jerry I. Holtrey, 1968
B.S., Indiana University
Chairman, Physical Education
Department
Director of Athletics

Patricia C. Hosmer, 1970
B.S.Ed., Kent State University
M.A., John Carroll University
Third Grade

Katherine B. Howard, 1988
B.A., Ohio University
M.A., Cleveland State
University
Psychologist

Robert J. Kachurek, 1980
B.S., Bowling Green State
University
Science 8
Chairman, Science
Department

Sandra L. Kahn, 1985
B.S., Bowling Green State
University
Physical Education K-8

Suzanne K. Kent, 1960
B.A., Ohio State University
Reading and Study Skills K-5
Director of the Lower School

Katherine A. Lawrence, 1984
B.S., Ohio State University
M.A., Cleveland State
University
Computer Education

James M. Lewis, 1988
B.S., Illinois Wesleyan
University
English 6

James E. Lowe, Jr., 1967
B.S.Ed., Youngstown
University
English 5,

Lynn M. MacArthur, 1974
B.S., Bethany College
Second Grade

Douglas MacDonald, 1954
A.B., B.S.Ed., Kent State
University
M.A., State University of Iowa
Art 4, 6, 8
Chairman, Art Department

Lori A. Morris, 1988
B.A., Ohio Wesleyan
University
M.Ed., John Carroll
University
Mathematics 4, 6, 8

JoAnne A. Moser, 1987
B.S., Ohio State University
M.Ed., Cleveland State
University
Physical Education K-8

Lawrence E. Nelson, 1969
B.S., M.A., Ohio State
University
English 7, 8
Advisory Coordinator

Patricia O'Donnell, 1988
B.A., Ursuline College
M.Ed., John Carroll
University
Computer Education

Bonita A. Oviatt, 1970
B. Music, Lindenwood College
for Women
Music
Sabbatical Leave 1989-90

Constance L. Palmer, 1967
B.S.Ed., Ohio University
English 4, Mathematics 4

Virginia K. Petrie, 1970
B.S.Ed., Case Western
Reserve University
Science K-4

Ann Ella Rasper, 1980
B.A., Ursuline College
B.S., Miami University
English 4, History 4

David A. Rosenzweig, l967
B.F.A. Music, B.F.A. Music
Ed., Carnegie Institute
M.A., Case Western Reserve
University
Chairman
Lower and Middle Schools
Music Department

Brian J. Ross, 1980
B.A., M.A., University of
Michigan
History 8
Chairman, History
Department

Mary I. Rule, 1989
A.B., Connecticut College
History 5, 6

Anne C. Smith, 1974
B.S.Ed., Miami University
English 5
Sabbatical Leave 1989-90

Genevieve B. Swan, 1966
B.E.P.S. Ecole Primaire
Superieure
French 7, 8
Chairman, Foreign Language
Department

Susan G. Szabo, 1984
B.A., M.A., Allegheny College
Library Assistant

Hugh G. Thompson, 1987
B.S., University of Denver
M.Ed., Antioch University
Mathematics 7, 8

Avis Thrash, 1989
B.A., Westmar College
M.A., University of Akron
Music, K-3

Inez Venning, 1989
B.A., Albion College
M.A., Columbia University
History 5, English 5

James C. Whiteman, 1981
B.S., Bowling Green State
University
M.Ed., Kent State University
Director of the Middle School

Rena L. Widzer, 1982
B.S., M.A., Case Western
Reserve University
Reading and Study Skills K-4

Sandra Wiebusch, 1972
B.S.Ed., Kent State University
M.A., Webster College
First Grade

Robert T. Wiemer, 1975
B.A., M.A., Cleveland State
University
Science 7

Susan C. Wilson, 1984
B.A., Lake Erie College
M.A., Ohio State University
Art l, 2
Director of Project CHARLIE

Pamela A. Win, 1988
B.S., John Carroll University
Science 6, Health 8

Laura R. Zappa, 1979
A.B., University of the
Americas (Mexico City)
Third Grade

Sally M. Zarney, 1972
B.S.Ed., Case Western
Reserve University
Reading K-3
Director of Admissions,
Lower and Middle Schools

Upper School

Roger J. Atwell, 1978
B.A., M.A., University of
Missouri, Kansas City
Theater Arts
Director of the Arts
Communication Building

Larry H. Banks, 1972
B.A., Simpson College
M.A., Kent State University
Ph.D., Case Western Reserve
University
Chairman, History
Department

Kelly Jones Benhase, 1986
B.A., University of Virginia
English

Jesse D. Bernstein, 1974
B.A., Simpson College
Ph.D., State University of New
York at Buffalo
Chemistry

Staci Ann Block, 1988
B.A., University of Wisconsin
M.A., University of Michigan
French

Phillip T. Blood, 1988
B.A., Northeastern University
English

Sandra Bohl, 1986
B.A., Oberlin College
M.A., John Carroll University
Dance

Frank P. Brandt, 1966-1969
B.S., Duquesne University
M.S., Oregon State University
Mathematics
Assistant Headmaster for
Admissions
and Special Programs

John G. Breisch, 1980
B.A., College of Wooster
M.A.R., Yale Divinity School
English
Associate Director of
Admissions, Upper School

James P. Bresnicky, 1964
B.A., Stonehill College
M.Ed., Duquesne University
M.A., John Carroll University
Latin, Practical Arts

Thomas J. Bryan, 1963
B.A., Baldwin-Wallace College
M.A., Kent State University
Physical Education

D. Bruce Carr, 1974-83, 1988
B.A., Miami University
M.A., Ph.D., Case Western
Reserve University
European History
Director of the Upper School

Merl B. Davis, 1977
B.S., Capital University
M.A., Colby College
Chairman, Mathematics
Department

Nadja M. Deighan, 1974
Coordinator of Individual
Advising

Randall R. Dlugosz, 1981
B.A., Hiram College
Biology

Sheldon Freedman, 1986
B.S., M.A., City College of
New York
M.S., Case Western Reserve
University
Biology
Chairman, Science
Department

Mary Ann Gaetano, 1985
B.S., M.A., Ph.D, Ohio
University
Education Specialist

Ronald Hall, 1986
B.S., M.S., Florida State
University
M.S., Yale University
Biology
Chairman, Computer
Department

Julie M. Handler, 1989
B.A., University of Michigan
M.A., Case Western Reserve
University
M.A.Ed., Case Western
Reserve University
English

Katharine D. Hartung, 1988
B.M., B.M.E., University of
Montana
M.M., University of Idaho
Acting Chair, Upper School
Music Department

Robert H. Hawkes, 1972
B.A, Yale University
M.A., Middlebury College
English
Director of Summer School

Rebecca R. Jones, 1989
B.A., Mary Washington
College
M.Ed., University of Virginia
History
Dean of Students

Eileen M. LaVerde, 1985
B.A., Hofstra University
M.A., Rutgers
Mathematics, Computer

Timothy C. Leslie, 1983
A.B., A.B., Miami University
M.A., Harvard University
French, History, Latin

Alan L. MacCracken, Jr.'54,
1963-70, 1978
A.B., Lafayette College
M.Ed., Kent State University
Ph.D., University of Akron
French
Acting Chairman,
Foreign Language
Department

Christian W. Marsh, 1985
B.A., Greenville College
M.S., Springfield College
Chairman, Physical Education
Department

David M. McCahon, 1972
B.S., Virginia Polytechnic
Institute
M.Ed., University of
Pittsburgh
Mathematics
Director of Senior Projects

Catherine S. McCants, 1989
B.S., North Carolina State
University
Mathematics Teaching Fellow

Allen McMickle, 1986
B.F.A., M.A., University of
Iowa
Art

Susan M. McNamee, 1975
A.B., M.A., John Carroll
University
Spanish, French

Jacqueline A. Meyer, 1989
B.A., Carleton College
English

Catherine A. Miller, 1983
B.S., M.Ed., Cleveland State
Univeristy
Reading and Study Skills
Specialist

Jennifer L. Mosse, 1988
A.B., Bowdoin College
Mathematics

Patrick J. Palumbo, 1987
B.S., Ohio State University
M.A., John Carroll University
Mathematics

Daniel T. Polk, 1985
B.A., Case Western Reserve
University
Theater Arts

Marla Robbins '75, 1986
B.A., Georgetown College
Physical Education

George A. Roby, 1969
B.F.A., Ohio University
M.A., Western Reserve
University
Chairman, Fine Arts
Department

Peter F. Scott, 1974
B.A., St. Lawrence University
M.A., American University
Chairman, English
Department

Jane E. Warner Seik, 1975
B.A., M.L.S., Kent State
University
Librarian

Lawrence M. Seik, 1981
B.S., Denison
B.S., Kent State University
M.S., Ohio State University
M.S., Case Western Reserve
University
Chemistry

Robert H. Shurtz, 1985
B.S., University of Michigan
M.A., Harvard University
Physics, Computer

Douglas L. Smith, 1987
B.A., University of North
Carolina
M.A., University of Western
Florida
Ph.D. University of Southern
Florida
History

James A. Snavely, 1965
B.A., Yale College
M.Ed., M.A., Western Reserve
University
English , Music

Fernando Soldevilla, 1986
B.S., University de Valencia
M.S., Kent State University
A.B.D., Case Western Reserve
University
Spanish

Joaquin Soldevilla, 1989
B.S., Universidad Politeonica
de Madrid
M.A., University of Akron
A.B.D., Georgetown
University
Spanish

W. Richard Stacy, 1987
B.S., M.A., Ball State
University
Ph.D., University of Wisconsin
History

Anne J. Thompson, 1987
B.A., University of
Massachusetts
Mathematics

John Loftus Tottenham, 1979
B.A., M.A., University of
Michigan
History

Clifford T. Walton, 1978
B.A., Concordia Teachers
College
M.A., Kent State University
Physical Education

Robert C. Wilhelm, 1988
A.B., Pomona College
Ph.D., Cornell University
College Counselor

Marcella M. Yedid, 1979
B.S., Indiana University
M.A., Brown University
French
Director of Educational
Planning

Faculty and Staff Emeriti
Listed by date of retirement

Charles A. Poutasse
Science Teacher and Primary
Grades
Chairman Emeritus: 1948-
1980

Herbert F. Furst
Middle School Mathematics
Teacher Emeritus, Lower
School: 1945-1984

Mildred L. Smith
Secretary Emerita to the Head
of the Lower School: 1968-1985

Inez T. Budd
Administrative Assistant
Emerita
to the Headmaster: 1968-1986

Leonard R. Carey
Physical Education Teacher
Emeritus,
Lower School: 1956-1987

Zoann L. Dusenbury
English Teacher Emerita,
Upper School: 1974-1987,
Lower School: 1961-1974
1961-1987

Charles L. Stephens '46
Middle School Director and
History Teacher Emeritus,
Lower School: 1960-1987

Dorothy E. Williams
Secretary, Mailing Office

Alice A. Zimmerman
Lower School Admissions
Secretary
and Receptionist Emerita:
1956-1987

Martha Brown
Middle School Director of
Admissions
1977-1980, 1988-1989
English Teacher Emerita:
1969-1988

Elizabeth McCullough
KindergartenTeacher
Emerita: 1963-1973
History Teacher Emerita:
1978-1989

Office Staff

Office of the Headmaster
Donna Drummer
Secretary to the Headmaster

Lower and Middle Schools
Kathleen Burgess
Secretary to the Director of
the Lower School

Rosetta Pavlik
Secretary to the Director of
the Middle School
Mary Podmore
Secretary
Lower and Middle School
Admissions

Upper School
Carolyn Miller
Secretary to the Director of
the Upper School

Kathleen Carr
Secretary
Upper School Admissions

Janice Davidian
Receptionist, Upper School
Secretary to the Director of
Athletics
Switchboard Operator, Gates
Mills Campus

Jeri Parks
Secretary to the College
Counselor/Registrar; Senior
Projects Secretary

Administrative Services
Cynthia Kovach
Secretary to the Associate
Headmaster for
Administrative Services

Financial and Support
Services

Joyce Brinkerhoff
Secretary to the Assistant
Headmaster for Financial and
Support Services

Kathleen Burgess
Transportation Coordinator

Cheryl Morris
Switchboard Operator and
Operations Secretary

Donna Nista
Bookkeeper
Margaret Widmar
Accountant

Development
Delores DiNero

Development Assistant for
Systems and
Special Programs

Jackie Gillespie
Secretary, Central Mailing

Fran Rose
Development Assistant for
Systems and
Special Programs

Summer Programs, Special
Programs and Financial
Assistance
Deborah Dykstra
Day Camps Assistant

Jackie Gillespie
Financial Assistance Secretary

KINDERGARTEN

Jonathan S. Adelstein
Lisa Suzanne Babin
Geoffrey Beck
Christine Sarah Divoky
Mark Aaron Elinsky
Rachel Elisabeth Estrin
Anthoni Fazio
Harry E. Figgie IV
Paul Franklin
Kelly Lavelle Friedlander
Elizabeth Anne Genovese
Jesse Golenberg
Hunter Haas
Peter Jacob Harrold
R. George Hawwa
Aaron Daniel Hoffmann
Megan A. Iammarino
Mervyn L. Jones II
Andrew Jeremy Kaplan
David Korngold
Brittany Marsh
Meagan Mauter
Duncan S. McCreery
Jamie Leigh McLaughlin
Paul R. Jecklenburg
Catherine Ross
Stefanie Lin Schwartz
Brendan Shanahan
Justin D. Steinhouse
Anna Strohl
Dustin Tallisman
Ameet Thaker
Jenna Rachael Walsh
Jonathan Watkins
Douglas Wiemer
Marguerite E. Wincek
Andrew Wolfort
Stepyhanie Joy Wyse

Allison Yang
Rachel M. Young

FIRST GRADE

Johanna M. Alperin
Andrea Erika Ament
Michael James Arendt, Jr.
Kerri E. Aveni
Scott Blackburn
Isabelle B. Bolton
Gina Christine Borsellino
Bonnie Duncan
Carl Fazio
Chase Foster
Justin Fry
Martha S. Fusco
Brett Goulder
Ian Thomas Greenwalt
Philip Hicks
Joshua Abbott Hirshman
Philip Tyler Holder
Elizabeth Soo Hyun Hong
Nicholas Iammarino
Justin R. Kahn
Jennifer Alyse Lane
Alexander C. Leslie
Stephanie Liff
Meredith Mackey
Brian Eric Martin
Celeste Alyssa McMickle
Geoffrey N. Milson
Christopher B. Morgan
Michael Osenar
Christopher S. Reech
Jed Marcus Rich
Corey K. Rubin
Maya M. Sequeira
Lindsey Stevens

Martha Ann Taplin
Elliot Arthur Shackelford
   Toms
Barry John Watt
Vashon W. Williams
Craig Sean Zeltner

SECOND GRADE

David A. Andrzejewski
Jamie Rochelle Babin
Scott Michael Bacon
Bradford Lawrence Baker
Meredith Lynn Belman
G. Bradley Bookatz
Andrew Bruner
Theophilus "Chip" Caviness
Emma Jane Church
Meredith Collins
Britt Lindsay Cosgrove
Dara Renee Cotler
Julia Dery
Eugene Dubick
Matthew Fuller
Scott Gordon
Jordan Greenberger
Christopher J. Hall
Stephen Matthew Hall
Natalie Hawwa
Peter Hoke
Barbara Shuyler Hoyt
Heather Humphrey
Megan A. Janicki
James E. Janis
James Martis
Peter Gibbs Oviatt
Erica Lara Rose
Jessica Ross
Andrew Rosskamm
Marni Santoro
Aaron Schwartz
J. Kearney Shanahan, Jr.
Srikanth Sivashankaran
Edward Smith

David Strickler
Nicholas Strohl
Samir Thaker
Roseanne Wincek
Chad Howard Young

THIRD GRADE

Kristen M. Aveni
Nathaniel H. Berk
Jennifer Bernstein
Anthony Salvatori Borsellino
Michael Andrew Cassara
Margaret Davis
James Dempsey
Jason Phillip deRoulet
Jessica Fusco
Monica-Kaye Gamble
Ryan Clayton Gillmore
Timothy Seth Goldberg
Rachel Goldstein
Amelia Rachel Haas
Josiah A. Haas
Christopher Martin Hoke
Christopher W. Horsburgh, Jr.
Ross Kinder
Jeremy Kuhlman
Joseph Langholt
Andrew Hann Martin
Nikil Mehta
Alexandra L. Milsom
Lara Sarah Nochomovitz
Adam S. Ours
Timothy Kent Oviatt
A. Aysegul Ozsoyoglu
John Hodge Peacock
Ann Elizabeth Redford
Brian Charles Roberts
Wesley Durham Roj
Laura Ashley Rose
Jeremy John Sager
Maryn S. Silverberg
Tiffin Annemarie Staib
Megan Ann Strobel

Alexis Tallisman
Scott VerMerris
Jeffrey T. Walton
Allison Minda Weinberger
Michael Wiemer

FOURTH GRADE

Jordan Alperin
Adam John Bass
Lauren Bass
Elizabeth Berman
Emily S. Bolton
Vikram Brahms
Billy Brown
Danielle Brown
Amanda Bruner
Chad Callaghan
Elizabeth Carr
James Phillip Church
Nicole Cosgrove
Noah Cox
Galen Brent Davis
Kathryn Dery
Charlynn Dubinsky
Haley Eppler
Thomas Finley
Matthew Fox
Christian Gauderer
Emily Golenberg
Julian P. Gratry
Jonathan R. Hausman
George Howard
Jacob J. Karimpil
David R. Jezek, Jr.
Scott Johnson
Bennett M. Kaufman
Erin Cathryn Koeblitz
Sonya Martin
Daniel Charles Matisoff
Tripper McCreery
Alexander P. Ogan
David Osenar

Brendan Quigley
Meghan Rogers
Brian Rothstein
Allison Schulman
Zachary Siegal
Caroline Smith
David Paul Soldevilla
Jeffrey William Stacy
Lauren Elizabeth Stark
Evan Walsh
Melissa Williams
Colette Helen Wiseman
Jonathan Yang

FIFTH GRADE

S. Clayton Bain
Christelle Lurene Bates
Joshua Berezin
Matthew E.D. Besser
Allayne Ernst Bole
Sam Anthony Borsellino III
Holly Elizabeth Bosley
Mari Boss
Samantha M. Bruce
Caroline G. Calfee
Joseph Caputo
Jeffrey Christian May
Michael Ciuni
Elizabeth Collins
Emmanuel Crouvisier
Michael Davis
Julie Eisenberg
Katherine Fiordalis
Jamieson Fry
Elizabeth Goldsmith
Richard Gordon
Luke Greicius
Jordan Haas
J. Walker Hall
Jarrett Hicks
Jason Hoagland
Callie Hoyt
Dudley Humphrey III

Afrika Jimerson
Matthew J. Lazar
Charles M. Lombardy III
Jeffrey Manners
Theodora Martis
Paul J. Murphy
Amanda Nicol
Scott O'Brien
Alice Ours
Alana Rezaee
James C. Rogers III
Allison Rosen
Michael Rosskamm
Erika Sandor
Brian Schaefer
Peter Schwartz
Zachary Schwartz
Moira Shanahan
Ryan M. Staib
Courtenay O. Taplin, Jr.
Steven Van Deusen
Andrew Wiemer
Sara E. Woomer
Brie Zeltner

SIXTH GRADE

Gregory Adler
Jeffrey Brett Bacon
Atusa Baghery
Brianna C. Baisel
Bowman Beeman
Dennis Bernstein
Richard Bole
Frances B. Bolton
Jeffrey Boxx
Latham Boyle
Joseph Cole II
Naomi Cotler
Elizabeth Davis
Jason Michael Davis
Lauren Dubick
Catherine Fazio
Vincenza Fazio

Anthony V. Fernando
Megan Fusco
Robert Thomas Gale
Abigail Gelfand
Brianna Teal Gerrity
Alan Gillmore
Andrei Gnepp
Michael Gutmacher
Edward Harvie
Lydia Holzman
Mahogany Jimerson
Matthew Kazdin
Jesse Kleinman
Joscelyn Langholt
Gabrielle C. Lentsch
Joshua Perkins McHamm
Ellen Mecklenburg
Brooke Milstein
Angeli Murthy
Celina Renee Nichols
Patrick Oppmann
Kimberly Rice
Shoshana L. Ross
Jonathan Rutman
Aaron M. Salomon
Rachel Siegal
Hugh Slater
Elizabeth Mae Stromberg
Jordan Michael Sumers
Scott Matthew Trilling
Daniel Walton
Tonya D. Werner
James Wilson
Tamara Louise Wiseman
Drew Zeltner
Gabriel Michael Zelwin

SEVENTH GRADE

Khalid Abdelrasoul
Artis Arnold III
David Aymat
Heather Baggott
Ardeshir Baghery

Joshua Benghiat
Allison Borkowski
Adam Borland
Shoma Brahms
Claudia Brittenham
Daniel Carr
Juliet Castrovinci
John G. Chapman, Jr.
Eli Davis
Deborah Dinner
Edward Dutton
Ursula Sue Fernandez
Melissa Fox
Kevin Gillespie
Jennifer Goldberg
Daniel Greene
Michael J. Gunn, Jr.
Alfreda D. Hall
Stephen Wales Hall
Joshua Harrold
Kaori (Lee-Ann) Honda
Eric Katz
Priya Khosla
Jenny Kim
Blake Kleinman
Daniel Kuhlman
Barbara Kwon
Kate LaRiche
Jason Lieberman
Christopher Mann
Neil Moffett
Kelley D. Murch
John W. Ours, Jr.
Emily Jane Oviatt
Eric Jayson Paul
Daniel Rosskamm
Brandon Santoro
Nicholas J. Schwegel
Brian J. Scott
Michelle Shafran
Sandeep Shekar
Lori Shulman
Eric Simms
William R. Stewart

Antoya Nicole Stovall-
  Leonard
Michael Strazzanti
Christopher Van Deusen
Darshan Variyam
Heather Williams
Lawrence D. Wilson, Jr.

EIGHTH GRADE

Lisa M. Antonelli
Jeffrey Beacham
Stephanie C. Behrens
Rachael Berezin
Jeremy Bilsky
Karen Elaine Childs
Jennifer A. Choich
Karen Cook
Christopher Davis
Nicholas A. DiCello
Charles Fiordalis
Joi Camille Foreman
Andrew Greenwalt
Anik Guha
Daniel Gutmacher
Elizabeth Hammack
Brandon Harrison
Douglas Harvey
Raymond Hwang
Carwil James
Sarah Janicki
Andrew Jawa
Margot Kahn
Lige Kaplan
Aneal Kohli
Joshua Leavitt
Bradley Lefkowitz
Monica Lehmann
Beth Levy
Erica Lieberman
Brinton C. Lincoln
Marci Lorber
Scott Martin

Suzanne Martis
Danielle Matta
David Munford, Jr.
Alexsis Pecuch
Lauren Peterman
Kenneth Peterson
Patrick Quigley
Larry Richmond
Joel Peter Rose
Jacob Scott
Molly Segelin
Scott Seidelmann
Colleen Shanahan
Veena Shankaran
Anoop Shekar
Ian Shrallow
Larysa Simms
Abhimanyu Singh
Arun Sivashankaran
Eric Starr
Jennifer Stevens
Heather Stuckey
John Szabo
Shahrad Teimouri
Peter Tomecki
Jennifer van Dijk
Divya Variyam
Lindsay B. Vilas
Ethan John Vlah
Benedikt von Dohnanyi
Stephanie Walters
Marren Weber
Katherine Wilson
Laura Woodburn
Korry O'Neil Wright
Billy Zaffiro, Jr.

NINTH GRADE

Macy Allatt
Holly Artz
G. William Bare
Allan Trent Bates

Brandi Sherrice Baylock
Allison Becker
Jennifer Bilenker
Evan Bishop
Clint Bradley III
Michael Brand
Scott Burns
Jodi Chesler
Tracy Cook
Anthony Cowsette
Cecilie Davis
Melanie deHaan
Nicole Dutton
Michael Dybbs
Daniel Egleston
Joseph Henry Elton
Kenyon Farrow
Meredith Fee
Heidi DeMott Fowler
Carrie Franklin
Ravi Goud
Hollis Grdina
Aaron Greicius
Christopher Gresham
Scott Hahl
Kevin Hanz
James Hardiman, Jr.
Michael Wayne Hawkins
Jessica Hawley
Nolan Hecht
Candice Huang
James Izanec
Kelly James
Robin Lanette Johnson
Karen Joseph
Elisa Karp
Anne Kelly
Rohit P. Khandekar
Aran Kim
Natalie Kirilcuk
Lily Koo
Ethan Korngold
Matthew J. Krug
Todd LaRiche

Sharon Lee
Josiah Russell Madar
Robert W. Mallett III
Indrani Mallik
William Mann
Steven Manners
Wendy Marston
Kristopher McCahon
Brian M. McEwen
Margaret Anne Miller
Joseph Patrick Morse
Cari Moskowitz
Elizabeth L. Murphy
Eilzabeth Neuman
Kristine Michelle Newton
Emily Beth Neye
Laura E. O'Neill
Laura O'Neill
Michael Paddock
Kelly Palchick
Timothy Peppard
Geoffrey Piper
Andrew Presby
James Redford
Garth Robins
Jordan Rohler
Heather L. Roote
Dauri Rosenfield
Lauren Rosenfield
Carmen Ruiz-Davila
Naomi Sandor
Charles E. Saulino
Laura Schwartz
Chalana A. Seward
Justine Siegal
Gretchen V. Skok
John Andrew Smith
Winston Stromberg
Julie Suh
Jonathan Talbot
Jennifer Thompson
Alicia Times
Mark A. Travassos
Jennifer Byrne Varanese
Scott Walton

Hannah Widzer
Michelle Wilker
Sckylor Williams
Jamie Wilson
Kevin Wilson
Joshua Zaremba
Ryan Zeltner

TENTH GRADE

Nicole Adler
Michael J. Antonelli
Amanda Ballew
G. Lynette Bennett
Scott A. Bilsky
Paul Breen
Erika Ginae Brown
Alexander Calfee
Faith Chiang
Kimberly G. Crone
Vanessa Crouvisier
Kathryn Diehl
Aimee Discenzo
Christopher Fowler
Kirk Framke
Beth Frankel
Courtney Galin
Carly Denee Gerrity
Teresa Gillespie
Durvelle D. Grissett
Nicole Guth
Paul R. Hairston III
Caroline Hardy
Kathleen Hawley
Miriam Huang
Nina Stewart Ingalls
Andrew Jimerson
Ravi Kalhan
Adam K. Katz
Eric Klein
Kim Koontz
Virginia R. Kuechle
Mark Allyn Lang
Jillan Lankford

Julie Lorber
Alan M. MacCrackin III
Yasmin S. Mahmoud
Michael Lavelle Martin
Jennifer Melsher
Jessica Messer
Matthew Miller
Ryan Edward Morgan
Craig Morman
William Morris
Bryan Payne
Jacques J. Payne
Edward C. Pembroke III
Dionna R. Peoples
John Eric Poulos
Leon William Pryor
Malcolm G. Pye
M. Timothy Quigley
Milakshmi Rajapakse
Kevin Reese
Scott Johnes Reik
Adam Rich
Courtney Jane Rogus
Jason A. Ross
Laurel Sahley
Matthew A. Salerno
Surekha Samal
Jason Santoro
Michael Schaefer
Amy Michelle Schick
Amanda Schulman
Mara Schwartz
Katy Louise Sheterom
Katy Sheterom
Michael Shulman
Andrew Simms
Aaron T. Smith
Sarah Smith
Heather Sooy
Jeremy Stephens
Susan Leigh Stewart
Liza Studen
Christy Taddeo
Lisa Takaoka
Reed Tepper

Virginia C. Theis
Priya M. Travassos
Jeremy Earl Tuss
Nicole Villafana
Traci Vitonis
Sara L. Wald
Andre Walter
Robert S. Weller
Andrew J. Wengerd
Rebecca Wheeler
Justin Wyatt
H. Spencer Young
Kathleen Young
Jessica Zellner
Oliver Zeltner

ELEVENTH GRADE

Alison Ainsworth
Marcia Karen Bates
Stacy John Behrens
Sam Borsellino
Harlan Bruner
William Burns
Shaalein Carroll
Rebecca Chesler
Laura Christie
Elizabeth Commes
Susan Currier
Caleb Davis
Cameron Dovgan
Eric Dubinsky
Betsy Eisenberg
Allegra Fogt
Tyler Forstner
David Friedman
Amy Beth Goldberg
Clate Reeves Grunden
Erik Gzibovskis
Sarah Haberman
Peter Hammack
Melissa Hexter
Prajakti Jayavant
Aziza Jimerson

Effram Kaplan
Daniel Karp
Michael Kerek
Alexandra Kirilcuk
Lea Koonce
Christopher Lacey
Matthew Leavitt
Erin Ayn Lee
Michael Lehmann
Kevin T. Lie
Todd Lieberman
Carol Lipscomb
Nina Longino
Michael Longley
John Malloy
Mary McCahon
Currier McEwen
Kathleen Merrill
Todd Moore
Daniel Moskowitz
Carl Hans Christian Muller
Kevin M. Neebes
Ian Osborn
Jonathan Osborn
Sean Peppard
Amy Rand
Stuart Resnick
Matthew Ricchetti
Liz Richmond
Chris Ristau
Marc Rivitz
Ashley Rogers
Jamie Rosenfield
William Shawn Sanders
Julie Marie Schick
Douglas Schiller
Joseph Todd Schmelzer
James Schonitzer
Erica Lynn Schutter
Daniel Sheahan
Irene Olivia Mei-Wai Siu
Thomas Slater
Kevin Smith
Andrew Smyser
Socheat Som

Teri Marie Starr
Katherine Szabo
Shahram Teimouri
Matthew Tien
Bronwynne Tuss
Antonio L. Twymon
Shefali D. Ujla
Brian Weiss
Daniel Weiss
Amanda E. Wrobel
Christopher Wyatt
Jonathan Wyman
Jeremy Zinn

TWELFTH GRADE

Paul E. Austin III
Michele Ballou
Tonia Bates
Thomas Bercu
Joshua Bilenker
Kimberly Bird
Matthew Boyle
Melissa Burovac
Anthony Calabrese
Jennifer Carr
Michelle Carr
Kathleen Cook
Alyse Daberko
Shawn Darr
Matthew Davis
Rufus Davis
Ramin Doustdar
Lamont Dozier, Jr.
Amanda Ellis
William Ernest
Thomas Feldman
Robert Alan Fellinger
Amy Frankel
Joshua Franel
Marni Friedman
Ross Galin
Bindi Narra Gerrity
Heather Gerwin

Zachary Goldberg
Jennifer Gordon
David Grano
Jessica Guertin
Christine Hanz
Gregory Harper
William Hayden
David Hexter
Matthew Hoagland
Shanon Hoffman
Mirie Hosler
Megan Hunter
Peter Izanec
Robyn Cathy Joseph
David Kendra
Rebecca Kickel
Elizabeth Kirby
Jonathan D. Kolb
Sonia Lee
Kenneth G. Lie
Ms. Marion Lloyd
Christine Logar
Christopher Mahovlic
Polly Marston
Ingrid Perkins McHamm
Andrew Montlack
Damond Moodie
Dean Moyar
William Mulligan
Maynard Murch
Ajay Murthy
Nicholas Nardi
David Nau
Douglas Neye

Shawn Nickens
Christopher Pacini
Gregory Poulos
Griffin Ralston
Jennifer Rankin
Pamela Rice
Iris Rodriquez
Courtney Rohler
Kevin Roll
Megan Schoff
Brett Shaheen
Vijay Shankaran
Stacy Singerman
Michal T. Slominski
Leonard Spacek
Benjamin Sterling
Neil Stormer
Aaron Studen
Tyson Stuelpe
Tricia Tatalick
Kevin Thomas
Amy Times
Win Joseph Travassos
Amy Lynn Tucker
Ilya Vilinsky
Gerald Walker
Shari Waxman
David Widzer
Eric Wilker
Jonathan Williams
Sarah Wilson
Sasha Yevzlin
Tamera Zelwin

Appendix XII: Hawken Alma Mater

To Hawken School we sing a song of praises loud and clear.
Fly high the glorious banner of this our school so dear.
We're pledging our allegiance, to serve her faithfully.
So Hail to Alma Mater; proud we will ever be.

And when in future years we roam far from these hallowed halls.
We'll ne'er forget the happy hours we spent within her walls.
We always will remember and pray we ever may
Keep high the Hawken Standards.
Keep bright the Red and Gray.

Now the day is over
Night is drawing nigh,
Shadows of the evening
Steal across the the sky.

Grant to little children
Visions bright of Thee;
Guard the sailors tossing
On the deep blue sea.

Through the long night watches
May Thine angels spread
Their white wings above me,
Watching round my bed

When the morning wakens
Then may I arise
Pure, and fresh, and sinless
In Thy holy eyes.

Amen

Statistical Analysis of Hawken Applications, Acceptances, and Matriculations at Various Universities and Colleges, 1985-89

COLLEGE/ UNIVERSITY	APP	ACC	MAT
Allegheny	26	21	5
American	15	8	2
Amherst	14	5	3
Bates	28	8	3
Boston College	15	4	2
Boston University	21	16	5
Bowdoin	25	9	1
Brown	41	6	5
Bucknell	30	14	4
Carleton	11	3	2
Carnegie-Mellon	9	6	2
Case-Western	23	18	3
University of Chicago	12	9	2
Cincinnati	14	11	3
Colby	18	8	3
Colgate	31	8	1
University of Colorado	15	9	3
Columbia	9	1	0
Connecticut	10	4	1
Cornell	52	26	14
Dartmouth	35	10	8
Denison	41	25	12
Depauw	30	16	3
Dickinson	11	5	0
Duke	24	3	1
Emory	15	7	3
Georgetown	19	4	1
Hamilton	15	5	2
Harvard	37	10	8
Indiana	18	10	2
Johns Hopkins	11	2	1
Kenyon	41	25	7
Lafayette	20	8	1
Lehigh	15	8	1

COLLEGE/ UNIVERSITY	APP	ACC	MAT
Macalaster	10	3	0
Miami (Ohio)	108	64	21
University of Michigan	61	25	8
Middlebury	13	2	0
M.I.T.	10	4	2
University of New Hampshire	11	2	0
Northwestern	49	22	8
Notre Dame	10	6	4
Oberlin	16	10	2
Ohio University	27	18	4
Ohio Wesleyan	12	10	2
University of Pennsylvania	42	17	8
Princeton	33	12	4
University of Richmond	18	7	1
University of Rochester	34	28	5
Skidmore	21	15	6
Smith	11	7	2
Stanford	22	2	1
Syracuse	17	12	3
Trinity	13	8	3
Tufts	38	18	9
Tulane	9	4	0
Vanderbilt	16	8	1
Vassar	17	9	3
University of Vermont	36	16	5
University of Virginia	16	6	5
Wake Forest	12	0	0
Washington University	47	32	7
Wellesley	12	10	4
Wesleyan	22	10	4
Williams	15	3	1
University of Wisconsin	25	12	4
Wittenberg	16	9	2
Wooster	16	12	3
Yale	36	7	3

Sources

The major sources for the manuscript are the substantial archives in the development office on Hawken Upper School campus in Gates Mills, Ohio; interviews with faculty; faculty emeriti; administrators; alumni; former support staff, and students. Among the archives an important source is the Hawken board of trustees minutes.

Chapter 1. Most of the information is found in a printed memoir by Charles R. Stephens filed under his name in the Hawken archives; in letters from James Hawken to his staff filed under his name; in two small printed brochures addressed to parents and prospective parents, explaining the objectives and the methods. We also received much information from interviews with Charles L. Stephens, son of Charles R. Stephens; from interviews with senior alumni who were in the first class.

Chapter 2. This information comes from periodical clippings about Congressman Frances Bolton; from a biography, *A Long Way Forward,* by David Loth (Longmans, Green and Company, 1957); and from alumni interviews.

Chapters 3, 4, and 5. Largely from correspondence: James Hawken to Chester Bolton, to Frances Bolton; Chester Bolton-Henry Sheffield in the Hawken archives; interviews with alumni; various Lower School publications by the boys; minutes of the Hawken School endowment association.

Chapters 6–7. Minutes of the Hawken board of trustees; *The Red and Gray Book* for 1928; alumni interviews; an article by David Russell and Elmer Sipple, filed under Russell in the faculty drawer in the archives.

Chapter 8. Minutes of Hawken board of trustees; alumni interviews.

Chapter 9. Board minutes; Bolton biography, *A Long Way Forward;* periodicals featuring Liv Ireland, filed in archives under Ireland.

Chapters 10–11. Periodicals in possession of Mrs. Nancy Boles; board minutes; alumni interviews.

Chapters 12–13. Alumni interviews; board minutes; class yearbooks of the period.

Chapter 14. Alumni interviews.

Chapters 15–16. Alumni and retired faculty interviews; correspondence, James Hawken-Richard Day; board minutes; board interviews.

Chapter 17. Ireland address to faculty; Meacham Hitchcock correspondence; alumni interviews.

Chapter 18. Alumni and former trustee interviews; issues of *The Affirmative No* for the time period.

Chapter 19. Alumni interviews; board minutes; *The Hawken Review* and *The Affirmative No* for the time period.

Chapters 20–25: comprising Book III and covering 1976 to December 1989. The sources are largely as stated in the text: *The Affirmative No; The Hawken Review;* class yearbooks. Additionally—interviews with students, faculty, administrators, former faculty, and alumni; board minutes.

Notes

Notes

Notes

NOTES

NOTES

NOTES

NOTES